DO FOR ME

A True Crime Story of Politics
and Corruption in New York

Bill Sanderson

MANHATTAN SQUARE PRESS · NEW YORK

Contact the author at wpsanderson@gmail.com

Paperback print edition ISBN 979-8-9870503-0-9

Front and back cover design by Shaun Johnson

Front cover photo of Sheldon Silver
by Mary Altaffer/Associated Press

Back cover photo of the Great Western Staircase
in the New York State Capitol
by Bill Sanderson

Table of contents

Chapter 1 – A favor

As speaker of the New York State Assembly, Sheldon Silver was one of the most important people in state government. He had a say in everything the state did, from public transit funding to state education policy to legalizing same-sex marriages. "He was a prominent public official, whom I trusted and who I thought would know people who would refer work to me," said Jay Arthur Goldberg, a lawyer who specialized in handling New York City property-tax appeals and who grew up with Silver on Manhattan's Lower East Side.

In the mid-1990s, Silver pursued a new client on Goldberg's behalf. Glenwood Management built and operated luxury apartment buildings in wealthy Manhattan neighborhoods—properties that made it a potentially lucrative client for Goldberg's law firm.

Glenwood, a family-owned company, was run by Leonard Litwin, whose father began investing in real estate in the 1940s. The details of how Litwin and Silver came to meet remain unclear. But Brian Meara, a Silver friend who made his living lobbying the state Legislature, said he introduced Silver to Litwin. Glenwood was one of Meara's lobbying clients. At Litwin's request, Meara said, he arranged for the men to share a meal.

Litwin and Silver lunched at Ratner's, a kosher restaurant on Delancey Street on the Lower East Side legendary for its onion rolls, blintzes, latkes, and split pea soup. They had similar backgrounds—both were born to Jewish immigrant parents. They talked about politics and the city's future. It's unclear how many times they got together. Silver's appointment books confirm two sit-downs, in November 1995 and October 1996.

Around the time of these meetings, Silver summoned Goldberg to his Manhattan legislative office. Silver called his friend Yaacov, which is the Hebrew version of Jacob, Goldberg's formal first name.

"He said, 'Yaacov, I think I'm going to be able to refer Glenwood Management.'"

Goldberg was delighted by this news. "They were very prominent real estate owners and renters and managers in the city," he said.

Goldberg was happy to pay Silver for the referral by giving him a share of the fees Glenwood would pay on the account. This arrangement would last as long as Goldberg kept Litwin's company as a client—perhaps for many years. But he wondered if this setup was legal, given that Silver was the speaker of the state Assembly.

"I've known Mr. Silver for a long, long time, and I trusted his judgment," Goldberg explained. "He was always a trustworthy person. I had given referral fees before in my professional life, but I never gave one to the speaker of the Assembly. So I just wanted his assurance as my friend and as a trusted person."

Goldberg asked, "Is this all right, Shelly?"

"Of course, Yaacov," Silver answered. "I'm a lawyer."

That was good enough for Goldberg to decide the fee was OK, and to accept the favor Silver offered his firm.

Goldberg said he gave credence to Silver's remark, "I'm a lawyer."

"I took that to mean that he knew the law and it was OK to refer cases to a lawyer no matter what position he held," Goldberg said.[1]

Under the deal, Glenwood agreed to pay Goldberg's firm fees of 25 percent of whatever reductions it won on Glenwood's property taxes. Separately, Goldberg agreed to pay Silver 25 percent of Glenwood's fees.

This fee-sharing agreement was a significant turn in the life and political career of Sheldon Silver.

Silver was a rarity—a lifelong Manhattanite. He was born in 1944 in the Lower East Side, the same neighborhood where he and Litwin lunched, and where Silver's political and personal lives were rooted.

Silver was the youngest of four children in an Orthodox Jewish family. His parents emigrated from

6

Russia. When Silver was a child, a men's clothing store on the Lower East Side might have called itself a haberdashery, and the Silvers could have bought rugelach and braided loaves of challah bread at Gertel's kosher bakery. Silver's father owned a wholesale hardware business, which provided a career to Silver's oldest brother. Another brother became a physician and was the chief of orthopedic surgery at New York Methodist Hospital in Brooklyn. A sister became a teacher in London.

It is hard to imagine the family wanted for anything.

Silver attended the Rabbi Jacob Joseph School, an Orthodox Jewish institution that taught boys from kindergarten through high school.

During his youth, Silver's mother wanted him to learn to play piano. It didn't work out.

"I was a dropout at Henry Street Music School," Silver once told an interviewer, referring to a program run by the Henry Street Settlement, a Lower East Side educational organization. "My mother enrolled me in piano lessons when I wanted to play the trumpet. They told her until I was 13 they wouldn't let me play a wind instrument but I should learn music and play piano."

Then Silver learned about a youth basketball league operated by another community organization, the Educational Alliance, still in existence today. The league played at the same time his music lessons were scheduled.

"I never went to Henry Street," Silver said. "I played basketball there in Gulick Park [in the Lower East Side] every Sunday, every Friday afternoon after school. That was the place. At the Educational Alliance, before they had the big gym, I played on the roof," he said. "The ceiling was about 11 feet. You learned how to shoot line drives at a basket up there."[2]

He was a good athlete. In high school, Silver captained the Rabbi Jacob Joseph basketball team. He wasn't good enough for the varsity team at Yeshiva

University, a Jewish institution with roots on the Lower East Side that established a campus in Washington Heights in upper Manhattan when it was also a Jewish neighborhood. But in his senior year at Yeshiva, Silver was named most valuable player in the university's intramural basketball league.

A contemporary, David Mandel, recalled playing hockey with Silver. "He was much better than I was," Mandel said. As a politician, Silver played up the athletic prowess of his youth and was sometimes photographed holding a basketball. Yeshiva's varsity men's and women's basketball teams visited Silver on the Assembly floor during a legislative session in 2010.

In Silver's time there, Yeshiva was a politically liberal campus. Most students were too young to vote—New York's voting age wasn't lowered from 21 to 18 until 1971, when the Twenty-Sixth Amendment passed. But a survey found that if Yeshiva students cast ballots in the 1964 presidential election, liberal Democratic incumbent Lyndon Johnson would get 90 percent of their votes, and conservative Republican Barry Goldwater just 10 percent. At Silver's graduation in 1965, New York State Appellate Division Judge Bernard Botein lauded Silver's classmates who participated in the civil rights movement, which he found preferable to the "sullen silence of the 50s."

Silver enrolled in Brooklyn Law School in what would have been his first significant time at a non-Jewish educational institution. He earned his law degree in 1969, soon passed the bar exam, and began practicing personal injury and product liability law.

Many Jewish families moved out of the Lower East Side from the 1960s onward, but Silver stayed. He and his wife, Rosa—they met in high school—worshipped at the Bialystoker Synagogue, a congregation founded by Polish Jews in 1878. They raised four children in the same apartment complex in which Silver grew up, and which remained his home during his entire time in public office. He was known to maintain the traditions of Orthodox Jewish life. News reporters and everyone else in the city knew better than to seek out Silver from sundown Friday to sundown Saturday, the Jewish Sabbath.

In the early 1970s, Silver moved from practicing law to a government job. He worked as a law secretary to a civil court judge in Manhattan, performing legal research and helping the judge write opinions. Courthouse jobs come with a lot of downtime, some of which Silver used to strike up a friendship with Brian Meara, who before his lobbying days was a New York City court officer. "We spent time in the same courtroom and talked quite a bit and talked basically about sports and politics and maybe some comparative religion," Meara remembered.

The late 1960s and early 1970s were a time of ferment in Manhattan politics. In 1966, Carmine DeSapio—the last leader of the infamous Tammany Hall political machine to wield real power—was pushed from his perch atop the Greenwich Village political organization by future mayor Ed Koch. President Richard Nixon's hawkish republicanism was popular nationally, but in Manhattan politicians were liberal.

Bella Abzug was an exemplar of the liberalism that carried the day in Silver's neighborhood and in much of the rest of Manhattan.

Abzug ran for Congress in 1970 against Leonard Farbstein, the incumbent and a fellow Democrat, who represented a liberal district that stretched from West Eighty-Third Street on the Upper West Side south to bohemian Greenwich Village, and then east to Silver's Lower East Side turf. In 1966 and 1968, Farbstein turned away strong primary challenges from City Council member Ted Weiss. Abzug was a far tougher foe, and she ran to Farbstein's left, complaining among other things that he was too slow to oppose the Vietnam War, which took tens of thousands of American lives.

A *New York Times* story about the race called
Farbstein "liberal but unexciting." Abzug toppled him in
the primary by about 2,700 votes. In a fundraising ad in
the *Village Voice*, Abzug labeled her general election
opponent, radio host Barry Farber, as "a Nixon-Agnew
Republican hawk who's got a pile of money to spend and
an outspoken peace candidate—Bella—to shoot at."
Abzug beat Farber by 8,690 votes.

In this milieu, Silver launched his political career.

He ran in 1974 in a Democratic primary for a City
Council seat that covered a swath of lower Manhattan.
The incumbent, Miriam Friedlander, won the seat the
year before but had to defend her job in a special election
because a court ruling changed the district's boundaries.
Friedlander was so far to the left that Ed Koch—at the
time a congressman—described her as "an old-time
Marxist, a member of the Bronx Communist Party." This
was at a time in America when being labeled a
Communist was an epithet. Yet Friedlander's political
philosophy fit her East Village base. Silver's base in the
Lower East Side was liberal and a birthplace of the
American labor movement. But Silver's neighbors
weren't as far to the left as East Village voters in the
neighborhood next door.

Silver, one of six candidates for the seat, finished
second in the early tallies, which variously put him
between 30 and 143 votes behind Friedlander. The
differing counts put the outcome in doubt. Six days after
the election, Silver and six campaign workers showed up
at a New York City Board of Elections warehouse in
Manhattan near the Holland Tunnel, where they hoped
to figure out the correct election result by inspecting the
180 voting machines used in the contest. "We're taking
down every number," Silver said in a voice described by
a *New York Times* reporter as having "more
determination than hope."[3]

The final, official count put Friedlander at 4,237 votes
and Silver at 4,142, a margin of 95 votes. The other four

candidates trailed well behind. Silver sued, and several weeks later a judge ordered a new vote because the instructions given Spanish-speaking voters "were in part incorrect and were generally confusing." Silver and Friedlander also agreed that, somehow, 303 people who voted should not have, either because they were not registered or because they were registered with other parties.

Alas for Silver, the judge's order for a new vote was overturned. The original result stood. Friedlander kept her seat in the November general election. She served on the City Council until 1991.

Silver didn't give up. Two years later, in 1976, he ran for the state Assembly seat in the district that covered his neighborhood. Silver won the primary by 1,300 votes. He trounced his Republican opponent in the general election by more than 10,000 votes.

In Albany, the state capital, Silver soon came across his old friend Meara, who had moved on from being a court officer to being a lobbyist for the State Court Officers Association. "I hadn't even known he was running for the Assembly, because we had lost touch a little bit," Meara recalled. "I don't want to say I showed him around, but we spent time together."

The hotel where Silver stayed during Assembly sessions had a TV in its lobby. "I would go there with other people and eat kosher pizza and watch ball games," Meara said. One of Silver's colleagues in his early Assembly years was fellow Manhattanite Jerrold Nadler, who years later became a Democratic congressman and, after the 2018 election, chairman of the House Judiciary Committee. Another was Chuck Schumer of Brooklyn, who became the Democratic leader of the U.S. Senate and, after the 2020 election, its powerful majority leader.

Silver built his political career in the state Assembly. Albany isn't as glamorous as Washington—but state government has as much or more influence on Americans' lives than the federal government. Silver took interest in its details. He could talk at length about the minutiae of state laws and legislation, and he made his way in part by staying attuned to his constituents.

During his first weeks in office in 1977, Silver and Nadler worked on a bill to require 60 days' notice before the closing of any New York City subway station. In 1981, Silver attended a press conference outside a shelter for homeless men in the East Village to urge the city not to build another. "This community is already shouldering its responsibility. ... Put them elsewhere," he said.

Silver advocated stronger state gun-control laws and expanded drug treatment in state prisons. As chairman of the Assembly Elections Committee, he pushed reforms to political campaign finance rules.

He could not steer clear of a big New York political scandal in the mid-1980s that was his first public brush with ethical trouble.

Silver was reported in 1986 to have invested in CitySource, Inc., a company run by Bronx political boss Stanley Friedman. CitySource was accused of fraudulently obtaining a $22.7 million city contract to produce handheld computers for the city Parking Violations Bureau. Traffic agents used the computers to write parking tickets. It was the biggest political scandal of Mayor Ed Koch's administration and was thought to be one reason for the March 1986 suicide of Donald Manes, a former Queens borough president and Democratic power broker.

Friedman was convicted of bribing a state National Guard official in an effort to sell some of the handheld computers. Three of Friedman's business associates were convicted of related charges. Silver was among several prominent politicians who invested in the company; another was former New York governor Hugh Carey. Silver said a stockbroker persuaded him to buy 500 CitySource shares. He decided later to buy another 700 shares. He said he didn't know Friedman was involved in the company until after he bought the stock, and that, in any event, he lost money. Silver was not charged in the case.

Five years later, another politician's scandal helped advance Silver's career.

In December 1991, Assembly Speaker Mel Miller was convicted in federal court in a complicated real-estate-fraud scheme that involved using inside information to profit from buying and selling co-op apartments in Brooklyn. Miller eventually won his appeal. But in the short term, the conviction forced him from office.

By this time, Silver was chairman of the Assembly Codes Committee, which considered matters related to the state's criminal and civil justice system. Knowledge of the state's civil and penal codes was one of Silver's qualifications for the chairmanship. His loyalty to Miller was another. As speaker, Miller decided who led Assembly committees. That Silver attained an important chairmanship showed he was playing a smart inside game. As a member of the Assembly leadership's inner circle, Silver was one of several Assembly members in a position to take Miller's post as speaker.

Silver quickly decided against seeking the speakership and cast his lot with Saul Weprin, a longtime Assembly member from Queens. When Weprin was elected speaker in December 1991, he reciprocated by naming Silver chairman of the Assembly Ways and Means Committee. That position gave Silver a big say in state spending and boosted his political power.

Ill health shortened Weprin's speakership. In January 1994, barely two years after he won the office, Weprin suffered a stroke that left him unable to speak. Because Weprin could not speak, he could not resign his job or give any instructions about how he wanted the Assembly to proceed. For two days, his family and staff kept his illness a secret from everyone except his closest political allies. Silver used that time to maneuver himself into position to take Weprin's place.

13

News of Weprin's illness finally broke on Thursday, January 20. By the next day, Friday, January 21, Silver had buttoned up enough support from other Assembly members to be elected interim speaker. By the time Weprin died on February 11, Silver was firmly in power. He was now one of the "three men in a room"—the governor, the Assembly speaker, and the Senate majority leader—who controlled much of what happened in Albany.

George Pataki's election as governor in November 1994 brought Republicans new power in the state capitol. For the first time in decades, they controlled the governor's office as well as the state Senate, which was led by Majority Leader Joseph Bruno. Silver was the only Democrat left among the three men in a room.

Democrats were on the ropes. Also, the state party was $800,000 in debt. By New York political tradition, if the governor was not a Democrat, leadership of the state party fell to the next-ranking state office holder—who in this case was Sheldon Silver.

Silver recruited Judith Hope, a Long Islander and former aide to Governor Hugh Carey, to help raise money to get the party back on its feet. Hope came to see Silver as an advocate of strong political and governmental ethics.

"Judith, we are going to build a firewall between government business and political business. Do you understand?" Silver told her.

"He went on to say it was his observation that most political people got in trouble when they confuse the two, and when they use one to advance the interests of the other," Hope wrote in 2015. "He specifically cautioned me never to 'ask any favors' of him in his role as Assemblyman and Speaker, and added that he would do me the same courtesy.

"True to his promise, over the seven years that I knew and worked with him, he never once asked me to do anything inappropriate or questionable," Hope wrote.[4]

But Silver's request of Hope was at odds with his practice. He had no trouble seeking the kind of questionable favors he asked Hope to avoid. This was proven by the deal he arranged early in his speakership between Jay Goldberg and Leonard Litwin.

Litwin may have known that by giving property-tax-appeal business to Goldberg, he was doing Silver more than a simple favor.

Litwin gave some of his company's tax-appeal business to Goldberg as the Legislature battled over the state's rent-control laws in 1997.[5] Glenwood owned more than 20 buildings subject to the rent laws. The outcome of the fight mattered greatly to Litwin's business.

Pataki's election as governor threatened the regulations that governed the rents of millions of New York City residents. Pataki's Republican colleague, Senate Majority Leader Bruno, vowed to end the rent regulations, which dated to the 1940s. As the only Democrat among the three men in a room, Silver had to stop the two Republicans from having their way.

In public, Silver supported tenants. But rent-control advocates came to believe that, in 1997, Silver didn't push back hard enough against Bruno—or against Pataki, who countered Bruno's vow to end rent regulation with a plan for a gradual phaseout.

One day, as that year's final rent bill was being drafted, tenant advocate Michael McKee saw Glenwood lobbyist Meara shuttle 17 times between Silver's office and the Senate offices on the other side of the state capitol, where Bruno worked. "We were wondering what the hell Brian was doing," McKee recounted.[6]

He realized later that Meara was probably working to make the final bill more to the liking of Glenwood and other landlords.

Most of the 2.7 million tenants of rent-regulated apartments in the state were not directly hurt by parts of the new law that weakened their protections. But some of them were.

The new law said tenants paying $2,000 or more per month in rent would have their apartments decontrolled if they earned more than $175,000 per year. That income level—down from $250,000 per year in the previous statute—was a win for landlords like Litwin, whose luxury buildings were filled with high-income tenants. But it didn't matter much to a majority of rent-regulated tenants, whose incomes were much lower and whose average monthly rents were around $600.[7]

The new law also let landlords raise rents on some vacant apartments by 20 percent—another landlord victory.

Some tenants might have seen the new law as a mixed bag. But tenant advocates viewed any changes to the law—even those that only affected higher-income people—as a step backward. A newsletter issued by a tenant advocacy group quoted Joseph Strasburg, a lobbyist for the Rent Stabilization Association, a landlord group: "The new law provides the most sweeping benefits and relief measures for property owners in the history of rent law negotiations. Never before has the housing industry gained so much without giving up anything in return."[8]

Michael McKee was convinced Silver betrayed tenants. "He sold us out big time, and it was a shock," he said.

Silver didn't limit his relationship-building to Glenwood and other residential landlords. Around the time he regularly lunched with Litwin and engaged in the 1997 rent-regulation battle, Silver met Steven Witkoff, a downtown Manhattan real estate developer. Downtown Manhattan is home to Wall Street and was once the center of the United States' financial business. It was also in Silver's Assembly district. Downtown's fortunes were important to Silver's political fortunes.

Witkoff recalled that he met Silver through Merryl Tisch, a philanthropist and politically-connected heir to the Loews Corporation fortune who from 2009 to 2016 was head of the New York State Board of Regents, which oversees education policy.

At lunches and meetings, Witkoff and Silver talked about the late 1990s revitalization of downtown Manhattan. "I thought we needed to promote downtown Manhattan as a 24-hour city," Witkoff said. Even in the years before the devastating September 11 attacks, downtown's growth was an iffy proposition—as Witkoff put it, "It was 50-50 as to whether it was going well or not."

Witkoff said that, when they met, he always found Silver "cordial and professional." He hoped his relationship with Silver would help him promote downtown—and help the success of his own business.

Silver was a presence in the Financial District, on the Lower East Side, in Chinatown, and in other parts of his district. He helped people with housing or medical problems and was involved in school issues. More than a few of his constituents kept the number for Silver's office by their kitchen telephones. "He met with people. Shelly was at the street fairs, to [sic] job fairs and CUNY [City University of New York] fairs to encourage people toward higher education," longtime Silver aide Judy Rapfogel wrote in 2016. "He was in his mobile 'office,' he visited the housing projects so that he could talk to people and listen to the issues that made a difference to them."[9] He was also a presence through his involvement in the Bialystoker Synagogue and his longtime relationships with neighbors.

Some Silver constituents could not deny his interest in their problems. One of his regular causes was the state's Loft Law, which lets people living in abandoned commercial buildings convert them to residences. Many lofts existed in Silver's district.

The Loft Law had to be renewed every few years, and sometimes legislative negotiations over its extension dragged on late at night. One night in 1999, Chuck DeLaney—a member of the city's Loft Board, which oversees disputes between landlords and loft tenants—got a call from Silver. "He wanted to discuss what he saw as the likely progression of events," DeLaney said. It was past 11 p.m., and, because the negotiations were going poorly, the Loft Law would have to be allowed to expire for a short time. At the end of the conversation, DeLaney thanked Silver for the late-night call.

"That's OK," Silver said. Then he asked, "Guess what I'm doing?" He paused, then answered his own question: "I'm eating lunch."

But his stance on issues like housing, transit, schools, and homelessness was just part of Silver's political life. His constituents didn't know he'd leveraged one of his political relationships to get fees from Glenwood Management through Jay Goldberg.

As his power grew, Silver looked out more for himself.

Chapter 2 – Power

Power in the state Legislature is a matter of "survival of the fittest," said Alfred E. Smith, the storied early 20th-century governor of New York. "The man who fights best and accomplishes most for his constituents and his party gains positions of leadership," Smith wrote in *The Citizen and His Government,* a 1935 book meant to instruct readers in the workings of politics.[1]

As Assembly speaker, Sheldon Silver accomplished the most for his constituents and his party in negotiations with the governor and Senate majority leader—the "three men in a room." Joseph Bruno, the Senate majority leader for much of Silver's speakership, told the story of the 1995 budget negotiation in a memoir.

Silver, who at the time was the only Democrat among the three men, negotiated that year's budget with two Republicans, Bruno and Governor George Pataki. Silver was outnumbered. The two Republicans in the room controlled the Senate and the governor's office. But neither Pataki nor Bruno could get anything done without the approval of Silver and the Assembly Democrats. So the three men sat down to work things out.

Some of Silver's fellow Assembly Democrats wanted to build a library in Brooklyn. This was outside Silver's Manhattan district. But to keep his job as speaker, Silver heeded requests like this from other Democratic Assembly members.

"I need $62 million for a library in Brooklyn," said Silver.

"Done," said Pataki.

"Hell no, it's not OK with me!" said Bruno, whose power base was in the Albany area. He didn't care about the wants of Silver's colleagues in New York City. "I'm not going for that just to make him happy," he told the governor. Bruno wanted his share too.

"What's it going to take for you?" asked Pataki.

"How about $62 million?" Bruno asked. If the Assembly could get an extra $62 million for its pet projects, he didn't see why the Senate should not have the same amount. Bruno wanted to spread the money around. He demanded $40 million for upgrades to the Albany airport and $11 million for infrastructure projects sought by Senate Republicans from Long Island. The remaining $11 million he'd divide among the pet projects of other Republican senators.

That was the deal. Silver, Bruno, and Pataki walked out of the negotiations happy. In his memoir, Bruno made it seem like he got the better end of the bargain. [2] But remember: Silver was the only Democrat in the room. If Silver hadn't spoken up, he never would have gotten money for the Brooklyn library. He pulled it off by getting two Republicans to go along with his plan.

When Silver cut that year's budget deal with Pataki and Bruno, he pursued policies his members wanted. "What becomes important is whether the leadership is in touch with the rank and file and is reflecting their goals in the negotiation," said Richard Brodsky, a Westchester County Democrat who served in the Assembly with Silver. "Shelly is always viewed as essentially representing the view of the rank and file."

That Silver had such control over the Assembly's decisions on important issues seemed right to many legislators. Brodsky felt Silver's handling of things wasn't much different from what went on in the other 49 states. "You do not have rank and file negotiating large issues anywhere," he argued. Even when Silver dealt with a Republican governor, Brodsky said, "things that the Assembly really wanted, he [Silver] got delivered in the budget. ... And the members knew it."

Yet Silver expressed willingness to give up some of this power and reform the three-men-in-a-room system. "The era of 'three-men-in-a-room' budget-making is over. As one of those three men, I say, 'Good riddance,'" he claimed in an April 1998 op-ed in *Newsday*, the Long Island newspaper.

Silver promised in the op-ed to be more open and consider other officials' views in setting policy. He also promised to give more power over spending to legislative committees. "In the past, too many of these decisions were left to legislative leaders," he wrote. [3]

Silver's op-ed idea ran up against a reality of politics and politicians: it required him to cede some power. No politician cedes power unless they must. Silver's constituents in lower Manhattan did not clamor for this change. And giving up the power he shared with the governor and Senate majority leader would make it more difficult for Silver to keep his fellow Democrats happy. Silver had no incentive to cede his influence as one of the three men in a room.

It was true, as Silver wrote in his op-ed, that Assembly and Senate committees pored over the details of the state budget. But the real decision-making power stayed in his hands, and in the hands of the Senate majority leader and the governor.

Silver had other cards to play besides making sure his members got what they wanted in the state budget. He also controlled a pot of state money that he could allocate as he pleased. Most of the money was doled out to Assembly members' pet projects, or to community organizations in their districts. Silver used this power as another means to maintain his grip on the speakership. If other Democrats didn't toe Silver's line, they would lose access to the money he doled out.

But there was a side to his control over this and other little details that irked his Democratic Assembly colleagues. "His shortcomings were largely that he was remote and somewhat controlling. ... That did him no good. Shelly didn't have any friends in the membership," said Brodsky. [4]

Silver's fellow Democrats saw him as aloof and uncaring. They complained they got little to no face time with him—and came to think of themselves as sheep merely following orders. They went to the capitol, voted for bills the leadership wanted, and went home. They wanted more say about the laws they passed but felt Silver and the other two men in the room hoarded the power. "I thought we were so leadership driven. ... I would drive home from Albany and I would say in my head, 'I don't need to be here. They just want my vote 'Yes.'... I was ready to quit," recalled Assemblywoman Sandy Galef, another Democrat from Westchester County.[5]

His quiet nature didn't help. For such a powerful man, he was not always noticeable. He was known for saying little. A former colleague in the Assembly called Silver "sphinx-like." Arthur Luxenberg, who became Silver's law firm colleague eight years into his speakership, called him "very reserved" and "very quiet and guarded."[6]

Sometimes, silence is good strategy. The less Silver said—the fewer opinions he expressed—the freer he was to act when the time came to decide an issue. But his quiet nature kept him from developing friendships with his Democratic allies.

Silver's fellow Assembly Democrats also complained he spent too much time with lobbyists. Even Assembly committee chairs couldn't get one-on-one time with Silver. "It was hard to get a meeting with Shelly about anything," said Edward Sullivan, a former legislator from Manhattan's Upper West Side who chaired the Assembly Higher Education Committee. "You would put in a request for a meeting and two weeks later you'd hear, 'We'll get back to you.' Which is very bad."

In his failure to get along personally with many Assembly Democrats, Silver ignored one of Al Smith's maxims: "The legislator who wishes to get many of his measures successfully through both houses [the Assembly and Senate] must be ... an organizer and promoter of good will at the State Capitol. ... He must make himself liked and respected by other members of the Legislature."[7]

One Assembly member with issues about Silver's rule was Michael Bragman, a moderate-to-conservative Democrat from a district near Syracuse, in upstate central New York. Bragman was the Assembly majority leader early in Silver's time as speaker. Bragman and Silver were once allies—they both backed Saul Weprin's election as speaker in 1991. But a few years after Silver became speaker, Bragman began maneuvering to unseat him. A *New York Times* story in November 1997—three and a half years into Silver's speakership—noted that Bragman made no secret of his wish to take over. "Mike is obviously campaigning for the job. Shelly has told him flatly that he is not going anywhere, and to cut it out," an anonymous source told the newspaper. At the time, the story said, Silver was in no danger.[8]

Silver's standing with his members deteriorated in the two and a half years after the article appeared.

Assemblywoman Galef was unhappy enough with the system that she became interested in how legislatures in other states worked. Galef organized a trip to Boston to learn about the Massachusetts Legislature, which suffered a scandal in 1996 when the speaker of its House—equivalent to New York's Assembly—resigned after pleading guilty to charges involving tax evasion and accepting gifts from lobbyists. "They seemed to be doing a lot of very interesting things," Galef recalled—such as giving legislators more say in committees and televising legislative sessions.

Silver labeled Galef's Boston trip a "junket."

"A few of my colleagues went, but because he said it was a junket, people were not interested in going," Galef said. She was disappointed her reform ideas were quashed. "Shelly Silver—he turned his back on me."[9]

Assembly members' frustrations boiled over one night early in 2000 when Bragman attended a New York Knicks game with about a dozen of his colleagues.

The event turned into a gripe session about Silver and his leadership. Among those at the game was Thomas Manton, a former congressman who was then the leader of the Queens Democratic Party. Manton was not an Assembly member, but, as a political boss, he had heard the stories. He and Bragman talked. Bragman thought Manton would back him if he moved against Silver.

In the following weeks, Bragman gradually and quietly built his support. By May 18, he was ready to move. "Many Assembly colleagues have come to me with great concern over the leadership in our house," he wrote other Assembly members in a letter that day. "I have shared their views and concerns and have finally decided to respond to their call for new leadership."

His language was stronger in a news release issued the same day as the letter. It said Democratic Assembly members "want a more meaningful role in the legislative process. They want to be more informed and participate fully in decision making. Most of all, they want an end to secret deal-making by three men in a room."

"At best, Assemblyman Silver's style as speaker has been secretive and aloof," the news release said. "Many times, he has placed his own personal interests ahead of the interests of the Majority Conference and the Democratic Party."

"He has surrounded himself with paid lobbyists and other non-legislators who are seeking to influence members on how to vote on this matter," Bragman said. "Working through these agents, he has sought to portray our effort as an upstate versus downstate conflict. This is wrong. We have a solid majority of Democratic members representing all parts of the state who share an overwhelming desire to effect this change now."[10]

Edward Sullivan was to Bragman's left on most issues. Nonetheless, he aligned himself with Bragman's coup effort. When Bragman went public, Sullivan called Silver to explain himself.

"This is not personal," Sullivan told him.

"Ed, it is very personal," Silver replied. Sullivan said Silver was offended he would back someone trying to oust him from his job.

Brodsky, though a Silver supporter, also recognized the speaker's shortcomings. He saw an irony in the leadership fight: Bragman was just as aloof as Silver, and "not personally warm and likable." Bragman also wasn't popular with his colleagues. "It was a sign of Shelly's unpopularity that a guy as unpopular as Bragman got as close as he did." And like Silver, Bragman "was viewed as very close to the lobbying community." Yet, like Silver, Bragman was "smart, and an effective operative." In the end, Brodsky believed, not much would have changed if Bragman became speaker.

In the days before the Assembly debate and vote on his coup attempt, Bragman claimed to have "50 rock-solid [Democratic] votes." But he went public early enough to give Silver plenty of time to counter-organize.

Silver called in his chits with political leaders like Tom Manton, the Queens political boss, who abandoned Bragman's candidacy. Bragman also failed to get support he wanted from Carl McCall, then the state's leading Black politician—even though Bragman was an early backer of McCall's 2002 gubernatorial candidacy.

When it came time on May 22, 2000, to debate whether Silver should remain speaker, Assemblyman Martin Luster, a Democrat from the upstate Finger Lakes area— his district included Ithaca, home to Cornell University— argued that one of Silver's excesses was holding too much control over some corners of state spending.

"We need an accounting of funds that are controlled by the Speaker, funds that are appropriated in the budget and for which we have no mechanism of tracing," Luster said in a floor speech that day.[11] There was no public disclosure of the specific expenditures Luster worried about. All anyone knew was the total amount of the spending printed in the state budget.

During the debate, Galef said she was angry about an article on the New York Legislature in the March 2000 issue of *Governing* magazine. Its headline was, "Yesterday's Legislature: In the old days, legislatures were secretive and autocratic. In Albany, the old days continue." The article said the three men in a room ruled Albany too tightly, and that other legislatures had more open processes for discussing issues and considering legislation. New York's Legislature was "not member-driven in the way that most of the other 49" were, the article said.

"I'm embarrassed by this," Galef said on the Assembly floor. "How do I stand up and talk about this secretive and autocratic system?"

When his turn came, Bragman made an argument about the way Silver doled out favors. "Everyone here has felt the frustration and the dissatisfaction with the current situation," he said. "Member after member is forced to go to this speaker to ask for everything from paper clips to chairmanships, from parking spaces to staff needs. And you feel like your requests are being kept in a favor bank. ... Either you do what the speaker wants, or you never get what you're entitled to."

Democratic conferences—meetings at which Assembly Democrats discussed policy priorities and Assembly business—were no longer a place to seriously hash out issues, Bragman said. They were "meaningless and don't provide the opportunity for debate. And we all know that those who dare disagree with the speaker in conference are admonished for their actions and encouraged to never do it again."

But by the time Bragman spoke, most of his support had fallen away, and Silver had brought enough members back into the fold to keep his job. Silver's allies spoke up in the floor debate. Brodsky, always a Silver supporter, alleged that Bragman and his backers sought to "turn anger and ambition into institutional change."

26

Ronald Canestrari, whose district was in the Albany area, pointed out that Silver ably represented the Assembly before the Republican governor and Republican Senate majority leader. His comments reflected the view among many Democrats that Silver had done a good job looking out for them while they were in a weakened, minority position. "Sheldon Silver has advanced proposals that we, as a conference, have espoused, have fought over," he said. "And maybe that does not please all of us all of the time, but there has to be a leader taking direction from his or her members. We do have that."

Catherine Nolan, a Silver ally from Queens, said Bragman's takeover try was "an unfair attack" on Silver, who she believed helped Democrats accomplish a great deal. She quoted Al Smith from *The Citizen and His Government*: "He said, 'The officeholders come and go and some of them, only some, are able to leave an imprint on the statute books.'"

"But the Democratic Party has left that imprint," Nolan said. "This Democratic majority has left that imprint in education and in labor and in transit." Her argument was that Silver had won a lot for his party— and she didn't want to risk those accomplishments by toppling him from power.

In the end, Bragman had 19 Democratic votes, including his own. Silver had 78 Democrats on his side, more than enough to retain power. The final tally, which included the votes of Democratic and Republican legislators, was 85 to 63 in Silver's favor.

Most legislators who opposed Silver went unpunished. Sullivan stayed on as chairman of the Assembly Higher Education Committee. At the last minute, Sullivan realized Bragman would lose, so he supported Silver in the final vote. "Most of the people who were on the Bragman side, the vast majority of them, kept whatever positions they had that were at the hands of the Speaker," he said.

Sullivan and other legislators argued that the coup attempt made Silver a better and stronger leader. Over the following months, Silver built up his relationships with legislators who felt ignored by him. Sullivan asked for a sit-down with Silver, thinking it would be no more than 15 minutes. "We talked for an hour and a half," he recalled. The two men spoke about what they had wanted in their lives when they were younger. Silver admitted he had hoped for a pro basketball career. "His dream as a kid was to be point guard for the New York Knicks," Sullivan said.

"Shelly is Orthodox Jewish. I was—am—a not really active Catholic. We talked about how that affects our work. It was a good meeting, a meeting you would have with friends. It was the first meeting I had with Shelly, even though we were both elected at the same time."[12]

The coup attempt was such a close call Silver feared it might happen again, said a former staffer. Silver and his staff took notice whenever groups of as few as four or five Assembly members went out to dinner or socialized together, this person said. After all, Bragman's coup got rolling when just a dozen Assembly members attended that Knicks game. Silver didn't want to take any chances.

Retribution fell hard on Bragman. Silver made sure he was shunned. He lost his position as majority leader, and the extra pay that went with it. He also lost all the power and staff he'd amassed in 20 years in the Legislature, and was moved to a smaller office. He remained popular in his district. Bragman's Syracuse-area constituents reelected him by a wide margin to another two-year term in November 2000. But the loss of his influence in the capitol was hard to bear.

Amy Paulin was elected to the Assembly from Westchester County for the first time in November 2000, after Bragman's coup attempt fizzled. When she took office that January, she was assigned a seat in one of the back rows of the Assembly chamber. Bragman, banished to the back of the chamber as part of his punishment, sat next to her.

"Don't talk to me," Bragman would tell her. "Because that's not good for you."[13]

Bragman quit the Assembly in December 2001, in the middle of his term.

In the end, Bragman's coup attempt came to naught. Though Silver was forced to improve his relationships with his fellow Democrats, the system didn't change. It was as dysfunctional as ever. It still lacked enough public input and openness, and it still lacked accountability. Silver called the shots. He tended to tell his members, "This is what we are going to do," Sandy Galef recalled years later.

Silver kept the $79,500 salary and $41,500 bonus he earned as speaker. He kept control over who became legislative committee chairs and got leadership jobs, which also paid bonuses. And he kept control over tens of millions of dollars in state taxpayer money he could dole out to Assembly members' pet causes and programs.

From 1997 to 2001—a period that included the time Silver fought to remain speaker—just one major bill passed by the Assembly had a committee hearing.[14] "I never felt like the committees really worked," said Galef. As before, members of the Assembly and Senate left major policy decisions to their leaders, who cut deals with each other and the governor in private meetings. Despite Silver's vows of reform, the three-men-in-a-room system lived on.

Silver curbed his relationship with lobbyists by making it harder for them to meet with him. "Until 2000, I could go see him any time I wanted," said lobbyist Brian Meara about his old friend. Because of the Bragman coup attempt, "my access became an issue." Instead of walking into Silver's office when he liked, Meara had to make appointments. He still saw Silver "daily, or almost daily."[15]

Otherwise, Silver's dealings with Albany's lobbyists and influence peddlers were largely unchanged.

Lobbyists and pressure groups understood how the system worked and played it to their advantage. A notorious example in the Silver-Bruno-Pataki era was the Health Care Workforce Recruitment and Retention Act of 2002, which awarded $1.8 billion in raises to hospital workers represented by Service Employees International Union 1199.

The law passed after it was agreed upon by Silver, Bruno, and Pataki. Perhaps health-care workers deserved better pay. But they didn't have to make a case before the Assembly and Senate committees that dealt with health and insurance issues—those committees held no hearings on the matter and never even saw the bill before it reached the Assembly and Senate floors. The bill cleared the Legislature late at night, "without any chance for legislators to even read it," said a report by the Brennan Center for Justice, one of a slew of good-government groups that has complained about New York state government for decades.[16]

The lack of hearings and the speed with which the bill became law didn't matter to Governor Pataki. He didn't care that the Legislature conducted so much business in secret. "The process is the process," he said. "But what I'm interested in is the results."[17]

Chapter 3 – The firm

As Sheldon Silver built his political career in the 1980s and 1990s, two men who eventually became his good friends—Perry Weitz and Arthur Luxenberg—were building legal careers.

Before they teamed up to start their own firm, Weitz and Luxenberg worked for Morris J. Eisen PC, named for its lead lawyer and headquartered in the iconic Woolworth Building in lower Manhattan. Morris Eisen was one of New York's biggest personal injury law firms, and in 1986 it employed 40 lawyers and grossed about $20 million in contingency fees. [1] The firm's caseload included "motor vehicle accidents, trip and fall cases, construction cases like when somebody falls from a building. Things like that," Weitz explained. [2] Weitz, Morris J. Eisen's son-in-law, began working for the firm while he studied at Hofstra Law School on Long Island.

When Weitz passed the bar exam in 1985, he joined Morris Eisen as a trial lawyer. Luxenberg, who also passed the bar in 1985 after graduating from Benjamin Cardozo Law School, worked at Eisen in a legal research role.

The Eisen firm often made headlines. It brought the first lawsuit against the Palestine Liberation Organization for the 1985 Mediterranean Sea hijacking of the *Achille Lauro* cruise ship, during which 69-year-old wheelchair-bound Leon Klinghoffer was shot dead and dumped overboard. The hijacking made headlines around the world. Eisen's firm sued on behalf of people traumatized by the two-day ordeal. Its lawyers handled the case with skill. When the Italian company that owned the MS *Achille Lauro* tried to get the suit dismissed, Morris J. Eisen PC fought all the way to the U.S. Supreme Court. The justices ruled in Eisen's favor in 1989, allowing the case to continue.

But by the time the *Achille Lauro* case was settled in 1997, Morris J. Eisen PC was long out of business, brought down by federal prosecutors who found the firm routinely paid off witnesses and faked evidence. Many Eisen lawyers were crooked to the core.

One Eisen specialty was suing the City of New York in motor vehicle cases. In 1978, Shmuel Aboud was hurt when his car hit a pothole on the city-owned Queensboro Bridge. Morris Eisen sued on Aboud's behalf, with help from a witness named Arnold Lustig. The case went to trial in May 1984. But before the jury reached a verdict, two Eisen lawyers negotiated a $700,000 settlement with the city.

At another trial—in October 1984—Eisen lawyers called Lustig to testify in a suit against the city by Naomi Schwartz, whose husband was killed while changing a tire on the Whitestone Expressway in the Bronx. The jury in that case awarded Schwartz $2 million, which was reduced on appeal to $1.2 million.

The city's lawyers thought it odd that, in the span of a few months, Eisen called the same man to testify in two traffic cases originating in different parts of the city. They also thought it odd that in the Aboud case, Lustig testified under the alias Harlow Lustic. Even stranger were records showing that on the day Naomi Schwartz's husband died changing his tire in the Bronx, Arnold Lustig was jailed on Rikers Island on what officials said was a charge involving stolen bonds.

It turned out that Lustig, a used-car salesman from Brooklyn, was paid $2,500 for his false testimony in both cases.

Suspicious city lawyers took the case to local prosecutors, and eventually the U.S. Department of Justice got involved. A federal grand jury indicted Eisen and seven colleagues on racketeering and conspiracy charges.[3]

In one case discussed in the indictment, Eisen's firm represented a woman named Carmela Pietrafessa who said she was hurt when she fell on a dangerous sidewalk outside a Grand Union supermarket in Manhattan. When her suit was tried in 1984, Eisen lawyer Evan Torgan called to the witness stand Helen Gaimari, who testified that she had tripped on the same sidewalk earlier, and that she had complained to the supermarket's staff to no avail. The jury awarded Pietrafessa $40,000.

Gaimari's daughter was Geraldine G. Morganti, the Eisen firm's office manager. Federal prosecutors said Morganti enlisted her mother to lie on the witness stand in the case.

Asking witnesses to lie was just one Eisen tactic. Eisen investigators and lawyers also faked evidence.

One of the firm's tricks involved making a photocopy of a 12-inch ruler. The copy machine would be set to shrink the copy of the ruler by several inches. Then the photocopy of the 12-inch ruler—reduced so that it was perhaps eight inches long—would be photographed next to a pothole where a Morris Eisen client allegedly tripped or fell. Next to the shrunken ruler, the pothole looked a lot bigger and more menacing in the photos offered as evidence in court.

A shrunken ruler wasn't the only way the Eisen firm made a pothole look bigger. In 1984, an Eisen employee filed a lawsuit that claimed he was hurt when he tripped over a pothole at Aqueduct Racetrack in Queens. Eisen investigator Marty Gabe went to the track's parking lot to find a suitable pothole. Once he found a good one, Gabe used a pickaxe to make it bigger. Morris Eisen himself negotiated a $15,000 settlement in the case.

In another case, an Eisen employee whacked a tire rim with a sledgehammer to exaggerate the damage the rim incurred in a car crash.

A prime example of the Eisen firm's gaming of the legal system was its handling of a December 1979 car crash that injured a woman named Beth Mulnick.

Mulnick was crossing a street near the intersection of First Avenue and East Fifty-Sixth Street in Manhattan when motorist Peter Kardaras struck her. Kardaras had borrowed the car from a friend, who had leased it. Kardaras's friend had an insurance policy on the car; so did the leasing company. Kardaras was also insured by a policy held by his father, a lawyer. It was a lot more car insurance than most people carried. Together, the insurance policies could pay hundreds of thousands of dollars in damages—a lot more than the money available from most car crashes.

Even the insurance company lawyers believed Mulnick was seriously hurt and deserved payment. Nonetheless, Eisen lawyer Joseph P. Napoli felt obliged to tip the scales in Mulnick's favor. Eisen paid a witness in the case to not show up in court. The firm paid another witness to lie. In the middle of the trial, before the case went to the jury for deliberation, the insurance companies negotiated with Morris Eisen himself a $1 million settlement.

Perry Weitz was not charged in the criminal case that brought down the Morris Eisen firm. But the indictment named him in connection with a medical malpractice suit tried in Manhattan Supreme Court. The plaintiff represented by the Eisen firm in that case was Susan Ippolito, who alleged that Dr. Walter Pizzi had failed to properly treat an injury to her leg. Napoli tried the case for Eisen. Napoli put on the witness stand Jody Weitz—whom he identified as an expert witness—to testify about the harm Ippolito had suffered at Dr. Pizzi's hands. Federal prosecutors said Jody Weitz's testimony was "false and misleading." They also noted that Napoli and others in the Eisen firm concealed "the fact that she was the sister of Morris J. Eisen's son-in-law Perry Weitz, an Eisen Firm attorney." The jury awarded Ippolito $1 million. Pizzi's lawyers settled the case with Eisen's firm for $650,000 rather than risk losing on appeal.

Morris J. Eisen and two other lawyers with the firm, Napoli and Harold M. Fishman, were convicted in March 1991 of racketeering and conspiracy. Morganti and two private investigators were also convicted of racketeering and conspiracy; a third investigator was convicted of conspiracy. A fourth investigator charged in the indictment pleaded guilty before the trial to the lesser charge of aiding bribery.

The prosecutors crowed about their big win, which came after a four-month trial. "I'm not aware of any comparable conviction involving a law firm in New York City or anywhere else," said Jerome C. Roth, who was the case's chief prosecutor.

All the convictions were upheld on appeal. Eisen served three years of a four-year prison sentence. Napoli and Fishman were also sentenced to prison. All three lawyers were disbarred.

The prosecutors weren't done. They pursued a case against Frank J. DeSalvo, a fourth Eisen lawyer. DeSalvo lied to a federal grand jury by saying it was pure coincidence that his cousin was an eyewitness on behalf of two Eisen clients in unrelated personal injury cases. He also said that when he'd called Helen Gaimari to testify in one of his cases, he had no idea she was Morganti's mother. DeSalvo was convicted of perjury and obstruction of justice and sentenced to 30 months in prison. He was disbarred too.

Perry Weitz worked about three years as an Eisen lawyer. Like his colleagues, he handled plenty of personal injury cases. He also took an interest in lawsuits by people sickened by asbestos, which for years were effectively banned in New York state courts.

Before 1986, New York state law required people sickened by asbestos to file lawsuits within three years of being exposed. This posed a problem for people with mesothelioma and other asbestos diseases, who get sick decades after they breathe in asbestos fibers. Their diagnoses cannot possibly be made within three years of their exposure. Because of this law, it was impossible for New Yorkers sickened by asbestos to seek damages in the state's courts.

After years of pressure by the AFL-CIO coalition of labor unions, New York's Legislature passed a law in 1986 that let people sickened by asbestos, or other materials or chemicals, sue within three years of their diagnosis. The law—a priority of then-governor Mario Cuomo—passed the Assembly and Senate by unanimous votes. Sheldon Silver was among the legislators who voted for the bill. Cuomo called the bill's passage "long overdue" and "a victory for justice."[4]

The new law was a boon to people unknowingly exposed to asbestos decades before they became sick. But Weitz recognized it would still be hard to bring asbestos cases in New York courts. Asbestos lawsuits were complicated and expensive and could ruin law firms that mishandled them. "The unions were having difficulty finding a plaintiffs' lawyer that wanted to handle the cases," Weitz said. "Most of these personal injury firms were small law firms, only 5 or 10 lawyers, and they had to sue some of the biggest corporations in the country."

One of Weitz's law school friends was the son of an AFL-CIO lawyer. He connected the union group with Weitz. "They came to me and asked me if I would be interested in pursuing some of these cases." Weitz realized he had a lot to learn about asbestos litigation and how it worked. "So, I went around the country to other states where they allowed asbestos cases to go forward," Weitz said. He traveled to Texas, Ohio, and North Carolina. "I met with some lawyers who had handled these cases and read some of the transcripts of those trials and saw some of the documents."[5]

Weitz was outraged by what he read in court papers and learned from other lawyers. The companies knew for decades that asbestos was killing their employees. In Weitz's view, corporate executives made a cruel cost-benefit analysis. The companies preferred to "continue to not tell anybody that asbestos caused these terrible diseases because they were making so much money." They profited greatly from selling dangerous products—and were content to do so.

"I was a young, ambitious lawyer at the time—I was in my late 20s, and it inspired me," Weitz said. "These families had been ruined as a result of this terrible exposure to asbestos and these terrible illnesses."

Back in New York, Weitz took his ideas to colleagues at Morris Eisen. He saw opportunity. The cases could pay big to lawyers who figured out how to present them to judges and juries. But asbestos litigation was complicated, and far different from the accident and personal injury cases the firm handled. Morris Eisen lawyers were skeptical, Weitz told an interviewer in 2014.[6] "So I decided to go out on my own and begin this asbestos practice."

Arthur Luxenberg was one of Weitz's closest colleagues at Eisen. "He was a law guy; I was a trial guy," Weitz said. "We were both the bottom guys on the totem pole."

Luxenberg worked in the background, as a legal researcher. His job was to solve legal puzzles in hope of putting the best spin on the firm's cases. "I was the guy who had answers, the guy who could figure solutions," Luxenberg said. He was sometimes invisible to clients even though he was essential to their cases. Weitz had a more up-front role, bringing in clients and trying cases. "He had an uncanny ability to get business," Luxenberg said in a 2006 interview.

By 1989—around the same time a federal grand jury was deep into its investigation of the Eisen firm—Weitz and Luxenberg were fully on their own. They sublet office space from the law firm Mudge Rose Guthrie Alexander & Ferdon, where future president Richard Nixon practiced law in the early 1960s. "Those were tumultuous times. We worked 15, 16, 17 hours a day," Luxenberg said. They brought in another Morris Eisen lawyer, Gary

Klein, who over the years grew into a managerial role in the firm.

Weitz & Luxenberg started out mainly as an asbestos firm—and thanks to the change in New York law, it got plenty of asbestos cases.

In 1991, Weitz & Luxenberg reported getting a $76 million verdict for 36 men exposed to asbestos while working at the Brooklyn Navy Yard in the 1940s and 1950s. If Weitz & Luxenberg took its usual one-third fee, it would have kept $25.3 million of the award. If the remainder of the award was divided equally among the plaintiffs, each of them would have walked away from the case with about $1.41 million.

In June 1995, Weitz & Luxenberg won a $45 million jury verdict that was split among the estates of several asbestos victims. One of them, George Adinolfi, died of mesothelioma at age 52. He told his wife, Sandra, that after he graduated from high school in 1958, he spent several years packing asbestos insulation in walls of new buildings all over New York City. "He said, 'San, that's what I worked with,'" his wife told *Newsday*. "I said, 'Not everybody gets it, right, George?' He said, 'No. Not everybody.' But it was in the back of his mind all the time."[7] Perry Weitz said the verdict was the largest awarded by a New York state jury to that date.

In 1996, Weitz & Luxenberg won a $64.65 million verdict that was shared among four asbestos plaintiffs. Business boomed. By 1998, Weitz & Luxenberg claimed a portfolio of 10,000 asbestos lawsuits. VerdictSearch, a company that studies legal verdicts and settlements, told the *New York Post* that from the 1980s up to 2003 Weitz & Luxenberg won its clients at least $280 million in asbestos jury verdicts.[8] Figuring the fees at one-third of the awards, out of that $280 million, Weitz & Luxenberg would have been paid $93 million.

And that was just the beginning. The $280 million figure undoubtedly represented just part of what Weitz & Luxenberg got for its clients, and didn't come close to telling the story of the firm's asbestos-related income. VerdictSearch's data did not include numerous cases settled before trial. It didn't include what the firm got clients from claims made with asbestos trusts, or from product liability or personal injury suits.

Other lawyers sought Weitz & Luxenberg's expertise. John Dearie, a personal injury lawyer and former state Assembly member, began taking his asbestos cases to Weitz & Luxenberg in the early 1990s. Weitz & Luxenberg's knowledge of asbestos claims meant the verdicts and settlements won by the firm's lawyers were "superior to anybody anywhere," Dearie said.[9] He knew Weitz & Luxenberg would do a better job with asbestos cases than he could. And when he referred a case, he collected a third of Weitz & Luxenberg's fee. If Weitz & Luxenberg got a $300,000 fee in a case, Dearie would get $100,000.

In 2002, Weitz & Luxenberg won a jury verdict of $53.5 million for a single plaintiff—one of the biggest such verdicts ever. Stephen Brown was likely first exposed to asbestos when he worked fixing automobile brakes at a gas station in the 1960s, his family said. In 1968, Brown joined the Coast Guard, where he was also exposed to asbestos while working in engine and boiler rooms. He was diagnosed with mesothelioma in June 2000 and died six months later. Brown's family hired Weitz & Luxenberg to sue 47 separate defendants—one or several of which might have caused his cancer. The cost of the award by a Manhattan state court jury was to be split among the defendants and their insurance companies.

Weitz & Luxenberg took on some personal injury cases, including one involving the 1994 carbon-monoxide-poisoning death of 40-year-old tennis star Vitas Gerulaitis in a pool house at a luxury home in Southampton, New York. In 2002, Luxenberg told a *New York Times* reporter that the case was headed to a confidential settlement.

The firm also began filing lawsuits on behalf of people hurt by the drug industry—"where people had heart attacks and strokes or diabetes as a result of drugs given [them], and improper warnings for the drugs," Weitz said in 2015. [10] Weitz & Luxenberg also represented 4,000 women who sued over defective breast implants made by several manufacturers. In 1994, it was among several law firms that negotiated a $3.7 billion settlement in the case.

But asbestos was always Weitz & Luxenberg's mainstay. By 2015, asbestos cases provided more than 60 percent of the firm's revenue. [11]

In the 2000s, Weitz & Luxenberg was outgrowing its headquarters in Manhattan's Financial District. A limited liability company that gave its address as Weitz & Luxenberg's offices bought a building at 700 Broadway in trendy NoHo, near Greenwich Village and New York University's campus. The building was constructed in the 1890s as a department store; a century later it was the headquarters of the National Audubon Society. When the law firm moved in, it was renamed the Weitz & Luxenberg Building. A plaque at the entrance calls the firm headquartered inside "the champion of the common citizen and protector of the inalienable rights of the individual."

By 2015, Weitz & Luxenberg had over 100 lawyers and 500 staff spread across several offices, including one in New Jersey and another in Los Angeles. Weitz lived a luxe life beyond the means of the common citizens his firm claimed to champion. He came to own a 190-foot yacht and a corporate jet, which he used to travel to his ranch in Aspen, Colorado, where Weitz & Luxenberg maintained a branch office.

Luxenberg once admitted he wasn't as ambitious as Weitz. "If a genie had come down and said, 'Sign here, and you'll make $75,000 every year for the rest of your life,' I'd have taken the offer," Luxenberg said. "Perry wouldn't have. That's why Weitz and I make a good team."[12]

Weitz's and Luxenberg's different approaches to business and their profession meshed well. It helped that Weitz and Luxenberg hit it off personally. "It was a love affair that hasn't ended," said Weitz. The relationship, Luxenberg said, was "like a marriage."

If it was a marriage, then Weitz was the lead partner.

"Did you flip a coin to decide whose name came first?" a federal judge once asked Luxenberg.

"It wasn't much of a choice, judge," Luxenberg answered.[13]

Fees from the firm's big asbestos verdicts and other cases gave it money to burn—some of which Weitz and Luxenberg spent hiring a new employee they expected would do little work.

For years, Sheldon Silver was associated with the law firm Schneider, Kleinick, Weitz, Damashek & Shoot—which as it happened had offices in the Woolworth Building, the same neo-Gothic skyscraper that once housed Morris J. Eisen PC. Like Eisen, the Schneider firm had been one of the city's premier personal injury law firms. But after the September 11 attacks devastated downtown Manhattan in 2001, the firm lost business, and its staff dwindled from 34 lawyers to 6. Silver needed a new gig.

Arthur Luxenberg had the idea of bringing Silver to Weitz & Luxenberg. "Sheldon Silver would bring prestige, honor to the firm, and help the name of the firm," Luxenberg said.

Weitz said Silver's role as speaker of the state Assembly was important to the decision. "He was a very prominent, prestigious guy in New York," he said. "It would help the prestige of the firm. ... We thought it would help with the brand of the firm."

Weitz gave another reason for wanting to hire Silver: "He grew up in the court. ... He knew everybody."

Weitz said Silver was not hired with the expectation he would draw new business to the firm. "We were not relying on him to bring in cases one way or another," he said.[14] Also, Silver was not expected to work directly on cases. He wasn't expected to appear in court. He wouldn't negotiate any settlements. In any case, he didn't have the skills to work in Weitz & Luxenberg's main line of business. "I did not understand that he had a background in asbestos," said Luxenberg.

Nonetheless, Weitz and Luxenberg were so eager to bring Silver to the firm, they gave up some cases involving state government, "to avoid any appearance of impropriety between the firm, the state and Sheldon Silver," Luxenberg said. In his view, giving up lawsuits for or against the State of New York wasn't much of an issue. He said Silver's employment at the firm cost it "a limited number" of cases.

Weitz & Luxenberg hired Silver in September 2002 at a salary of $120,000 per year—a pittance to a firm that reaped tens of millions yearly in legal fees. Within weeks of his hiring, Silver began boosting his income by reeling in two negligence lawsuits for the firm.

Yet it remained that all Silver needed to do for his $120,000 salary was let Weitz & Luxenberg put his name on its letterhead. Anything else was extra.

"We did not have an expectation that he would bring asbestos cases," Luxenberg said.

Chapter 4 – Pay dirt

Breathe in, breathe out. We do this between 17,000 and 23,000 times a day. Every breath we take is a chance to draw in something bad—chemicals, dust, smoke, pollution. An unlucky few breathe in things that will kill them. Some who breathe in asbestos dust will be stricken decades later with mesothelioma, an incurable cancer that usually brings death within a year or two of diagnosis.

Twenty, thirty, or forty years can pass between the day you breathe in asbestos fibers and the day mesothelioma strikes. You live a normal life, unaware death will come early.

"That's the scary part—there is nothing," said the widow of a maritime industry worker who died two years after his mesothelioma diagnosis. He was "healthy as a horse," his widow recalled. He never took pills for anything, and he enjoyed yoga and Zumba classes. "All of his physicals always came back normal, so he never suspected anything."

Then one day, when he was 61 years old, he was sick. Suddenly he could not climb stairs during ship inspections. Soon after that, he woke up in the middle of the night in intense pain. "It hurts. It hurts. I can't catch my breath. It really hurts," he told his wife. He figured he was exposed early in his career, before asbestos safety rules became strict. Doctors, surgery, chemotherapy, and drugs could not stave off death.

"It felt like a rolled-up towel was stuck underneath my skin, right up beneath the rib cage," said another patient, Chris De Santis. He was diagnosed with mesothelioma in 1998, when he was 28 years old. More than two decades later, he was extraordinarily lucky to be alive—his doctors thought he'd survive only 18 months. But his life was diminished. The disease cost him a lung, half of his diaphragm, and a couple of ribs. He needs an oxygen

43

generator to do housework, and he seldom goes outside without a portable oxygen tank. He had to give up the successful insurance agency he ran with his dad in eastern Long Island, New York. "It was our place. I didn't have a boss. I enjoyed it—I loved helping people out." The northern winters made him gasp—it was harder for his lungs to get oxygen from the cold air. De Santis moved to a home on a two-acre plot in Arizona, where the warm, dry air is easier to breathe.

Movie star Steve McQueen—best known for playing tough guys like Virgil Hilts in *The Great Escape* and the title role in the cop movie *Bullitt*—is probably the most famous mesothelioma victim. McQueen's symptoms included shortness of breath and night sweats. No one could say for sure how McQueen breathed in the asbestos fibers that killed him. It might have happened when he went to sea as a merchant mariner in the 1940s, when he was 16 years old. Or maybe he was exposed as a U.S. Marine in the 1950s, when he stripped asbestos off pipes in a Navy troop ship. McQueen loved to race cars, and he might have breathed in asbestos fibers woven into his fire-retardant driving suit.

Doctors at Cedars-Sinai Hospital in Los Angeles diagnosed his mesothelioma in 1979 and told McQueen he would die in a few months. The doctors "basically told us to enjoy the time we had left," said his wife, Barbara McQueen. "The doctors said surgery was out of the question and chemo didn't really work. It was a rare cancer and all their patients had died."[1]

People with mesothelioma usually have tumors in their pleural mesothelium, or pleura, which is a thin membrane that blankets the wall of one's chest, beneath the ribs. The pleura surrounds the lungs, which absorb inhaled asbestos fibers. In some cases, mesothelioma develops in the pericardium, which is the mesothelium surrounding the heart, or in the peritoneum, which is the mesothelium surrounding the abdominal organs. Some mesothelioma cases have been attributed to radiation treatments for other kinds of cancer, such as Hodgkin's disease. But asbestos is by far the leading cause of mesothelioma.

It's often impossible to figure out how someone gets mesothelioma. Raya Bodnarchuk, a Washington, D.C.-area artist, worked with a Baltimore law firm to make a list of asbestos-laden art materials she used. The lawyers asked exhaustive questions about her life. "They go back into the history of everything," she said. "It can get ridiculously detailed." The lawyers settled on the idea that Bodnarchuk was infected by materials she used early in her art career. "It was discovered that there was asbestos in these materials I used in art school and afterward—some ceramic products." [2] Some kinds of potter's clay have been found to contain asbestos. Pottery kilns were built with asbestos. Exactly what gave Bodnarchuk the disease was unknown.

Many who did not get sick working with asbestos exposed their spouses and children to illness by bringing asbestos dust home in their clothes. Chris De Santis suspects that when he was a child, he inhaled asbestos fibers from the clothing his father wore at work as an aircraft mechanic. Asbestos was once used in many kinds of aircraft parts, to reduce heat and dampen sound.

Asbestos has been around for centuries. It was a miracle to the ancient Greeks. They tossed dirty napkins woven of asbestos into fires and saw them come out "whiter and cleaner than they could possibly have been rendered by the aid of water," wrote Pliny the Elder, the Greek naturalist. [3] Pliny mistakenly believed asbestos was a plant—he thought it grew in the desert. In fact, it is a fibrous, silky rock, dug from mines.

Asbestos found countless uses in the industrial age. It is so fire resistant that U.S. building codes required it in many kinds of construction. Asbestos linings in ovens ensured even heat distribution. Asbestos was also woven into tabletop heat pads and oven mitts. Fibrous "spinning grade" asbestos dug from the Grand Canyon in the early

20th century was woven into fireproof theater curtains—a use that probably saved thousands of lives. Asbestos was mined in Georgia, North Carolina, and Washington State.

Some modern writers—including judges, in written court decisions—wrongly say Pliny and his contemporaries knew asbestos was dangerous. [4] But there is no doubt that the hazards of breathing asbestos dust became apparent as its use grew in the late 19th century. The first recorded case of asbestos disease came in 1899, when a man who worked 12 years in an asbestos factory was diagnosed at Charing Cross Hospital in London. He died a year later. By the 1920s, the disease had a name: pulmonary asbestosis. By the mid-1930s, as medical knowledge evolved, doctors determined that many asbestos workers were getting lung cancer. [5]

America's asbestos industry got wise to the danger and embarked on a decades-long cover-up. Just as in the tobacco industry—which dissembled for decades about the dangers of cigarettes—people in the asbestos business didn't want the public to know the truth about their product.

In 1935, R. S. Rossiter, the editor of the trade journal *Asbestos*, asked Sumner Simpson, head of big asbestos manufacturer Raybestos-Manhattan, if she could reprint British publications' articles about asbestos illness. "You may recall that we have written you on several occasions concerning the publishing of information, or discussion of, asbestosis and the work which has been, and is being done to eliminate or at least reduce it," Rossiter wrote Simpson. "Always, you have requested that for certain obvious reasons we publish nothing, and, naturally, your wishes have been respected."

Simpson took up the matter with Vandiver Brown, a lawyer with Johns-Manville Corp., another big industry player. "The magazine 'Asbestos' is in business to publish articles about the asbestos trade and they have been very decent about not re-printing the English articles,"

46

Simpson wrote to Brown. He felt that the less said about asbestos illness, "the better off we are."

Brown concurred, saying the industry's "interests are best served by having asbestosis receive the minimum of publicity." Besides, Brown wrote, an American doctor who studied asbestos "has frequently remarked, to me personally and in some of his papers, that the clinical picture presented in North American localities where there is asbestos dust hazard is considerably milder than that reported in England and South Africa."

Rossiter and her magazine were deep in the industry's pocket. *Asbestos* did not publish the British reports. The issue arose again in 1941, when *Asbestos* considered reviewing a new book on pneumoconiosis, a lung disease caused by breathing dust. Brown suggested to Rossiter that *Asbestos* subscribers—people who led and worked in the asbestos industry—might not appreciate seeing an article about the danger of the products they were making and selling. Rossiter kept the book review from her readers. As long as Rossiter suppressed the facts, asbestos industry executives had no reason to worry that their trade magazine would publish a critical article that might fall into the hands of someone who could widely expose their products' danger.[6]

Asbestos industry executives were cavalier for decades more about the hazards of their products—but doctors woke up to the danger. Dr. Irving Selikoff of Mount Sinai Hospital in New York led U.S. researchers in proving the hazards. Selikoff was the lead author of a pioneering 1964 study that showed New York–area members of the Asbestos Workers Union who installed asbestos insulation had far-higher-than-normal levels of asbestos illness. Selikoff's work also showed the long latency of asbestos exposure. He found some asbestos workers never got sick, while others got sick decades after their exposure.

In the 1970s, the Occupational Safety and Health Administration imposed rules meant to limit workers' exposure to asbestos. In 1973, the government banned spray-applied asbestos insulation. In 1975, it banned some types of asbestos used to insulate boilers and hot water tanks.

Also during the 1970s, lawyers for people sickened by asbestos came across a cache of Sumner Simpson's papers, which included his correspondence with Rossiter and with Johns-Manville lawyer Brown. [7] Simpson's papers and others discovered by lawyers clearly showed the industry's cover-up. Over the years, the anti-asbestos consensus mounted. In 1990, *The New York Times* quoted Selikoff: "There is no issue, no debate about asbestos."[8]

Asbestos was never completely outlawed in the United States—but tighter regulation of its use, worker safety rules, and worries about lawsuits effectively removed it from the U.S. marketplace.

The last American asbestos mine closed in 2002. Since then, all asbestos used in the United States has been imported. All 681 metric tons of raw asbestos fiber brought into the country in 2018 was used in filters needed to manufacture chlorine. The U.S. Geological Survey says it's possible some asbestos was also imported in "gaskets used to create a chemical containment seal in the production of titanium dioxide and brake blocks for use in the oil industry." Asbestos might also be imported in "automotive brake linings and other friction materials, cement products, knitted fabrics, other gaskets and packing, tile, and wallpaper." Yet the amount of asbestos used in the U.S. in the late 2010s was less than 0.1 percent of its peak in the early 1970s, the government said.[9]

As asbestos disappeared from the market, a new industry emerged. Lawyers found they could make big money suing on behalf of people sickened by asbestos. Jury awards and settlements in mesothelioma cases run to millions of dollars. A lot of that money can end up in lawyers' pockets: they keep 25 to 40 percent of whatever they get for their clients through trials or settlements.

Asbestos lawsuits first arrived at courthouses around the early 1970s. As state and federal laws evolved, more people claiming to suffer from asbestos sickness sued. By the early 1980s, asbestos manufacturers faced thousands of court cases.

Because it was hard to learn how and when someone acquired mesothelioma, lawyers cast a wide net in their quest for money damages. In August 2013, Baltimore's Peter Angelos PC law firm sued on Raya Bodnarchuk's behalf in Baltimore City Circuit Court against 35 corporations, trusts, and other entities. That may seem like a lot of defendants, but it's below average. One study found that in 2014 a typical asbestos case in Baltimore City Circuit Court had 48 defendants, and that the Angelos firm typically sued 52 defendants.[10]

Bodnarchuk's suit named ceramics firms, the CBS broadcast network, General Electric, International Paper, the Bayer and Pfizer drug companies, the Hasbro toy company, and the Metropolitan Life Insurance Company. The court complaint didn't specify what these companies had to do with Bodnarchuk's exposure. But other lawsuits have accused them of exposing plaintiffs to asbestos.

CBS once owned Westinghouse Electric, which used asbestos to make turbines, light bulbs, and welding equipment. General Electric used asbestos in many products—it built asbestos insulating panels into hot-running consumer items like radios. A company owned by International Paper distributed asbestos-containing materials to shipyards. A Bayer affiliate is the legal successor to several companies that made asbestos products. A Pfizer subsidiary made asbestos insulation used in steelmaking. Hasbro was accused of selling clay that contained asbestos. Metropolitan Life has been accused of aiding the cover-up of asbestos's dangers.

Probably only one of the 35 entities named in Bodnarchuk's lawsuit was responsible for her illness. But there's no way to know for sure, and it's common in asbestos litigation for several companies to end up sharing responsibility. Under the legal principle of joint and several responsibility, a company found partly responsible for someone's exposure to asbestos can be found fully responsible for damages. In cases that go to trial, judges, lawyers, and juries figure out how much each company must pay. In the end, companies or insurance companies can agree to share the costs of a jury verdict or court award.

Bodnarchuk's lawyers likely knew which 35 companies to sue because asbestos law firms invested millions to build databases about the history of asbestos use. Lawyers have amassed a great deal of information about what products were made with asbestos, and how their clients might have encountered them.

Weitz & Luxenberg, the law firm that gave Sheldon Silver a job, has such databases. It was accused in a March 2012 lawsuit of stealing from another law firm a database that contained 988 "easily used and highly organized" files about asbestos use on U.S. Navy ships.

Navy ships contained lots of asbestos, and the database shows how it was used. Picture a valve that might control a shipboard steam or hot-water pipe. Asbestos from one manufacturer might have been used in gaskets bolted between the flanges connecting pipes to a valve. A different kind of asbestos from another manufacturer might have been packed around the outside of the valve.

If Weitz & Luxenberg believes one of its clients was exposed to asbestos from a valve on a Navy ship, the firm might need to file cases or claims against each asbestos manufacturer whose material was used on the valve. A file containing such information for one ship would have cost at least $2,500 to obtain from the government, the lawsuit said. If that's true, then the 988 files Weitz & Luxenberg was accused of obtaining illicitly cost their original owner more than $2.47 million. The case was eventually dropped, and whether it resulted in Weitz &

Luxenberg compensating the files' purported original owner is not public record.

Jury awards in asbestos lawsuits taken to trial can make headlines. From 1993 to 2011, a typical mesothelioma case tried by a jury resulted in a $3.79 million verdict, a RAND Corporation study found.[11] From 2010 to 2014, jurors in New York City's Asbestos Litigation Court awarded $324.5 million to 14 plaintiffs—an average award of more than $23 million for each asbestos victim. In July 2013, a jury in New York City returned a verdict of $190 million to be split among five asbestos victims—which worked out to $38 million per plaintiff. [12]

Rarely do asbestos companies or their insurers pay out the full amount of a jury award. Under appeal or threat of appeal, awards are negotiated downward. One of the biggest jury verdicts ever, a $250 million award given in March 2003 to retired U.S. Steel employee Roby Whittington, was settled for less than $50 million. The jury in Madison County, Illinois, decided the case on a Friday. Whittington's lawyers settled with U.S. Steel the following Monday. A $250 million jury verdict is a good place for a victim's lawyer to start settlement talks. By settling for $50 million, U.S. Steel avoided the risk of losing on appeal and having to pay the full amount.

Lawsuits aren't the only way for mesothelioma victims and their families to seek damages. Raya Bodnarchuk and her lawyers also could have decided to seek money from one or several trusts set up to pay people sickened by asbestos. The trusts were funded by insurance money and the assets of asbestos companies forced into bankruptcy.

The trusts' story begins with Manville Corporation. The company—known for much of its history as Johns-Manville—was once America's largest asbestos products manufacturer. It was big enough to be part of the Dow Jones Industrial Average. By 1982, Manville faced 16,500 lawsuits from people who claimed to be sickened by asbestos. Lawyers filed more than 400 new suits against the company each month.[13] Together the suits sought more than the company could pay. Manville was forced into bankruptcy.

The bankruptcy court's solution to the problem was to put $869 million of Manville's assets into a trust. That sum included Manville stock and money paid out from its insurance policies. Instead of suing Manville, people sickened by the company's asbestos had to file claims with the Manville Trust. It seemed like a good arrangement for both the company and asbestos victims. People sickened by Manville products would have a way to be compensated. And Manville itself stayed in business. It later became part of Warren Buffett's Berkshire Hathaway conglomerate.

The Manville Trust's founders figured that over its lifetime, it would pay off between 83,000 and 100,000 people. But that estimate was way too low. The trust began taking claims in 1989. By the spring of 1990, the trust was named in over 90,000 lawsuits in state and federal courts. By October 1994—less than five years after it opened for business—the trust had taken in 240,000 claims. Of those, it had settled 30,000. The other 210,000 or so were pending.

Most of these claims weren't the multi-million-dollar kinds of cases that make headlines—but their size caught Manville Trust managers unprepared. The trust's founders figured an average claim would be $25,000. But an average claim filed with the trust in 1989 sought $40,000.

Nobody wanted the Manville Trust to go broke. So in 1995, federal judges in New York reorganized it. A new federal law helped: it let the courts establish trusts that would pay off people sickened by asbestos and protect Manville and other asbestos companies from further lawsuits. Thus protected in the statutes, the Manville Trust could sell its shares of the company's stock and diversify its investment portfolio. The Manville Trust was the model for about 50 similar trusts set up for bankrupt asbestos companies.

The trusts are a reliable source of compensation for mesothelioma sufferers. There is no to-the-penny estimate of the trusts' wealth, but the generally accepted figure in 2021 was around $30 billion. Studies found that legal fees take up about a third of the money the trusts pay out. That meant lawyers could end up with $10 billion of the trusts' money.

It is easy for lawyers to seek money from the trusts. They fill out a series of forms, usually online. The money is awarded to their clients—but the lawyers of course get their 25 percent to 40 percent cut. Thanks to the trust system, online filing, and the ever-growing knowledge of asbestos's dangers, lawyers do less to earn those fees than they did when asbestos litigation was new. But the lawyers' presumably lower costs are not passed on to their sick and dying customers.[14]

Critics say the $30 billion pot of cash available to asbestos victims and their lawyers is a tempting target for fraud. Lester Brickman, an emeritus professor at Yeshiva University's Benjamin N. Cardozo School of Law, told a congressional committee in 2011 that law firms hire friendly doctors to read potential clients' chest X-rays, and that these doctors report nonfatal asbestos illness in patients who have none. "Their error rates when subjected to testing by doctors who had no participation in the litigation were in the high 90 percent range," Brickman testified.[15]

Less fraud exists in mesothelioma cases—because it is easy to prove mesothelioma patients are sick, and because the disease usually kills them soon after diagnosis.

Awards appear to have declined over the years. In 2002, mesothelioma victims and their lawyers at Simmons Hanly Conroy, a law firm based in Alton, Illinois, typically reaped around $2 million or $3 million from lawsuits and claims filed to the trusts, said Gregg

Kirkland, who was the Simmons firm's chief executive officer. By 2015, a typical mesothelioma settlement shared by Simmons and its clients had declined to about $1 million, Kirkland said.[16]

But mesothelioma payouts are still bigger than payouts for other kinds of asbestos illness. A typical lung cancer case in 2015 brought in from $50,000 to $100,000 for Simmons and its clients, Kirkland testified in federal court. That was just 5 percent to 10 percent of a typical mesothelioma case's value.

Because mesothelioma patients' claims are much more valuable than other asbestos claims, lawyers work hard to find them. When Chris De Santis shopped for a lawyer after he was diagnosed in 1998, Weitz & Luxenberg offered him a limousine ride from his Long Island home to its downtown Manhattan offices. Soon after Raya Bodnarchuk was diagnosed in mid-2012, she got phone calls out of the blue from two law firms. She didn't know how they got her phone number. After they called, both firms sent lawyers to her door.

Simmons Hanly Conroy developed an elaborate protocol for handling phone calls and email queries from potential mesothelioma clients. "When an intake comes in that we suspect to be a mesothelioma case, it is critical that we do everything possible to schedule an appointment," the protocol said.

Lawyers were instructed to follow up with people who didn't want to make appointments. Simmons assigned a team of employees to deal with potential clients they suspected were talking to other law firms, and to strategize in situations where potential clients cancelled their appointments.[17]

Kirkland explained the need for the protocols: "It's a competitive environment to retain those clients. It's just super competitive," he testified in federal court. "The faster we can get into a person's living room and talk to them about our firm and sign them, the more successful you are."[18]

Law firms also spend big on advertising. In 2015, law firms spent $45.6 million on TV ads aimed at asbestos victims, the U.S. Chamber of Commerce's Institute for Legal Reform estimated. Mesothelioma and asbestos lawyers also spend heavily on internet ads. A 2016 study reported on the website Search Engine Watch found that Google charged $935.71 every time someone clicked on a search engine ad with the words "best mesothelioma lawyer."[19] Type "mesothelioma" into an internet search engine, and you'll see lots of paid law firm advertising and many links to information websites funded by asbestos lawyers.

Those millions' worth of TV and internet ads aim at a tiny bull's-eye—the roughly 3,000 Americans diagnosed every year with mesothelioma. Put another way, the ads' target audience is fewer than one in 100,000 people. Yet law firm mesothelioma ads are a staple of local late-night TV news, which in 2020 appeared each night on about 3.7 million TV screens. Figuring one person might watch each screen, ads saying things like, "If you've received a mesothelioma diagnosis, or a loved one died from this cancer, call us today," target fewer than 37 of the news programs' viewers each night.[20]

Kirkland said the Simmons firm spent more than $100,000 on advertising for each mesothelioma client it signed up.[21] If a case worth $1 million yielded the firm between $250,000 and $400,000 in fees, that $100,000 was likely well spent.

The best kind of client for law firms representing asbestos plaintiffs comes from the handful of doctors who specialize in mesothelioma. Because their patients face such a horrible diagnosis, they are always a good bet to win big money from juries or trusts.

But doctor referrals are rare. At Simmons Hanly Conroy, one of Weitz & Luxenberg's biggest competitors, fewer than 5 percent of cases came from doctors. So Simmons's leaders set up a foundation to support research on mesothelioma and other cancers, partly because they knew their charity boosted doctors' willingness to send them cases. "We hoped we would get referrals by promoting research," said Kirkland.[22]

Weitz & Luxenberg was not as willing to fund research. Its lawyers tried many asbestos cases to juries. Opposing lawyers often asked doctors testifying for Weitz & Luxenberg: Have you or your hospital or your clinic received Weitz & Luxenberg research grants? Perry Weitz feared juries "would have thought that if we gave all this money to the hospital, that the doctor's testimony wasn't credible." Maintaining the credibility of the doctors' testimony was important to getting maximum payouts for mesothelioma sufferers and maximum fees for Weitz & Luxenberg. "So we avoided giving any money to a specific doctor's research," Weitz explained.

Raya Bodnarchuk was diagnosed with mesothelioma in 2011. It forced her to reorganize her work as an artist. She cut back working on larger, heavier sculptures, and focused on easier projects. "I paint a lot every day, and I work on small things. No matter what happens, if I can do something every day in my field, that's really a nice way to go for me."

Bodnarchuk's art has long been appreciated around Washington, DC. In 1984, a *Washington Post* reviewer called her art "charming-chunky"—the display included sculptures of a bright red galloping horse, and dogs carved from hunks of wood. In 2005 Bodnarchuk contributed to a gallery of 1,328 paintings and drawings of U.S. soldiers killed in Iraq. Her portrait of Private Corey Small looked like a "stylized cartoon," the *Post* wrote—and it was greatly appreciated by the soldier's sister. "If it had been more realistic, it would have been even harder to take," the sister said.

Mesothelioma was a presence in Bodnarchuk's life. "Everything can change. It's terrifying, actually." Her art helped her face her cancer. "I'm walking," she said in 2017. "A lot of people have a very rough road, a very rough road, from the get-go. I had a hard road, but I'm making it so far."

Bodnarchuk died September 17, 2021, at age 74. She survived with mesothelioma for a decade after her diagnosis, far longer than most.

Chapter 5 – A connection

Robert Taub took offense when a lawyer asked him in court how much time he spent seeing patients in his job as head of the Mesothelioma Center at New York Presbyterian Hospital/Columbia Medical Center. It was not a job, Taub insisted. "It is a calling."[1]

Medicine and cancer research were Taub's calling. He graduated from Yeshiva University several years before Sheldon Silver. Taub was the first Yeshiva graduate to attend Yale Medical School, from which he earned his medical degree in 1961. After postgraduate work at Yale and at Tufts-New England Medical Center in Boston, Taub went to the University of London, where he earned a Ph.D. in 1969. For a few years, he taught at Mount Sinai School of Medicine in New York. After that, he was a cancer doctor at hospitals in Virginia.

Over the years, Taub saw every kind of cancer case. He focused on mesothelioma in his research and medical practice. "It's a bad disease to have, a terrible disease," he said.[2]

In December 1980, when he was around 43 years old, Taub was hired as a professor of medicine at Columbia University, which operates its medical school in conjunction with New York Presbyterian Hospital. His interest in finding a cure for mesothelioma came from his work with Dr. Karen H. Antman, a doctor at Boston University who conducted pioneering research into mesothelioma in the 1980s. Taub said she was a mentor. "She had cured something like six patients with a combination of chemotherapy and radiation," he recalled. "I thought that was a very interesting thing to have done."[3]

Taub's mesothelioma practice expanded during the 1990s. By 2000, mesothelioma cases were half of his patient workload.

In 2000, Columbia set up Taub in what it called the Mesothelioma Center. It was funded by a donation of several million dollars from New York's Milstein family, which made its fortune in real estate and banking. Someone in the Milstein family suffered from mesothelioma, Taub said. [4] The Milsteins have long supported programs at the hospital, known to New Yorkers as Columbia-Presbyterian, a shortening of its historic name. Their grant "was an endowment so that I could get people together and get doctors to cooperate—surgeons, pathologists, and other people," Taub said. The idea was to study mesothelioma and seek a cure.

Taub's calling was not the kind that required vows of poverty or obedience. He drew a salary of $300,000 a year. His desk was in the corner office of a patient care suite on the ninth floor of Columbia-Presbyterian's Herbert Irving Cancer Pavilion, 15 blocks south of the George Washington Bridge in upper Manhattan. The hospital is a few blocks from the Yeshiva University campus.

To reach Taub's office, you'd walk past his secretary and patient examination rooms. You might have found Taub at his desk in a lab coat and bow tie, as he was depicted on the front page of the Columbia Mesothelioma website. The website was separate from the hospital and university web servers—it let Taub promote his practice without interference from administrators. In 2015, records show, Taub worked with a staff of four people—his secretary, an assistant, and two lab workers. He also employed several part-timers.

Over the years, Taub estimated, he saw 2,000 patients with peritoneal mesothelioma, in which cancer grows on the membrane surrounding the abdominal organs. Peritoneal mesothelioma is a rare form of a rare disease. Taub said that when he began seeing peritoneal mesothelioma patients in the 1990s, most died within a year. By 2015, these patients lived an average of four years past their diagnosis. "Some of the patients just go on and on for 10 or 12 years longer than that," Taub said. "So there's been a big change in the actual survival of these patients and the quality of their life."[5]

Taub said his byline appeared on more than 150 scientific journal articles. He and his colleagues studied ways to make mesothelioma chemotherapy more effective. "Sometimes we devise new techniques for giving chemotherapy right into the belly, also into the chest," he said. He also devised a series of algorithms the hospital used to determine correct chemotherapy doses, and studied how radiation and chemotherapy could work together to treat pleural mesothelioma cases. In 2016, he coauthored a study of how online support groups could help mesothelioma patients cope with the hardship of their treatment. His research was backed by several drug companies, including Johnson & Johnson, Genentech, and Sanofi.

"I love the work that I do. That's the only thing I can say," Taub once said. "I really feel very privileged to be able to take care of these people. This is a very terrible disease. I feel that I'm good at it.

"I love teaching about medicine. I love doing research, and I'm very, very passionate about finding a cure for the disease and treating it well."[6]

Taub offered other glimpses into his work ethic during a court hearing in 2016 that arose from Columbia University's effort to remove him from his job. At one point, he stated that he spent more than 50 percent of his time seeing patients.

"It can't be," said the judge.

"Why?" asked Taub.

The problem, the judge noted, was that Taub said earlier that he spent 50 percent of his time teaching. It was impossible for him to spend 50 percent of his time teaching and more than 50 percent of his time seeing patients. That adds up to more than 100 percent. And that didn't account for the time Taub said he spent on mesothelioma research.

"OK," said the exasperated judge. "So no time for research."

"Fine," said Taub. "Zero." He seemed exasperated too.

Sometimes during the hearing, Taub was so eager to talk about his work that lawyers and the judge had to ask him not to speak unless he was asked a question. "Just relax," his lawyer advised him.

In another court proceeding, a lawyer asked Taub about his oath to put his patients above all else.

Q. "When you became a doctor, you also took a Hippocratic Oath; is that right?"

A. "Yes."

The Hippocratic Oath, taken by doctors when they enter the profession, is a series of medical ethics standards.

Q. "In doing so, you vowed to put your patients' interests first?"

A. "The specifics of the Hippocratic Oath are not quite that, but I do put the patients' interests first, yes."

The leading modern version of the Hippocratic Oath—written in the 1960s by Louis Lasagna, then a professor at Johns Hopkins School of Medicine—says in part: "I will apply, for the benefit of the sick, all measures which are required." It doesn't say specifically that doctors must put patients first.

Q. "I was going to say, Hippocratic Oath aside, you've always put your patients' interests first; correct?"

A. "Pretty much."

Q. "That included when you made suggestions about them seeing a lawyer; correct?"

A. "Yes."

By referring his mesothelioma patients to lawyers—with the patients' permission, so he wasn't violating their privacy—Taub could fulfill another part of Lasagna's Hippocratic Oath: "I will remember that I do not treat a fever chart, [or] a cancerous growth, but a sick human being, whose illness may affect the person's family and economic stability. My responsibility includes these related problems, if I am to care adequately for the sick."

Mesothelioma didn't just threaten the lives of Taub's patients. It also damaged their families' finances. "There are tremendous numbers of medical bills," Taub said. Helping his patients cope with their financial problems "is a very important part of their care."[7] Taub knew his patients and their families could get money by filing claims with asbestos trusts and suing companies that manufactured or used asbestos.

Taub observed that about two-thirds of his new mesothelioma patients already had lawyers. He advised the one-third of his patients without lawyers to seek them.

"I'm not fond of any firm," Taub said.

"He viewed them with disdain," said Mary Hesdorffer, who for several years was Taub's nurse. Taub called the mesothelioma lawyers "ambulance chasers, and he would chuckle about it."[8]

Taub believed law firms like Weitz & Luxenberg profited too much from the $30 billion in the asbestos trusts. "They are getting money from a trust which was meant to help mesothelioma victims," he said. "Weitz & Luxenberg, like all those companies that get money from patients … they in a sense are obligated to support research into the disease as well."[9]

Nonetheless, Taub suggested law firms to his patients. He did not regularly suggest Weitz & Luxenberg, even though some of his patients told him the firm served them well. Though Taub took issue with Weitz & Luxenberg's refusal to donate to mesothelioma research, he knew other firms supported work to cure the disease, including two of Weitz & Luxenberg's competitors in New York, Belluck & Fox and Levy Phillips & Konigsberg.

The Illinois-based Simmons Hanly Conroy firm poured millions into a nonprofit foundation that supported research on mesothelioma and other cancers.

Simmons's management knew that its philanthropy would persuade doctors to send cases to the firm.

This tactic worked with Taub, who bristled at Weitz & Luxenberg's refusal to support mesothelioma research. "The Simmons law firm is more socially responsible," he said. [10]

One day in 2003, Taub came across what seemed like a way to persuade Weitz & Luxenberg to pitch in. The firm sent him a letter seeking medical records of one of his patients. He spotted Sheldon Silver's name on the long list of Weitz & Luxenberg lawyers on the letterhead. Taub first met Silver in 1984, and they moved in some of the same social circles. Now and then, Taub and Silver saw each other at weddings or on vacation—they sometimes stayed in the same hotel during the Passover holiday. They also had a mutual friend—Daniel Chill, a lawyer and Albany political operative.

"I don't know whether he [Silver] knew exactly who I was," Taub said. "He knew I was a physician and a friend of Danny's."

Taub and Chill had been friends since their school days—"from the age of 12," Taub said. They were skinny youths, and sometimes a teacher made them share a chair "to look at the same book in class," Taub said. Chill attended Yale Law School at the same time Taub attended Yale Medical. Years later, Chill worked for Stanley Steingut, a Brooklyn politician who was the Assembly speaker from 1975 to 1978, when Silver was first elected.

After Taub spotted Silver's name on the stationery, he asked Chill to set up a meeting.

During their discussion, Taub told Silver of his work with the Mesothelioma Applied Research Foundation— known by the acronym MARF—which raised money for mesothelioma research. Taub recalled that he wasn't critical of Weitz & Luxenberg during the meeting. But he noted to Silver that Weitz & Luxenberg was getting a lot of business from a terrible disease without helping the fight against it. "I wanted to ask him to convince his firm or influence his firm to contribute to MARF," Taub said.

Silver answered that "he just could not do that."

But Silver did not forget their conversation.

Chill contacted Taub a few days later. He asked Taub to start referring patients to Weitz & Luxenberg via Silver.

"Shelly wants cases," Chill told him. [11]

Taub began referring patients to Silver right away. The referrals were not his idea, he said. But he saw them as useful to his wish to help his dying patients. "My purpose was to incentivize Mr. Silver to be an advocate for mesothelioma patients and help raise funds for research," Taub explained. [12] He knew Weitz & Luxenberg would profit from the patients he sent them.

In September 2003, Catherine O'Leary of New Jersey was diagnosed with mesothelioma. She asked a friend to refer her to a lawyer. Thus she ended up on the phone with John Dearie, who after a 20-year run in the New York State Assembly quit in 1992 to devote himself to his personal injury law practice. O'Leary asked Dearie if he knew a doctor who could treat her disease. Dearie sent her to Taub's clinic.

Sending O'Leary to Taub's clinic was likely the best and only thing Dearie could have done to aid her health. But it cost him a big fee.

Taub's nurse, Mary Hesdorffer, saw Taub come out of his examining room with O'Leary. The doctor put his arm around O'Leary's shoulder. "Do you have an attorney?" he asked her. According to a Weitz & Luxenberg internal email, Taub told O'Leary that Dearie was "no good" as a lawyer, and that she should call Silver instead.

Seeing Taub urge a lawyer upon one of his patients made Hesdorffer livid. "It was a turning point— something different," she said. She and Taub worked for Columbia University—"an academic institution," Hesdorffer said. In her view, Taub's action was deeply wrong. She also believed patients were uncomfortable with the idea that their doctor would refer them to a law firm. "It was really bad practice. It was unethical. I couldn't understand." She yelled at him about it. "I told him it was slimy and it was unbecoming. ... I wanted nothing to do with it," she said.

Taub responded by calling her "a schoolteacher, a nun—I was too rigid."

Weitz & Luxenberg entered O'Leary's case in its records on November 6, 2003. A Weitz & Luxenberg employee told O'Leary and her boyfriend that had she retained Dearie, he would probably have referred the case to Weitz & Luxenberg anyhow. Dearie—who years later had only a vague recollection of O'Leary's case—said he referred many cases to Weitz & Luxenberg over the years, and that he was not angry about losing a fee to Silver.[13]

Within a few weeks, Weitz & Luxenberg lawyers were working on O'Leary's asbestos claims. "This is a new case—living meso—brought in by Sheldon Silver," one of the firm's employees wrote November 25 in a handwritten memo. O'Leary's case was the first of 48 mesothelioma cases Taub referred to Silver and Weitz & Luxenberg over the following decade.

Asbestos cases went on for years. Weitz & Luxenberg lawyers were still working on O'Leary's behalf in 2012, nearly a decade after she became the firm's client and six years after her death. Over time, her compensation for her illness totaled about $510,000, according to a Weitz & Luxenberg accounting. O'Leary and her estate got $344,000 of that sum. Weitz & Luxenberg collected a fee of $166,000 and handed a third of it—about $55,400—to Silver. That money would have gone to Dearie if Taub hadn't told O'Leary that Dearie was "no good."

Word got back to Taub that Silver was pleased with the referrals. "Mr. Chill told me that Mr. Silver expressed the thought that I was being a very good friend," Taub said.[14]

Taub talked up Silver and Weitz & Luxenberg with his patients. "I told them that Weitz & Luxenberg is a very good law firm and that Mr. Silver…because of his stature in the state and because he was a member of that law firm as well—that it would enhance their legal treatment at the firm. They would do better, they would have a good representation in the firm."

"I think it's automatic that if you have a very senior person in a firm bringing in a case that the case would be handled with a bit more care," Taub said.

Except that Silver was not a senior person at Weitz & Luxenberg—he was "of counsel," which meant that he was a consultant or part-timer, not a regular employee or partner. And there is no evidence Silver was involved in handling any of the mesothelioma cases he referred to Weitz & Luxenberg. He prepared no briefs, filed no papers, and never appeared in court. Rarely—if ever—did Silver even speak to the people Taub referred to him.

All Silver did was hand the information Taub gave him to Weitz & Luxenberg lawyer Charles Ferguson, who was the firm's manager of asbestos litigation. Silver's office at the firm was next to Ferguson's office. Taub would telephone Silver with a patient referral. Silver wrote down the information Taub gave him. Then he walked next door to Ferguson's office, and handed over the piece of paper.

"He gave me the name of the individual, the patient, the victim," Ferguson said. Silver also gave him "a telephone number, a very brief little history of when that person was diagnosed, maybe a little work history as well, how they might have been exposed to asbestos."

"From time to time," Ferguson said, "he [Silver] would ask if we were able to make contact with that individual to sign the case up, to start the investigative process." But beyond that, he said, Silver had "very little" involvement in the cases and never expressed any further interest in them.

Ferguson and his colleagues called the information Silver provided about a patient a "lead."

"What was the value of these leads?" a federal prosecutor asked him in court.

"They had potential value, certainly," Ferguson said.

"Potential to have significant value?"

"Potentially, yes."[15]

After Silver provided a referral, Weitz & Luxenberg's next step was to persuade that person to sign a retainer agreement.

Some of Weitz & Luxenberg's process of signing up clients would be familiar to anyone who understands selling.

In one case unearthed by federal prosecutors, a Weitz & Luxenberg attorney had trouble in 2011 getting in touch with Robert McKinley, a Taub patient and Silver referral who lived in San Diego, California. One lawyer suggested in an email it might be necessary to send a "closer" to McKinley's home—a word evocative of the hard-core salesmanship Alec Baldwin's character pushed in the movie *Glengarry Glen Ross*: "A, B, C. A, always. B, be. C, closing. Always. Be. Closing."

Despite their professed horror at the asbestos industry's cavalier attitude toward those sickened by its product—and despite their professed desire to seek justice—Perry Weitz and Arthur Luxenberg ran a business based on sales. Their lawyers sometimes focused on closing deals with sick and dying people.

It turned out McKinley did not require a hard sell. He was at his sister's home in Massachusetts, and when the lawyers found him, he readily signed up. Evidently, Taub did enough to steer him toward signing on what Alec Baldwin's character called "the line which is dotted."

Next, the lawyers needed to learn about McKinley's case. "There's an evaluation process ... there's a lot that goes into it," Ferguson explained. The lawyers sent McKinley a questionnaire designed to help them determine what companies to sue, or which asbestos trusts to petition for money. The questionnaire asked for McKinley's "exposure history," "asbestos containing products that you recall from your work history as well as the sites you recall using these products," and military history.

Weitz & Luxenberg asked McKinley for information about his income and financial status, which an economist could use to help determine the value of his case. McKinley was also asked to read through a list of companies that made products that might have exposed him to asbestos. He checked off National Gypsum on the list. National Gypsum made wallboard and other building materials said to contain asbestos. McKinley later realized he had not been exposed to National Gypsum products—"he must have checked it off on accident," a Weitz & Luxenberg lawyer wrote. The lawyer decided not to pursue a claim against the company.

The case was still being processed when McKinley died in June 2013 at age 53. Weitz & Luxenberg took a fee of $244,527. Again figuring that the firm's fees usually—but not always—amounted to a third of a case's settlement, the total size of the settlement in McKinley's case was likely $733,581, of which McKinley and his family saw $489,054 before expenses were deducted. Silver's referral fee was one third of Weitz & Luxenberg's fee—in this case, $81,509.

All Silver did for that money was transmit McKinley's name and contact information from Taub to Weitz & Luxenberg. Neither Silver nor Weitz & Luxenberg paid Taub anything for the referrals.

Taub said he didn't know what financial arrangement Silver had with Weitz & Luxenberg, or how much money Silver earned from his patients' cases. "I knew it would benefit his standing in the firm," Taub said. "That was the way I thought about it, and I didn't know precisely how it would benefit him otherwise. ... I think he conveyed that he was pleased with the referrals he was getting."

But Taub got something he wanted from the arrangement: money for his research.

Soon after Silver handed Catherine O'Leary's name to Weitz & Luxenberg in late 2003, Chill asked Taub to write Silver a letter seeking state grant money.

So Taub wrote to Silver in January 2004. He called his Mesothelioma Center "a new gem in the proud crown of recognized exceptional medical care available in New York," and said it "should especially be considered for State support." Taub asked for an annual state grant of $250,000. He said $250,000 was his standard request from anyone he thought might donate to his center.

"It's always good to get funds," Taub said. "The center was pretty well funded at that time, so it was not crucial. But the more money you get, the more research you can do."

The first draft of Taub's letter said he'd heard from Chill that his program was being considered for state funding. But Taub struck Chill's name from the final version. "Mr. Chill asked me not to put his name in the letter," Taub said. This was in line with Silver's request that Taub not discuss the matter anymore with Chill. "I didn't know what to make of it, actually," Taub said of Silver's request. "He just wanted it kept between me and Mr. Silver, between me and him."

"I felt that I would honor that request. Why not?" Taub said.

The money Silver planned to send to Taub's clinic came from state taxes on health insurance and health services collected under a law called the Health Care Reform Act. The law evolved over the years. As it stood in 2004, the law allowed Silver as Assembly speaker to appropriate about $8.5 million per year to health-related pet projects without disclosing where any of it went. He could send money to Taub without the public knowing about it.[16]

Soon after Silver got Taub's January 4, 2004, letter, the state's bureaucratic wheels began turning—slowly.

First, the letter to Silver was passed to Dean Fuleihan, a top Silver aide. Fuleihan passed it on to several other Assembly aides, with a note scribbled on the top: "Shelly is very interested in this."

Nobody on the Assembly staff cared why Silver wanted the money. It was up to Silver how it would be spent, and the staff didn't question it. "The speaker was the ultimate decision maker," said Victor E. Franco, a staffer for the Assembly Ways and Means Committee, which handles budget matters.

Assembly employees checked that Columbia University—a member of the Ivy League and the fifth-oldest university in America, founded in 1754—was indeed a nonprofit organization eligible to receive public money. They condensed Taub's letter to a one-page form that was forwarded to the state Department of Health.

The matter stayed with the Department of Health for months. Finally, in July 2005—18 months after Taub wrote the letter—the Department of Health informed him that money for his grant was appropriated.

The next step was for Taub to formally apply for it. Taub, who had sought many grants before, thought this odd. "The process usually was the opposite, which is, first you filled out the application, then you got the grant," he said.

With Taub's application in hand, the Department of Health drafted the formal contract with Columbia University for receipt of the money. Bureaucrats in the state Attorney General's Office reviewed the contract "to ensure that it is in fact the typical state contract and that it meets all the legal requirements, in their view, for a state contract," explained Dennis Whalen, a former executive in the state Department of Health. [17]

The state Comptroller's Office also reviewed the contract. "They have audit and financial review responsibility," Whalen said.

The contract contained some bureaucratic absurdity. It prohibited Taub and Columbia from participating in "an international boycott in violation of the federal Export Administration Act of 1979." That law banned "any boycott fostered by a foreign country against a country which is friendly to the United States," and was aimed at countering the Arab League boycott of Israel that had largely fizzled by 2005. Taub's laboratory was also barred by New York law from using tropical hardwoods to comply with the contract, "unless specifically exempted by the State or any governmental agency or political subdivision or public benefit corporation."

Columbia also had to promise that the money would be properly spent.

Finally, in February 2006—more than two years after Taub and Silver started the process—the contract had the needed rubber stamps from the attorney general and the comptroller and was signed by everyone involved. The contract gave Columbia University $250,000 for expenses incurred by Taub's lab between July 2005 and June 2006.

Whalen said he would not be surprised if 20 different state officials were involved in reviewing Taub's grant. "We didn't have anything to say about who got the money or how much. We were just to process the contract," he explained. Silver made the request, and the contract was funded with state money Silver controlled. That was enough.

In November 2006, Taub and Silver started the process all over again. The second $250,000 grant was approved far more quickly, in June 2007.

Taub hoped that by giving Silver names of more patients, he'd be "incentivized" to keep the state money flowing to his research. He felt he was building a good relationship with one of the state's most powerful politicians.

Because of the referrals, Taub said, "a friendship was beginning to develop."

Silver transmitted dozens of lucrative cases from Taub's examining rooms to Weitz & Luxenberg. Over the years, these cases brought the firm millions in revenue. Weitz & Luxenberg paid Taub nothing. But Silver made sure Taub was compensated, through the $500,000 in state money to support his research.

Weitz & Luxenberg gladly paid Silver one-third of the fees it earned from the cases he brought in. That was its standard payment to any lawyer who brought in business, whether they worked for the firm or not.

Taub was a terrific unpaid salesman for Weitz & Luxenberg. His cases were a gift to the firm. They came without advertising or marketing costs, which—going by the experience of Weitz & Luxenberg competitor Simmons Hanly Conroy—could run $100,000 or more for each mesothelioma sufferer it signed as a client. And because Taub was one of the few doctors in the country specializing in mesothelioma, his referrals were a sure thing. They were the cases of people dying of mesothelioma who, under the asbestos payment system evolved through years of litigation, brought the biggest settlements and legal fees.

Mary Hesdorffer was bothered that her boss handed the names of their patients to law firms that made big money off their cases. She talked with patients about the referrals in a way she felt Taub would not. "My relationship with patients was different—I would have longer conversations with patients," she said. The patients told her they were uncomfortable that Taub referred them to lawyers.

Aside from her ethical concerns, Hesdorffer feared Taub was breaking the law. "I told him they would take him out in handcuffs."

Chapter 6 – Extra money

Albany power plays—such as his vanquishing of Michael Bragman's effort to depose him as speaker— were one way Sheldon Silver held his spot in the political elite. Another was building relationships with businessmen via rich-guy activities like golf outings and steakhouse lunches.

One Silver businessman pal was Jordan Levy, a wealthy investor in upstate real estate and other businesses, and an advocate for Buffalo's economic development. One day on the golf course, probably around 2003—years later, memories were hazy on this point—Silver and Levy learned they had a mutual friend when one of Silver's mobile phones rang.

"It was Arthur Luxenberg," Levy said. "He, Shelly, explained that he was playing golf in Buffalo. I assume on the other end [Luxenberg] asked with who; he said it was me."[1]

Silver wasn't a good golfer, Levy said—but that didn't hurt their friendship. "We played golf again and I saw him frequently in New York City." Levy said he may have met Silver at group lunches he regularly attended at Weitz & Luxenberg. They attended sporting events together, and shared meals. "I would consider Sheldon Silver a close friend," Levy said.

Silver also worked to improve his relationship with Steve Witkoff, the downtown Manhattan real estate developer whose fortunes were important to Silver's Assembly district. Witkoff's properties in and around downtown's Financial District struggled in the years after the September 11, 2001, attacks. Also, the neighborhood was changing—the center of the city's finance industry for years had been moving north to Midtown Manhattan. Witkoff and Silver were both concerned about the Financial District's recovery.

In 2004, Silver asked Witkoff for a favor on behalf of Jay Goldberg, his longtime friend. The request came as the men lunched at the Prime Grill, a kosher steakhouse in Midtown. Silver asked Witkoff if he employed specialized lawyers to handle his New York City property-tax appeals.

"Of course I do," Witkoff replied.

As he had with Leonard Litwin and Glenwood Management years before, Silver pitched to Witkoff the services of Jay Goldberg's tax certiorari law firm.

Silver called Goldberg *haimish*—a Yiddish word that means friendly or homey.

Witkoff didn't know how to spell "haimish." "I'd have to have my grandmother here," he explained.

"He said to me he had a friendship with this man. He was a good, decent man."

"As it was explained to me, he was a man who needed help and was trying to earn a good, decent living," Witkoff said. "He needed some help, and would I consider using him for tax certiorari work on buildings that we owned or controlled?"[2]

Silver's statement to Witkoff that his friend's law practice "needed help" was something of a lie. Goldberg indicated that his business was doing fine at the time.[3]

Witkoff decided sending some of his tax-appeal business to Goldberg was a good idea. "It was an easy favor for me to do," he said. Witkoff's company, The Witkoff Group, wasn't as affected by state government as Glenwood. But Witkoff saw that a connection with Silver could be useful. He hoped he and Silver would have a "positive relationship." He admitted being motivated by "a combination of looking to create good will and not alienate Mr. Silver."

"He was one of the most powerful politicians in state politics," Witkoff said. "In the event that I wanted to discuss things with him or have access to him about things that might be relevant to my business, I wanted to be able to have that—to be able to approach him as needed."[4]

Witkoff explained further: "It was an easy favor to do and I didn't want to run the risk of alienating him for such an easy favor. He didn't need to threaten me."[5]

After the steakhouse lunch, Witkoff spoke to one of his employees, Sarah Parnes, who oversaw his firm's tax-appeal lawyers. He asked her to consider hiring Jay Goldberg, and advised her "that she should look into his background. And, if all things were equal and if his fees were consistent with fees that we paid other lawyers or in fact lower, and if he was a good certiorari lawyer, that she should consider using him."

Witkoff did not see his tax-appeal lawyers as highly skilled. "It's pretty much pro forma stuff in the filing of the documents and hopefully getting some sort of reduction," he said. "You're entitled to it, or you're not." In his view, Goldberg was probably no better or worse than any other tax certiorari lawyer.[6] So if he was qualified to do the work, Witkoff saw no downside and maybe plenty of upside to giving him some tax appeals to handle.

After several weeks of back-and-forth, Goldberg in January 2005 sent Parnes a contract for tax-appeal work on five of the Witkoff Group's Manhattan properties. Goldberg wrote in the contract that his fee was 25 percent of any tax savings his firm won for the buildings. That was Goldberg's standard fee, and it was what Glenwood Management paid. But Witkoff didn't want to pay so much. Someone in Witkoff's office crossed out Goldberg's stated fee and wrote instead that it would be 15 percent.

Goldberg took the deal with the reduced fee. Over the following years, his law firm came to represent five to 10 Witkoff buildings, said Goldberg's law partner, Dara Iryami. Goldberg handed Silver 15 percent of the fees Witkoff paid.

Witkoff said he had no idea Goldberg was sharing his fees with Silver.

At the same time Silver took fees from the Witkoff Group and Glenwood Management, he continued to rake in money from the dead.

Robert Taub's mesothelioma patients, who tended to be in their late 60s, usually lived around 18 months after their first visit to his office—but their legal cases went on for years. It was normal for Weitz & Luxenberg to collect money on their behalf seven, eight, or nine years after they died. Whenever the firm collected money on behalf of Taub's patients—living or dead—Silver got a cut.

Since Silver needed to keep secret the money he earned aside from the $121,000 state salary he earned as Assembly speaker, it was just as well for him that Taub's patients didn't live long. Dead people don't talk. If Silver got in trouble, his clients could not be brought to court to testify.

The families of Taub's patients were also in the dark about Silver's involvement in their cases.

Federal investigators found that survivors of Taub's patients knew nothing about Silver's referral fees. An investigator who called the daughter of Taub patient Walter Bernabe learned that neither the daughter nor Bernabe's widow knew who Silver was. Silver earned $121,400 in fees from Bernabe, who signed up with Weitz & Luxenberg in 2005.[7] None of the former Taub patients or their surviving relatives contacted by federal investigators "was aware of any role played by Silver in providing legal services to himself or herself or a family member," an investigator wrote. [8] Some surviving relatives had never even heard of Silver.

One of the dead people who helped fill Silver's investment accounts was Vincenza Lala, a New Jersey woman who ran a retail lawn and garden business with her husband, Jim, in Sayreville, in suburban Middlesex County. She specialized in the flower arranging part of the business, which was called Artistic Flowers by Jean— Jean was the name by which her friends knew her. Her obituary depicts her as a respected member of her community. She belonged to the Ladies Auxiliary of the local Elks Club and attended a Catholic church. Though she and her husband had no children of their own, they raised money for children with brain injuries. "She was a talented and creative person who won many awards for her porcelain dolls, ceramics, and cross stitching at the Middlesex County Fair," said the *Home News Tribune*, the local newspaper.

Lala was diagnosed with mesothelioma on February 17, 2004, records show. She and Jim followed Taub's advice and let him give their names to Silver.

In turn, Silver gave the Lalas' names and phone number to his colleagues at Weitz & Luxenberg. In an email dated February 20, a Weitz & Luxenberg lawyer complained to Silver that he was having a hard time contacting the Lalas because their phone had no answering machine. This obstacle was soon overcome. By February 25, the Lalas agreed to retain the firm. Lala was the second case Taub gave to Silver.

There was no way to be sure how Vincenza Lala came to inhale deadly asbestos fibers. Weitz & Luxenberg lawyers sought money for the Lalas from asbestos trusts and companies it believed might be responsible for her illness. Over the following year, the Weitz & Luxenberg lawyers reached two settlements on Lala's behalf.

One settlement was with Crown Cork & Seal.[9] Among other things, Crown Cork made cans for food, drinks, and aerosols. In 1963, Crown Cork bought a company in New Jersey called Mundet Cork, which made cork-lined bottle caps. Mundet Cork had a subsidiary that used asbestos to make insulation. Within about three months of acquiring Mundet Cork, Crown Cork sold off the insulation subsidiary's assets. But that brief period of ownership stuck Crown Cork with Mundet Cork's asbestos liability.

No one could say exactly how Crown Cork's former subsidiary was involved in causing Lala to contract mesothelioma. But under the law, if Crown Cork was found partly liable for Lala's illness, it could be forced to pay most or all of the money damages she would be owed. Crown Cork settled Lala's case in January 2005 for $300,000, Weitz & Luxenberg records show.

Another settlement was reached with Owens-Illinois, one of the world's largest makers of glass bottles and containers. Owens-Illinois is more clearly connected with the asbestos industry than Crown Cork. Early in its history, Owens-Illinois manufactured and sold asbestos insulation. Lawyers connected the company to the decades-long cover-up of asbestos's dangers. Weitz & Luxenberg records show that in February 2005, Owens-Illinois settled its case with Vincenza Lala for $226,206.

Together the Owens-Illinois and Crown Cork settlements were worth $526,206. Weitz & Luxenberg took $16,022 off the top to cover expenses. That left $510,184 as the settlement to Lala. Of that sum, Weitz & Luxenberg took one-third—$170,061—as its fee. Silver netted $56,553 for the referral, about one-third of Weitz & Luxenberg's fee.[10]

Weitz & Luxenberg combined Silver's fee for the Lala case with his fees for four other mesothelioma clients Silver also obtained from Taub—Catherine O'Leary and Stanley Levinson of New Jersey, Donald Pieper of Minnesota, and William Zimmerman of Pennsylvania. Thus Silver got a check dated March 18, 2005, for $176,048.

That check was the first of the $3,057,901 in fees Silver collected over the next decade for taking Taub's mesothelioma cases to Weitz & Luxenberg. The $56,553 portion of the fee that came from Vincenza Lala's first two settlements was just the beginning of the money Silver made from her. By January 2015, Silver's one-third cut of fees from Lala's case added up to $214,401.

Lala died on August 1, 2006, at age 75. Her obituary said she succumbed "after a courageous battle with mesothelioma, a rare lung disease." She was Taub's patient for two and a half years. Weitz & Luxenberg

David McCluskey

2/25/23

Dear President Cheng,

This book came out late last Fall and I thought you'd enjoy it!

The author is a Daily News writer and it is a quick read.

Nard

Encl.

P.S. I met Shelly in '86 before he became Speaker and he introduced me to Kosher Pizza.

251 Westpoint Terrace ♣ West Hartford, CT 06107

lawyers worked on Lala's case at least until mid-2013, seven years after her death, and around the time her husband Jim died at age 78. Records are unclear on whether the lawyers' work on Lala's file at that late date brought any money to the trust in which the Lalas held their assets. But it is clear the case still produced paperwork. [11] Silver continued to collect fees from the case simply because he had transmitted Lala's name and contact information to Weitz & Luxenberg.

The most lucrative case Silver brought to the firm was that of Donald Pieper.

Pieper—whose case amounted to $32,670 of Silver's first check in March 2005—died in October 2008. Weitz & Luxenberg lawyers also worked on Pieper's case for years after his death, at least until late 2013. Over the years, Pieper's case netted Weitz & Luxenberg more than $1.38 million in fees. By January 2015, Silver had been paid $461,775 simply for transmitting Pieper's name from Taub to the firm.

Weitz & Luxenberg's internal emails confirm that lawyers knew Silver's cases came from Taub.

They knew how William Zimmerman's case came to them. "He was diagnosed with... Mesothelioma and has most recently been treating with Dr. Taub at Columbia Presbyterian.... Please note that this potential case is a direct referral to Sheldon Silver," said a June 25, 2004, email by Charles Ferguson, the firm's manager of asbestos litigation.

Zimmerman died in October 2004 at age 59, just six months after he first showed up in Taub's patient records. Weitz & Luxenberg lawyers worked on his case until 2012. Over time, Zimmerman's case brought Silver $58,252 in fees.

The lawyers also knew Taub and Silver got them Stanley Levinson's case. A note in Levinson's Weitz & Luxenberg file dated July 30, 2004, says, "Shelly S. called with this new case that called him after a recommendation by Dr. Taub." Levinson died in March

2005 at age 84. Weitz & Luxenberg lawyers kept working on his case up to at least 2012. By 2015, Levinson's case had brought Silver $176,005 in fees.

Early in March 2005, Ferguson had a hard time reaching a potential client named Henry Ross. He emailed one of the firm's administrative staffers: "Nancy, would you please relay a message to Shelly. Please tell him that the phone number he got from Dr. Taub for Henry Ross ... continues to ring off the hook; I tried to call Mr. Ross periodically over the weekend and throughout the day to no avail. Does Shelly want to speak with Taub to see if there is another contact person?" Ferguson knew the case came from Taub. If Silver didn't know how to reach Henry Ross, he figured, maybe Taub had his number.

Ross died in January 2007 at age 79. He was Taub's patient for 21 months. Weitz & Luxenberg lawyers worked on his case until 2014. Over the years, Ross brought Silver $98,179 in fees.

Silver got so much cash from Weitz & Luxenberg and Jay Goldberg's law firm that managing it was a problem.

For one thing, the money took time to reach his bank account. Silver was "upset or annoyed" that the checks Weitz & Luxenberg wrote him took too long in the mail, said top Weitz & Luxenberg manager, Gary Klein. It wasn't that Silver faced any financial emergencies. "He just said he was annoyed at the delay," Klein said. Eventually Silver and the firm worked out a system whereby a secretary deposited the checks at the bank on Silver's behalf.

Another problem was what to do with all his cash.

Silver wanted his money to work hard. Many people of his income might have put the cash in mutual funds. If Silver put his money in plain-vanilla stock index funds that tracked the S&P 500, he might have averaged an annual return of around 10 percent—some years more, some years less, and in some years he might have lost money.

Silver wanted more.

His relationship with Jordan Levy—his sometime golfing partner from upstate—offered a solution to the problem Silver described to Levy as his "extra money."

Around 2006, Silver told Levy he wished to invest in his businesses. The request posed some difficulty. Though Silver was one of New York's most powerful politicians, his personal wealth was peanuts compared to Levy's other investors. Levy testified that the people whose money he handled were "high net worth." "Most all are friends," he said.

But Silver was a friend too, and Levy found a way to accommodate him. He decided to let Silver put some money into what he called Clover Communities Fund I, which invested in senior citizen housing, mostly in upstate New York. "I thought it would be a good investment for him to be in," Levy said. He added, "It was fairly safe and ... very solid returns."

In fact, the Clover I fund paid a lot better than the stock market—in "the mid- to upper-teens," Levy said. In other words, somewhere around 15 percent to 20 percent per year. The only investors were friends or associates of Levy and his partner, Michael Joseph—the funds were not open to the public. At the time Silver got in, the fund was closed to all new investors. But Levy and Joseph reduced their own investment in the fund to make room for $100,000 of Silver's "extra money."

Over time, Levy got Silver into other investments. "I would go to him and tell him that I had something that I thought would be good for him to invest in," Levy said.

He never asked where Silver's money came from.

Silver put $175,000 into other Clover housing funds. Levy also helped Silver invest in Synacor, a company that provides internet content to telephone and cable companies; NewSat, an Australian satellite company that collapsed in 2015, costing investors around $150 million in U.S. currency; and venture capital and hedge funds.

The biggest investment Silver made with Levy's advice was with Counsel Financial, a company that loans money to plaintiff law firms like Weitz & Luxenberg. It was another way Silver could make money off legal cases, including those brought by people with mesothelioma.

Counsel Financial loans money to law firms in anticipation that the firms would win fees from their cases. When the firms' cases pay off, they repay Counsel Financial. Silver didn't own stock in the firm. Instead, he provided money for Counsel Financial to loan out. In return, he got a cut of the interest the company earned from its lending.

Perry Weitz and Arthur Luxenberg were among Silver's fellow investors in Counsel Financial. Weitz chaired the company's board of directors, and Luxenberg was the vice chairman. According to Levy, Weitz and Luxenberg were not involved in Silver's investment. Instead, documents show, Silver invested in Counsel Financial via Levy's venture capital firm, Buffalo-based SoftBank Capital.

"My staff would handle all the paperwork and documentation and work directly with Sheldon Silver or his accountants on these investments," Levy said. Silver was spared the kinds of fees buried in the publicly available mutual funds used by many of his constituents: Levy did not charge Silver for his company's work in setting up the investments.

Silver first invested in Counsel Financial in January 2007 by writing a $25,000 check. [12] He followed up in March 2007 with a $75,000 investment. [13]

People who provided Counsel Financial money to lend to law firms got between 9 and 15 percent interest, said Paul Cody, the company's president. [14] Levy told Silver he would earn 11 percent interest on his money—and promised that by letting the interest accrue, he'd do a little better. "We will keep an eye on the investment and we are also accruing the interest so that it should build and deliver a yield well north of 12 percent for you," he wrote Silver.[15]

Counsel Financial typically required a minimum investment of $250,000. Silver's initial $25,000 and $75,000 investments were far less than that sum. Asked how Silver was able to invest less than $250,000, Levy answered: "Because I made those arrangements."

Levy bent the rules for Silver. He also helped Silver get into other investments.

Arthur Luxenberg told Silver about Alpha Orbit, a Dallas hedge fund in which Levy and a group of investors planned to place $5.2 million. Levy told Silver he should invest in Alpha Orbit, "but it is a little riskier" than most of the other investments he suggested. A statement Levy's firm prepared in 2014 said Silver's stake in Alpha Orbit was $25,000—less than 0.5 percent of the $5.2 million Levy gathered for the investment from his friends and associates.

Levy also helped Silver invest $25,000 in Lerer Ventures, a Manhattan venture capital firm. "I asked him if he would like to participate. ... If I thought it was something he should do, he would," Levy said.

Like Counsel Financial, none of these investments were available to the general public. They also weren't normally available to people of Silver's net worth, which was much lower than that of Levy's usual investors.

It's hard to say what Levy got from helping Silver. It may have cost him money—after all, he and a partner gave up part of their investment in the closed Clover Communities Fund I to make room for Silver's contribution. Silver may have advanced Levy's work as a Buffalo civic booster. From 2007 to 2012, Levy was chair of the Erie Canal Harbor Development Corporation, a public agency that worked on developing Buffalo's Lake Erie waterfront. Silver was a member of the Public Authority Control Board, which controlled state money spent on Erie Canal Harbor projects. Silver told Levy he'd support his agency's work. No one ever said Levy benefitted personally by his efforts to help his hometown.

There was also the friendship. Levy said he and Silver usually spoke several times a week. They golfed. They attended Buffalo Sabres and New York Rangers hockey games. Levy met Silver's family and visited his Lower East Side apartment. When they talked, Silver never mentioned Jay Goldberg or Robert Taub. Levy knew Silver was associated with Weitz & Luxenberg. But he said Silver never told him about any of the mesothelioma patients he referred to the firm.

"Would you agree that sometimes Mr. Silver could be hard to read?" asked defense lawyer Justin Shur.

"Definitely," Levy replied. [16]

And, he said, Sheldon Silver had a good poker face. He was not a man who easily gave up his secrets.

Chapter 7 – The builder

Moneyed New Yorkers paid rent to Leonard Litwin. Six of his big luxury apartment buildings were on York Avenue in Manhattan's well-to-do Upper East Side. This got him an admiring nickname in some real estate circles: the Duke of York.

The Litwin family likes gardens and forests. Leonard Litwin's grandfather was a forester in Ukraine for Czar Nicholas II. Leonard's father, Harry, emigrated to the United States and opened a nursery on Long Island. Harry Litwin was also a writer. In 1955, he published a book of poetry and gardening advice, *The Green Kingdom*, under the nom de plume Harry Woodbourne. A *New York Times* reviewer said the book was written in a "sensitive, philosophical vein."

After the publisher shipped 3,000 copies, Harry Litwin asked that its type be destroyed.

Over the years, New York City real estate became the Litwins' focus. Harry Litwin began investing in real estate in the 1940s. In the early 1950s he opened a 105-unit apartment building in Briarwood, a neighborhood in central Queens. In 1960, Harry teamed up with his son Leonard to open a 402-unit apartment building in the Bronx's upscale Riverdale neighborhood. The company they founded, Glenwood Management, still owns that complex today.

Harry Litwin died in 1963 as he and Leonard were building their first Manhattan project, the 800-unit Pavilion, on East Seventy-Seventh Street just off York Avenue. Leonard Litwin took over the family business. He focused on building luxury Manhattan apartment towers with hundreds of units, marketed to high-income tenants. Besides the Bronx complex, Glenwood's website listed 30 luxury buildings in Manhattan in 2020. Leonard Litwin was the principal owner of Glenwood when he died in 2017 at age 102 in a house next door to the family nursery's trees and shrubs. Upon his death, his daughter Carole took over the company.

Unlike many Manhattan developers, Glenwood didn't build out its entire lots—the Litwins always left a little space for landscaping. Glenwood's 45-story building at 10 Liberty Street in Manhattan's Financial District—in Sheldon Silver's legislative district—is surrounded by shrubs, and even has trees on parapets atop its lower floors. The building went up in 2002 and was the first big construction project in lower Manhattan after the September 11 attacks on the World Trade Center several blocks away.

Typical Glenwood apartments have marble bathrooms and stainless-steel appliances. Twenty-four-hour doorman service is standard. Some Glenwood buildings have concierges, gyms, swimming pools, and landscaped roof decks. "We pride ourselves on being able to offer residents everything that they truly need in order to live the Manhattan lifestyle," the company's website said.

Because of New York's complex housing-finance and zoning rules, some luxury Glenwood buildings also house low-income tenants. Glenwood prides itself on treating high- and low-income tenants the same. Glenwood buildings lack what New Yorkers call "poor doors"—separate entrances for low-income renters. Apartments for high- and low-income tenants have the same appliances and fixtures.

Politics was key to Litwin's business plan. State government had a big impact on Glenwood's profitability and its ability to construct new projects. Its executives did not believe the company was diverse enough to survive laws that would make its apartment buildings costlier to build or own. "We don't build shopping centers. We don't build office buildings," said Richard Runes, who supervised Glenwood's state capitol lobbying operation. Housing, Runes said, is "all we build."

New York's rent regulation law—which, during Silver's speakership, was typically renewed every four years—affects nearly all Glenwood buildings. The city's Rent Stabilization Board sets how much landlords can increase rent every year. State law sets the rules by which the Rent Stabilization Board sets rents. Landlords want to be rid of the laws so they can set rents in an unregulated, competitive market. But the Legislature and voters support rent regulation, and the laws are here to stay. So landlords like Glenwood lobby to reduce the rules' impact on their bottom lines. The less the state regulates rents, the better, said Glenwood vice president for finance Michael Hoenig. The state rent law "affects negatively," he said. He explained: "The more regulated apartments you have, the lower your income is."

Glenwood relies on state programs meant to encourage housing development. From 2000 to 2015, Glenwood obtained $1.09 billion in state financing for its buildings. Silver, as a member of a state board that approved the financing, had veto power over Glenwood's state financing requests. He voted in favor of all eight of Glenwood's requests between 2000 and 2014.

Glenwood also took advantage of a law known in Albany and in real estate circles as 421-a, which denoted its place in the state property tax code. The 421-a law cut property taxes for new housing developments, and was credited with facilitating the construction of 117,000 new apartments from 2010 to 2020.[1] Such tax breaks are controversial, but New York housing developers have relied on them for decades. Al Smith, who was governor for most of the 1920s, mentioned in *The Citizen and His Government* that state law in his time let New York City exempt new housing from real estate tax increases for as long as 20 years. Smith said the law was part of "a great forward step in the development of American social legislation."[2] The real estate industry sees such laws as part of its path to profit. "If those programs were altered or disappeared, it would be difficult for us," said Runes.

The possibility the Legislature might alter or wipe away the 421-a law or change the rent regulation rules to favor tenants more was a constant worry for Glenwood and others in the business of developing and operating rental housing.

"There are hundreds of pieces of legislation filed every year that have to do with housing. The Assembly passes many of them," explained Brian Meara, who besides being one of Silver's friends was a Glenwood lobbyist. The Democratic Assembly's bills were often pro-tenant. Pro-tenant bills went to the Republican Senate to die. "The Senate passes very few, if any of them," Meara said. Runes put it this way: "The state Senate Republicans were more compatible with the issues and opinions of Glenwood."

Litwin, his lobbyists, and others in the real estate industry dealt with the situation by buying as much influence in the Legislature as they could.

Litwin focused his political campaign donations on state Senate Republicans, who fought to repeal the rent laws. "Mr. Litwin was a firm believer that the Republicans needed to control the Senate. ... He was a big believer that the Republican Senate was the backstop to business interests and even more so when the governor's mansion became held by Democrats," said Charles Dorego, Glenwood's chief in-house lawyer. Asked how Republican control of the Senate ranked in Glenwood's political priorities, Dorego answered, "It was the number one priority." [3]

New York's state campaign finance laws were originally written to keep big corporations, and big donors like Leonard Litwin, from unduly influencing politics.

The laws are dizzyingly complex. One of their peculiarities is that in primary elections, contribution limits vary by party. Some limits are based on the number of registered members of a party, or on a legislative district's population. Candidates' relatives can give more money than regular folks—but within limits. For example, contributions from candidates' relatives for statewide primary election campaigns are capped at the "total number of enrolled voters in the candidate's party in the state, excluding voters in inactive status, multiplied by $0.025." [4] Thus the family of someone running for governor in a political party with 4,000,000 active registered or "enrolled" members could give a maximum $100,000 to a campaign. The limits are lower for campaigns for the Senate and Assembly, because senators and Assembly members run in smaller districts. And the limits vary in each legislative district, because their political party memberships vary.

To help candidates and their families follow the rules about legislative district population, the New York State Board of Elections each year publishes a district-by-district guide to family contribution limits.

Other laws apply to corporate donations. For much of the time Sheldon Silver was Assembly speaker, corporations could give no more than $5,000 to a New York political candidate each year. But corporations could give without limit to political action committees, which in turn could give without limit to candidates.

In his push to maintain Republican influence in the Legislature, Litwin had an edge over his political foes.

Remember Republican presidential candidate Mitt Romney's comment in 2011 that "corporations are people?" Under part of New York's campaign finance law, that is true. The state Board of Elections ruled in 1996 that limited liability companies—better known as LLCs—are not to be treated as corporations under the campaign law, but as people—humans—not related to a candidate.

The Board of Elections ruling effectively wiped away corporate campaign donation limits for companies like Glenwood Management, which conduct business via numerous LLCs.

In 2012, New York law limited an individual corporation to giving $5,000 to a political candidate. But thanks to the Board of Elections ruling, corporations could give a lot more money through any LLCs they might own. In calendar year 2012, a person—as well as LLCs, treated as persons under the law—could give $6,500 to a senator's primary campaign, and $10,300 to a senator's general election campaign. The limits for Assembly members were $4,100 in a primary, and another $4,100 in a general election.[5]

Yet another rule capped at $150,000 the total amount of money individual donors—including corporations and LLCs—could give to political campaigns in a year.

Leonard Litwin didn't worry about these donation limits. He didn't have to.

Glenwood's 27 or so apartment buildings were each owned by a limited liability company. Glenwood held dozens of other properties—such as parking garages and office suites—in other LLCs. From 2000 to 2015, Glenwood—and Litwin, its sole owner—gave politicians money under the names of 85 LLCs based at the company's main office on Long Island, New York state campaign finance records show.[6]

Each of those 85 LLCs could give campaigns $150,000, the cap for donations by individual donors. That meant Litwin could give up to $12.75 million per year to state politicians. All he had to do was make sure each of his LLCs stayed within the $150,000-per-donor limit on contributions.

The limits on donations to individual campaigns also meant nothing to Litwin.

Under the law as it existed in 2012, Litwin could use Glenwood's 85 LLCs to give $348,500 to an Assembly member's primary campaign, and another $348,500 to that member's general election campaign. Those sums exceeded by $344,400 the $4,100-per-candidate cap for individual donors in Assembly primary and general election campaigns.

Through Glenwood, Litwin could donate as much as $552,500 to a state senator's primary campaign, and $875,500 to a state senator's general election campaign. Those sums exceeded the $6,500 individual donor cap for Senate primary campaigns by $546,000, and the $10,300 individual donor cap for Senate general election campaigns by $865,200.

Glenwood's state political campaign donations never came anywhere near those legal limits. From 2005 to 2014, Glenwood gave $12.2 million to candidates for New York state office, state campaign finance records show. Over those years, Glenwood's total political contributions didn't even hit the $12.75 million legal limit that applied just in 2012.

So much Glenwood cash went to political campaigns that Runes, one of the company's lobbyists, couldn't keep track. He said Glenwood gave "approximately $10 million" to state political campaigns in the decade leading up to 2015. That was about $2 million below the actual total. In any case, Runes allowed that Glenwood's political giving in New York ranked "pretty much at the top."

There is no question Litwin's giving via Glenwood was legal. Reformers have complained for decades that New York law unfairly let companies like Glenwood give vast sums to politicians and candidates through multiple LLCs. Critics say donations like Litwin's are bad for democracy. But New York elected officials have no interest in changing the system that funds their campaigns.

Not all of Glenwood's donations went to Republicans. Litwin gave strategically to some Democratic campaigns. The New York Public Interest Research Group, an organization seeking campaign finance reform, calculated that "through various entities and campaign accounts," Litwin donated $1 million to Andrew Cuomo's 2014 campaign for governor.[7]

One day in March 2009, Litwin asked Michael Hoenig, his company's vice president for finance, to write three checks to "Friends of Silver." The group was "a political campaign, I would imagine," Hoenig said. It wasn't his job to know or care that the money was going to Sheldon Silver's campaign.

Usually the checks Hoenig wrote were drawn on the individual bank accounts of Glenwood-owned limited liability companies. One check Hoenig drew that day was from River York Barclay LLC. The second was from a company called Tribeca North End LLC, and the third was from 94th Realty LLC. Each check for "Friends of Silver" was for $1,250.

Why that sum? "I don't know," Hoenig said. "I'm usually told to draw several checks and given the amounts." Sometimes, Litwin told him from which limited liability companies he should draw checks. Other times Litwin let Hoenig pick the LLCs himself. "We tried to rotate so one particular LLC wouldn't get overly burdened," Hoenig said.

It is easy to see that $1,250 wouldn't make much of a dent in the finances of any single Glenwood building or LLC.

Take a close look at River York Barclay LLC, the company in which Glenwood held its apartment building at 1755 York Avenue on Manhattan's Upper East Side. The Barclay is 37 stories tall and has 329 units—a "wide choice of one-, two-, and three-bedroom apartments," according to Glenwood's website. A March 2009 study of Manhattan rents found that in Upper East Side doorman buildings, one-bedroom apartments went for $3,106 per month and two-bedrooms went for $5,143. Three-bedrooms were rare, but north of Thirty-Fourth Street in Manhattan they went for $8,964 per month.[8] The $1,250 check Hoenig wrote from the building's account to Silver's campaign would barely register in the revenue River York Barclay LLC took in from 329 luxury apartments every month.

Glenwood's Tribeca North End LLC owned a building at 450 North End Avenue in Battery Park City, which is one of Manhattan's wealthiest neighborhoods and part of Sheldon Silver's district. The building has 145 apartments, mainly two- and three-bedroom units. Again, a $1,250 donation to Silver from this building would barely be a blip—a fraction of one month's rent on one apartment.

The outlier among the three LLCs from which Hoenig was asked to draw a check was 94th Realty, which according to city records owned a five-story office building at 207 East Ninety-Fourth Street. 94th Realty was one of a number of Glenwood LLCs that operated parking garages, offices, and other properties, most of which were incorporated into its residential buildings. But it is hard to see how the third $1,250 check Hoenig wrote to Silver's campaign would have burdened such a building's finances.

Hoenig didn't question Litwin's instructions when he was asked to write checks. "He was hands on all the way," Hoenig said of his boss. "He made the final decisions in just about everything."

Runes mailed Hoenig's checks to the campaigns. He put each check into an envelope, and added his business card. Never did Runes write a letter, note, or anything else stating why the donation was being made—the envelopes contained only checks written out to the order of a campaign, and Runes's card. That, and the envelopes' return address of Glenwood headquarters at 1200 Union Turnpike in New Hyde Park on Long Island, was enough for the recipients to know where the money came from. "It was just the way we did it," Runes said.

Glenwood gave money all the time, even in years when rent control and housing finance were not before the Legislature. "You need to have good relationships and a good reputation with people all along," said Runes. "You can't just call them and say, 'Hi, I'm back. It's four years. Renew the laws.'"

It is important for lobbyists to be physically present in politicians' lives.

On days when the Legislature is in session in Albany, lobbyists schmooze with politicians in the foyer behind the Assembly's elegant chamber and in the lounges adjoining the equally ornate Senate chamber. Runes made a point of being in Albany on big days, such as the governor's annual State of the State address, a ritual that brings out everyone important in state government. By hanging around, Runes could see and be seen by senators, Assembly members, court of appeals judges, the attorney general, the comptroller, and lots of other people. For decades, the speech was held in the 19th-century Gothic revival Assembly chamber. Silver's office was nearby. "I would make it my business to be outside the speaker's office as all those people would come by," Runes said.

It was important to be there, and to make sure the "three men in a room"—the governor, the Senate majority leader, and the Assembly speaker—knew of Glenwood's interests. Assembly Speaker Silver, whoever led the Senate majority, and whoever sat in the governor's office would take a "fairly hands-on role" in deciding rent laws, Runes said. "I think those three people ... end up making the decision on how those laws are extended," he said.

Another facet of Litwin's effort to attain influence in Albany was his employment of Jay Goldberg's law firm to handle some Glenwood buildings' property-tax appeals.

In the years after Silver helped set up the arrangement around 1997, Litwin gave Goldberg's firm more and more of Glenwood's tax-appeal business. "I couldn't tell you why," said Hoenig, who also oversaw the company's tax-appeal efforts.

Hoenig's view of tax certiorari lawyers was in accord with developer Steve Witkoff, who had a similar arrangement with Goldberg's firm. Hoenig didn't think they did much for their pay.

Hoenig prepared for the real-estate-tax appeals by drawing up financial statements for each building Glenwood felt the city had overtaxed. The statements were then audited by an outside accounting firm. New York City real estate taxes are based on an assessment of a property's value. In the appeals, Glenwood used the statements to claim that the buildings weren't profitable enough to justify the city's assessment of their value in calculating their taxes. "We try to reduce the assessed value," Hoenig said. If the city agreed to cut the buildings' assessments, their property taxes would be lowered.

Goldberg and the other tax-appeal lawyers Glenwood hired had no role in preparing the financial statements. "We give them a complete form filled out, which is a financial statement. And they'll go to the city and file it," Hoenig explained. Hoenig could never tell the difference between the work done by the different law firms. "I never recommended one over another," he said.

In 2000, Goldberg's firm handled property-tax appeals of two Glenwood buildings. By 2005—eight years after he began working with Glenwood—Goldberg's firm had seven Glenwood buildings. In 2008, Goldberg had 16 Glenwood buildings.

The appeals saved Glenwood millions—and netted fees for Goldberg's firm that ran into the hundreds of thousands of dollars. Goldberg shared those fees with Sheldon Silver.

During the 2004/5 fiscal year, New York City figured the Regent, a Glenwood building at the corner of West Sixtieth Street and Ninth Avenue on Manhattan's Upper West Side, was worth $33.75 million for tax purposes. The following year, the city assessed the Regent's value as $34.65 million. With help from financial statements on the building provided by Hoenig, Goldberg's firm reduced the Regent's assessed value in both years to $31.6 million. Over the two years, the assessment change slashed the Regent's tax bills by $635,232.

On May 31, 2005, Goldberg presented Glenwood Management with a bill for $158,808, which represented 25 percent of the property-tax reduction Goldberg and Iryami won for the Regent.

Goldberg had good luck with several other Glenwood property-tax appeals that year. He got the city to cut the 2004/5 and 2005/6 tax bills at the Marlborough House at 747 Second Avenue in East Midtown by $632,178. He also got the city to cut the 2005/6 tax bill for the Belmont on East Forty-Sixth Street by $386,025.60. In mid-2005, he was able to bill Glenwood $639,507.60 for his work filing tax appeals.

Because Silver sent him his first Glenwood buildings, Goldberg handed his friend 25 percent of the fees he collected from the successful Glenwood tax appeals. Silver got 25 percent because that was the same percentage of the tax savings Goldberg's firm received. "It is the same percentage the client is paying," explained Goldberg's partner, Dara Iryami.

On July 11, 2005, Goldberg wrote a letter to his longtime friend, delivering happy news about six successful appeals—and a check for $159,876.90, some 25 percent of the sum he had recently billed Glenwood Management. Goldberg sent the letter and check to Silver's home address. "Love to the family," he wrote at the end.

Silver, ever sphinx-like, said nothing in public about what Goldberg & Iryami paid him. He didn't have to. The disclosure forms he filed with legislative ethics watchdogs are a model of legalistic obfuscation. They complied with the law without providing details of Silver's nongovernment work, or what he earned doing it. In any event, for years New York did not require Silver's statements about his outside income to be released to the public.

On his ethics disclosure form for 2005, Silver described his non-legislative job as "limited practice of law in the principal subject area of personal injury claims on behalf of individual clients and of counsel to law firm." Which was sort of true. Most of Silver's non-legislative income that year—$408,897—came from Weitz & Luxenberg. Most of that money was Silver's cut of Weitz & Luxenberg's fees for mesothelioma cases. Skilled mesothelioma lawyers may not see themselves as practicing the kind of personal injury law associated with handling car accidents or sidewalk slip-and-fall lawsuits. But Silver's explanation was probably close enough to satisfy New York's ethics laws. And Silver mostly told the truth when he wrote on the ethics forms that personal injury claims were his "principal" source of income, if you consider that his Weitz & Luxenberg pay was more than twice the $159,877 in fees Silver reaped for referring the Glenwood and Witkoff Group accounts to Goldberg.

Silver figured no one had to know any more than that about this outside income. Except for Goldberg, Iryami, Weitz & Luxenberg, and maybe Leonard Litwin, no one did.

Chapter 8 – The sheriff

By 2006, about nine years had passed since Jay Goldberg began sharing his fees from Glenwood Management's tax appeals with Sheldon Silver. And it had been three years since Robert Taub gave Silver his first mesothelioma referral for Weitz & Luxenberg.

Four state legislators were arrested in 2006. Ada Smith, a Democratic state senator from Queens, was busted in Albany on misdemeanor charges for throwing a cup of coffee in an aide's face. Three Assembly members faced various corruption charges. News stories about the arrests gave reporters a reason to ask Silver about his outside income.

Even his fellow Democrats weren't sure what Silver meant when he wrote on disclosure forms that his non-legislative work involved "Limited practice of law in the principal subject area of personal injury claims on behalf of individual clients and of counsel to law firm." Silver didn't give any detail beyond the law's requirement. His spokeswoman told a reporter, "The speaker is in complete compliance with the state's financial disclosure statute." Which was true, even though the statute offered the public no information about legislators' outside income.

Eliot Spitzer, the Democratic candidate for governor in 2006, signaled he might push for a law requiring Silver and other legislators to fully disclose their outside income. "I reveal my tax returns every year. I think it's the right thing to do," Spitzer said.[1]

Corrupt state politicians faced more media scrutiny on another front. The Albany *Times Union* newspaper began digging into what New York politicians call "member items"—pork slipped into the state budget on behalf of legislators and the governor, usually as a favor to constituents. Scrutiny of this kind of state spending was a threat to the money Silver earned from Robert Taub's mesothelioma patients.

Member items, which range in amount from a few thousand dollars to millions, usually go to government programs or nonprofit groups. In Silver's time, they were usually put in the budget at the behest of individual legislators. Silver, the Senate majority leader, and the governor—the three men in a room—decided which member items were put in the final budget.

Most member items go to innocuous projects hard to oppose. For example, in the 2006/7 fiscal year, the Cornell University Cooperative Extension program—which helps farmers—got $2,000 to build a yurt at a center on Long Island "to provide shelter for students who come to the Global Village Project to learn about important global and local issues related to food production, hunger and the environment." Several upstate Assembly members got $10,000 for the Syracuse school district "for athletic stadium netting to separate two fields and for other sports equipment."

Silver allotted $21,000 to a Manhattan group called the Chinese-American Planning Council "to continue support for a recreation/education worker and cultural arts worker, as well as for public transportation for the elderly and other operating expenses." Manhattan's Chinatown, next door to the Lower East Side, was an important part of Silver's legislative district.

Assembly member William Scarborough got $5,000 for a civic group "to support the economic development of Laurelton, Rosedale, and Springfield Gardens," neighborhoods in Queens. [2] Later, Scarborough was sentenced to 13 months in prison for filing $40,000 worth of false travel expenses with the state and taking $38,000 in campaign funds for his own use.

For years, thousands of member items like these were public record, detailed in the state budget. But the Legislature lacked unfettered power to bestow these gifts: New York's state constitution gives the governor power to veto individual items in the budget. After Republican governor George Pataki used his line-item veto power in 1998 to delete some member items, the Legislature pushed this spending underground. Instead of including member items as individual items in the annual budget, the Legislature approved them in one big lump sum that Pataki would have difficulty vetoing. Pataki played the game too—he padded out the budget with his own undisclosed spending ideas.

This arrangement made member items a secret. The Senate and Assembly leaders did not disclose or publish a list of member items, or report how much taxpayer money was spent on each one. By 2006, the member-items budget was $200 million per year—$85 million for the Assembly, $85 million for the Senate, and $30 million for the governor.

Times Union reporters didn't uncover anything in their member-items investigation that hinted at legislators' outside incomes. But their work raised plenty of questions about legislators' activities. Much of the spending uncovered by the newspaper benefitted legislators and their friends politically and financially.

One of the newspaper's discoveries hit close to Silver. *Times Union* reporters found that millions in state money went to the Metropolitan New York Coordinating Council on Jewish Poverty. "Its executive director, who earns $273,181 a year, is married to Silver's chief of staff," the newspaper reported. The reference was to William Rapfogel, the husband of Judy Rapfogel, a top Silver aide and confidante. In 2014, William Rapfogel pleaded guilty to helping steal $9 million from the council in a years-long kickback scheme.

The reporters also found that hundreds of thousands of dollars in Senate money was allocated to the North Bronx-Westchester Neighborhood Restoration Association, which was controlled by Guy Velella, a former Republican senator. The money kept flowing even after Velella was convicted in 2004 of taking $137,000 in bribes to help people win bridge-painting contracts.[3]

Senate Majority Leader Joseph Bruno was one of two Republicans among the three men in a room who decided what was in the budget. He gave $500,000 in taxpayer money to Evident Technologies, a company run by some of his friends and campaign donors, the *Times Union* discovered. The money was a gift to Evident—the state asked nothing in return. The $500,000 Evident Technologies grant may have been an undue burden on taxpayers, but it cost Bruno nothing—and it may have helped him access some perks. Evident Technologies' directors gave Bruno airplane rides and donated to the Senate Republican campaign fund.

The *Times Union* pressed on with a lawsuit meant to pry from the Legislature more information about which members sought which items. The newspaper won its case in October 2006. A judge said the Legislature "failed to articulate a rational basis for redacting the names" of legislators who sought the money. The Legislature did not appeal—but it opened its files grudgingly. The Republican-led Senate was especially slow. It released thousands of pages of material in computer files impossible to search electronically.

The lawsuit was yet another annoyance for political leaders who had no interest in telling citizens what they did in Albany. But Silver lucked out. The *Times Union*'s suit did not uncover information about Silver's grants to Robert Taub's mesothelioma lab. Silver allocated Taub's money under a law called the Health Care Reform Act. The *Times Union* lawsuit did not seek information about money appropriated under the Health Care Reform Act, and the state did not make the grants public.

Days after the *Times Union*'s court victory, the results of the 2006 election posed a new threat to Silver's extra money. Eliot Spitzer—Princeton grad, Harvard Law grad, scion of one of Manhattan's wealthy real estate development families—was voted in as governor partly because of his promises to fix Albany's corrupt ways. He got more than 65 percent of the vote.

Spitzer had positioned himself as a reformer during the previous eight years, when he was New York's attorney general. His crusade against financial industry excesses had mixed success. He succeeded in ending some hedge funds' ability to buy mutual funds at the previous day's lower price—a shady practice that earned Wall Streeters big money at the expense of small-time investors. His widely publicized fight to curb the huge salary of New York Stock Exchange CEO Richard Grasso failed. Spitzer believed Grasso's $187.5 million pay package violated state law governing nonprofit organizations such as the stock exchange. But in 2006 a for-profit company bought the Exchange. That meant Grasso's pay was no longer under the jurisdiction of nonprofit law, New York state courts ruled in 2008. Grasso kept it all.

Win some, lose some. Spitzer's battles against finance industry greed earned him the nickname "Sheriff of Wall Street."

Albany got a new deputy sheriff too. Andrew Cuomo—U.S. secretary of Housing and Urban Development during the Bill Clinton presidency, and son of respected former governor Mario Cuomo—was elected to replace Spitzer as attorney general.

Spitzer and Cuomo believed they could boost their careers by fighting the larcenous stench hanging over the Legislature. They knew all about the lobbyists and campaign financiers clamoring for special treatment in the Assembly and Senate, and the influence-peddling and greed that sent some legislators to prison.

Publicly, Cuomo acted first. On January 4, 2007—three days after he took office—Cuomo announced that his staff would review legislators' use of member items. "The taxpayers of New York must be assured that their hard-earned dollars are used for legitimate public purposes—period," Cuomo said. He assigned eight assistant attorneys general to review 6,000 individual member items included in the 2006/7 budget year. Their task was to make sure organizations getting state money were in "good legal standing," that the expenditures fit the New York State Constitution's requirement that money be spent only for public purposes, and that legislators had no financial interest in the organizations that got the money.[4]

Silver had to see he was being squeezed—but the politics of the situation required him to play along. Silver joined Spitzer, Cuomo, and Bruno when they announced an agreement on January 16 to fully disclose each member item added to the state budget. Silver issued a public statement welcoming the changes. "We will have a more transparent, more easily understood budget process," it said.

Before the end of January, the Legislature—prodded by Spitzer—passed a law that doomed the grants to Taub's clinic. The new law said all member items had to be published in the state budget. That meant if Silver wanted to continue sending state money to Taub, he'd have to make the grants public.

As Spitzer made rapid progress on legislative ethics issues, he undermined himself by showing an arrogant, ugly side. When Republican Assemblyman James Tedisco complained of being cut out of negotiations on ethics laws, Spitzer replied, "Listen, I am a fucking steamroller and I'll roll over you and anybody else." He also told Tedisco, "I've done more in three weeks than any governor has done in the history of the state." Spitzer didn't deny these comments.

Tedisco thought Spitzer's hubris would get him in trouble. "He has a different side to him than a lot of people realize. ... I think at some point he is going to lose it."[5]

But the scandals then enveloping the Legislature required its members to act. The Republican Senate and the Democratic Assembly promptly passed another bill Spitzer pushed called the Public Employees Ethics Reform Act of 2007. This bill strengthened rules about honoraria and gifts that lobbyists and others could give legislators, and prevented nepotism in state hiring. It also combined separate commissions that oversaw ethics rules for lobbyists and public officials into one commission—though despite the urgings of ethics advocacy groups, the new commission was still largely controlled by the Legislature. The new commission was given the job of collecting and publishing information from legislators about their investments and outside earnings. Spitzer signed the bill into law on March 27, less than three months after he took office.

As the 2007 legislative session neared an end later that spring, Spitzer deeply undermined his reputation as an ethics cop when he blundered into a conflict with Bruno.

Bruno—who became the only Republican among the three men in the room after Spitzer replaced George Pataki as governor—long had an odor of scandal about him. Anyone who carefully read the newspapers saw that Bruno's business success continued during his years as a part-time legislator. "I never wanted to be dependent on my government salary—the system would own you then—so I vowed that I'd always have an outside income," he said.[6]

One of Bruno's flaws was his enjoyment of the perks that he believed accompanied his high office, including the use of New York state aircraft for what he deemed official business. An investigation by Cuomo's office found he was one of the "primary" users of state aircraft—the other primary users were the governor and lieutenant governor. The governor's office scheduled elected officials' use of the aircraft. Early in his term, Spitzer ordered that aircraft users had to "certify" that they were flying on official state business. The rule meant that if Bruno knowingly lied about his use of the planes, he might be guilty of a crime.

Spitzer's communications director, Darren Dopp, looked for a way to capitalize on the possibility Bruno broke the new rule. In May 2007, Dopp and another Spitzer aide, William Howard, began nudging the state police for data on Bruno's travels. It turned out that the records showed some of Bruno's trips to New York City during the first half of 2007 coincided with well-publicized political fundraisers there—a sign that Bruno's certifications that the trips were for state business were not entirely true. On May 23, Dopp emailed a colleague about "a new and different way to proceed re media. Will explain tomorrow."

Dopp wanted to find a way to get this information into the news. He bided his time, and opportunity soon presented itself.

On June 3, the *Times Union*, Bruno's local paper, reported that federal prosecutors were "focusing on potential corruption in his [Bruno's] use of legislative earmarks, called member items, to funnel public money to a friend's business and his frequent dealings with thoroughbred horse breeding and racing." [7] Bruno was an avid horseman.

Bruno wasn't the only senator suspected of wrongdoing. Things were so bad that Senate staffers quietly advised legislators to hand in their expense reports in person. Putting the reports in the mail or sending them by fax or email risked bringing an indictment under the federal mail fraud statute.[8] Dopp thought Bruno's suddenly public trouble with the feds was a good opportunity to pile on. He wrote to a colleague, "Think a travel story would fit nicely in the mix."

Cuomo's staff investigated and didn't come to a public conclusion about what Dopp did next. But the clear implication was that Dopp's plan was to ask some media organization to seek records about Bruno's helicopter use via New York's Freedom of Information Law (FOIL). "Persons in the Governor's Office did not merely produce records under a FOIL request, but were instead engaged in planning and producing media coverage concerning

Senator Bruno's travel on state aircraft before any FOIL request was made," Cuomo's report said.

Invited by Dopp or not, the *Times Union* made a FOIL request on June 27 for data "on the use of the state aircraft by Gov. Eliot Spitzer, Lt. Gov. David Paterson, Comptroller Thomas DiNapoli, Senate Majority Leader Joseph Bruno, Assembly Speaker Sheldon Silver," and the Assembly and Senate minority leaders. Reporters' FOIL requests in New York can take weeks or months. Yet the *Times Union*'s request was turned around in three days—amazing speed. Spitzer's staff even gave the newspaper information about Bruno's schedule and movements in New York City, which the paper didn't specifically seek.[9]

The *Times Union* published its story on July 1. It began, "Three times this year, Senate Majority Leader Joseph L. Bruno has used taxpayer-funded state aircraft to fly to political fundraisers in Manhattan while certifying he was on official state business." [10] Most newspaper reporters would consider that a pretty good story. Bruno's use of the aircraft, legal or not, was a window into his view of himself and his office. Also, taxpayers might reasonably want to know if their money was being wasted on Bruno's trips.

But in the cauldron of Albany politics, it didn't matter whether state money was properly spent on Bruno's travel. Questions about Bruno's business dealings were also turned aside. Instead, the issue became, How did the *Times Union* get this information?

Bruno pushed back right away. His staff even blamed the *Times Union* for creating his need for state police transport. "As he has, and continues to receive, death threats and other threats to his safety, based on what people read in the *Times Union* and other negative reports, he is provided with State Police protection when traveling," his spokesman told the newspaper in the July 1 story.

That was just the first sign that Bruno and the Republicans felt they could turn the story in their favor and against the newspaper, Dopp, and Spitzer.

On July 5, Fredric U. Dicker of the *New York Post* reported that Spitzer "targeted" Bruno in "an unprecedented surveillance program" that led the story to be leaked to the *Times Union*. Bruno said he was "set up."

"This is like something you'd expect in a Third World country, where some dictator has his enemies followed to see how they could either do something to them or disgrace them. ... This is dangerous in a free country," Dicker quoted Bruno as saying.[11]

"The Feuding by Bruno and Spitzer Turns Bitter" was the headline on a *New York Times* story posted online on July 6. It quoted Bruno at a news conference calling Spitzer's aides "hoodlums and thugs."

Over the next few days, Dopp stated that he did no more than produce records in response to the *Times Union*'s FOIL request. It was an implausible claim. If the *Times Union*'s FOIL request was made June 27, why were the state police and the governor's office gathering material in May and earlier in June? And Dopp undermined his story when he told *The New York Times* that the state police didn't have complete records of Bruno's itineraries—so the troopers reconstructed some of them to meet the *Times Union*'s request.[12]

The story—which got the headline name Troopergate—caused Spitzer and his staff months of misery. Spitzer's fellow Democrat, Attorney General Andrew Cuomo, issued a withering report later in July about the scandal. "Senator Bruno's use of state aircraft was in accordance with state regulations and practices," the report said—undercutting the Spitzer team's point that Bruno misused his power and misspent taxpayer money. Cuomo's probers also found that "the Governor's Office planned to obtain information concerning Senator Bruno's use of state aircraft for the purpose of giving this information to the media." In sum, Cuomo acknowledged what Bruno suspected: Spitzer tried to pull off a media hit job on him. [13]

The Albany County district attorney began investigating, as did the state inspector general and the state Public Integrity Commission. Spitzer, who steamrolled into Albany as Mr. Clean, was under an ethical cloud.

Finally, in September, Albany District Attorney P. David Soares announced he'd uncovered no criminal conduct. Soon after that, Dopp quit his job and cooperated with the remaining investigations. The criminal probes in the end came to naught. Bruno's questionable use of the aircraft was forgotten. But the damage to Spitzer's reputation was done.

Nonetheless, some of the reforms Spitzer won in his anticorruption crusade squeezed Silver's biggest scheme—the fees Weitz & Luxenberg shared with him for handing over the names of some of Robert Taub's patients.

Silver carried on with his scheme during the 2007 legislative session even as ethics reforms were being discussed. Between January and March, he made his first $100,000 in investments in Counsel Financial. Between February and June, Robert Taub gave Silver the names of four more of his mesothelioma patients, which Silver handed to Weitz & Luxenberg. In July and September—after the session ended—Silver referred two more Taub patients.

He got lucky with Cuomo's investigation of member items in the 2006/7 state budget. The attorney general's Member Item Review Team—whose task included looking at money under the Health Care Reform Act—didn't examine the state's first $250,000 contract with Taub, because it had been approved in the 2005/6 fiscal year, outside the 2006/7 budget. The team also didn't review Taub's second $250,000 contract, which didn't take effect until July 2007, also outside the scope of the review because it was part of the 2007/8 budget. Silver's grants to Taub's clinic stayed a secret.

Taub wanted more research money. He pleaded his case for another $250,000 grant in a letter dated October 11, 2007. "Asbestos-related cancers, including mesothelioma and lung cancers, cause thousands of prolonged debilitating pulmonary illnesses and deaths each year, many among residents of New York," Taub wrote.

Asbestos illness had a potential to devastate Silver's legislative district. Taub noted that the first 55 floors of the World Trade Center's twin towers destroyed on September 11, 2001, contained asbestos floor tiles— "ordinarily quite safe, the tiles become toxic and extremely hazardous if they are disintegrated by pulverization or by fire." Thousands of people in Silver's lower Manhattan district were exposed to this dust in the aftermath of the terrorist attacks. Taub also wrote that a "very important aim of our studies is to develop blood tests which can be applied to healthy New York residents who were occupationally or geographically exposed to asbestos to detect and perhaps protect against the increased future risk of malignancy."

Taub noted in his letter that the money would be spent in the city—the trainee doctors he worked with were New York City residents. "We also hope the Legislature continues to review our progress and consider further support in future years," he wrote.

Taub wrote that his clinic's work was going well. "The Mesothelioma Center was very productive both in terms of its clinical trial and its publication record and its research," he later testified. Taub said some of the state grant money was spent to develop a new mesothelioma treatment he used in a clinical trial. But mesothelioma was far from being cured. "The work is never ending," he said.

Years later, Taub firmly believed the $500,000 in state money allocated to his clinic was well spent. "It went for the study of pathological correlations between what you see under the microscope and how you can predict how the disease will progress," he said. Taub was interested in how microscopic study of peritoneal mesothelioma patients' tumors could offer clues to how the cancer might spread. "If the tumor remains superficial, the patient has a much longer survival," he explained.

The state's money also supported research on how different kinds of chemotherapy might work. "We developed a technique for giving chemotherapy into the bellies of patients who had mesothelioma by having surgeons who worked with me put special tools into the abdomen, and pumping chemotherapy into them every couple of weeks," Taub said.

"I can tell you some very important data came out of it," Taub said of the state funding. He added—proudly— that it led to "some very significant advances." [14]

But Taub's research success didn't matter to Silver's decision to deny more money to the Mesothelioma Center's work. The real problem for Silver was that future grants to Taub's clinic would be public record. That might put at risk the fees Silver took from Weitz & Luxenberg for referring Taub's patients. It might even bring trouble from law enforcement.

Silver never formally answered Taub's letter. But a few weeks after he received it—probably sometime late in October 2007—he made a surprise visit to Taub's clinic.

"I can't do this anymore," Silver told Taub.

There would be no third $250,000 grant. State support for Taub's clinic would end.

"I was disappointed," Taub said. But he didn't ask why Silver couldn't come through. [15]

Helping the sick and dying with state money to research a deadly disease didn't matter to Sheldon Silver.

What did matter was, he couldn't get caught.

Eliot Spitzer did get caught. Hard as Troopergate was on him, a more sensational scandal wiped away his remaining political capital and credibility. His government career ended in lurid headlines.

On March 10, 2008, Silver held a strategy session with legislative staffers to discuss how the Assembly's proposed state budget would be presented to the news media. The room was crowded—there were twice as many people as chairs.

During the meeting, a secretary pushed open the office door and handed a piece of paper to one of Silver's aides. The aide read the headline on the paper and interrupted Silver as he was speaking. "You can stop," the aide said. "You need to read this."

It was a news bulletin from the *New York Times'* website. It said Spitzer was found by IRS agents to be patronizing a prostitution ring. The prostitutes were part of an organization called the Emperors Club VIP, and Spitzer met them in a stately hotel in Washington, DC.

After Silver read the *Times* bulletin, he and his aides canceled that day's budget press conference. Silver issued a typically anodyne public statement: "The allegations against the governor are before the public. I have nothing to add at this time."

Later, he told someone who phoned to ask about the Spitzer case, "I've been better." It was an odd thing to say. Silver was having a good day. Spitzer's downfall would let the extra money continue flowing to his bank accounts. Spitzer wouldn't be around to crusade for more laws that threatened Silver's corrupt side gigs.

Silver could grow even richer.

Chapter 9 – Fraudsters

Corrupt New York politicians have a muse. George Washington Plunkitt was a leader of the colossally crooked Tammany organization, a fixture in New York City politics from the late 19th to the early 20th century. *Plunkitt of Tammany Hall*, an entertaining, funny, and slim book—a recent edition runs to 127 pages—contains Plunkitt's observations on how he got rich in politics. Plunkitt knew Albany well. He served in the Assembly in 1869 and 1870, and off and on in the Senate from 1884 to 1904.

Plunkitt saw two kinds of graft. One was dishonest graft, which involved "blackmailin' gamblers, saloonkeepers, disorderly people, etc." That kind of graft could get you in trouble with the police, and Plunkitt said Tammany bosses avoided it. The other kind of graft Plunkitt called "honest graft, and I'm an example of how it works."

Say Tammany planned a public improvement in the city that might require buying land. Plunkitt might get a tip about these plans and put the information to work. "I see my opportunity, and I take it. I go to that place and I buy up all the land I can in the neighborhood," he explained. Then he'd flip the property to the city at a higher price.

Honest graft made Plunkitt a millionaire. He saw himself as akin to someone who profited by closely watching the stock or cotton markets. "Ain't it perfectly honest to charge a good price and make a profit on my investment and foresight? Of course it is," he reasoned. "Well, that's honest graft."[1]

Plunkitt would have understood Sheldon Silver.

Silver knew the city's landlords and developers needed help in Albany—so he saw an opportunity to put his relationship with them to work for his friend Jay Goldberg, who cut Silver in on the profits. Silver saw an opportunity to put his power and connections to work for himself and for Weitz & Luxenberg by getting $500,000 in state grants for Robert Taub's clinic. The state's money might or might not have helped cure mesothelioma, but prosecutors never claimed Taub wasted it. In return, Taub gave Silver the names of some of his patients. Those names were money to Silver and his law firm colleagues.

Silver saw his opportunities, and he took 'em. Plunkitt might have said it was perfectly honest for Silver to make money from Weitz & Luxenberg and Jay Goldberg's law firm by virtue of being in the right place at the right time.

There were never formal quid pro quos behind Silver's reaping of money from Weitz & Luxenberg and Jay Goldberg. Goldberg didn't tell Leonard Litwin or Steve Witkoff he was sharing their fees with Silver. Taub thought his arrangement with Silver was unspoken. It's also worth noting that Silver was never accused of pocketing taxpayer money. None of the $500,000 he sent to Taub's clinic ended up in Silver's pocket. His profit came from Goldberg's clients and Taub's patients, not from the public till.

Silver and other modern-day Plunkitts face a different set of legal issues than existed in Tammany's heyday. Laws against government corruption have evolved. A politician today would get in about as much legal trouble blackmailin' saloonkeepers and disorderly people as those in Plunkitt's day. Bribery—the idea that you could pay a politician to do something—also remains illegal. But Plunkitt never dealt with the concept of honest services fraud, an idea in federal law that prosecutors use against public officials like Silver who profit from their office.

Honest services fraud has roots in the federal mail fraud statute, which Congress passed in 1872 and which bars the use of the U.S. Mail in "any scheme or artifice to defraud." The law's initial purpose was simple. Its sponsor said it aimed "to prevent the frauds which are mostly gotten up in the large cities ... by thieves, forgers, and rapscallions generally, for the purpose of deceiving and fleecing the innocent people in the country." Then as in the 21st century, urban and rural Americans were culturally divided.[2]

Congress expanded the law in 1909 to cover "any scheme or artifice to defraud, or for obtaining money or property by means of false or fraudulent pretenses, representations, or promises." Over time, the law grew beyond schemes involving the U.S. Mail. Today it applies to messages conveyed by "any private or commercial interstate carrier," which can include phone calls, emails, and texts.

The idea of honest services fraud seems to have started in a complicated bribery case involving New Orleans politicians and bonds issued in 1936 and 1937 by a government body called the Orleans Levee District. One of the defendants in the case, Herbert Waguespack, was a member of the Orleans Levee District board and a lawyer. A jury convicted Waguespack of helping set up a scheme by which some of his pals got a sweetheart deal to buy bonds used to fund Levee District projects.

The federal appeals court judges said in 1941 that a scheme to get a favorable public contract by bribing a public official "would not only be a plan to commit the crime of bribery, but would also be a scheme to defraud the public."[3]

But in the case of Waguespack, the scheme went further, the judges found.

As a board member, Waguespack did not have the final say in the bonds' issuance. But as a lawyer, he could offer information and opinions to his fellow Levee District board members to sway their votes.

The appeals judges wrote, "No other member of the Board knew or suspected his interest in the matter. ... We think the jury could well conclude that in his position his conduct was so irreconcilable with public duty and private morality that neither he nor anyone privy to it could intend fairness and honesty."[4]

This decision got at the idea that crooked public officials could defraud the public by conduct "irreconcilable with public duty." In this view, corruption isn't just about bribery or theft of public money—it is also about politicians and public officials failing to do their jobs with "fairness and honesty." The appeals judges implied that Waguespack owed the public "honesty"—and whether or not he profited from the Levee District bonds, the public didn't get honest work from Waguespack when he worked on the issue.

Over the years, other federal appeals courts made similar rulings, thus lumping government officials who fail to do their jobs honestly with "rapscallions generally" as targets of the mail fraud statute.

Interpreting officials' dishonest behavior as a kind of theft under the mail fraud statute was fine until 1987, when the U.S. Supreme Court ruled 7-2 that judges and lawyers read the statute too broadly in political corruption cases. "The mail fraud statute clearly protects property rights, but does not refer to the intangible right of the citizenry to good government," the majority decision said. [5] If this reasoning had been applied to Waguespack's case, he might never have been convicted of acting in a manner "irreconcilable with public duty."

Congress responded in 1988 by directly inserting the concept of honest services fraud into the mail fraud statute. It updated the statute to cover "a scheme or artifice to deprive another of the intangible right of honest services."

So by the time Sheldon Silver began his scheme in the mid-1990s, federal law required him to give the state of New York his "honest services."

Silver was not the only criminal in New York's Legislature. Some of his colleagues were also accused under federal law of depriving the public of their honest services by carrying out greed-driven schemes.

Brian McLaughlin, an Assembly member from eastern Queens first elected in 1992, stole brazenly from 1995 through 2006. When he pleaded guilty, his statement admitting it all to a judge took 45 minutes.

McLaughlin was a prominent union official. He led Local 3 of the International Brotherhood of Electrical Workers (IBEW Local 3), whose members among other things maintained and installed streetlights and traffic signals. He was well-liked enough to be mentioned in 2003 as a possible candidate for New York City mayor in 2005. At the time, his political campaign had $962,000 in the bank.

Some of McLaughlin's cons had the makings of comedy. The government said that to cover his theft of more than $10,000 from a union bank account, McLaughlin asked an associate to destroy the checkbook "by immersing it in water, so that they could later claim that the checkbook was among materials damaged when the basement of McLaughlin's District Office was flooded."

McLaughlin even stole from children.

For decades, IBEW Local 3 sponsored the Electchester Athletic Association. The association's main business was a Little League for kids in the Pomonok Houses, an apartment complex in the southern part of the Kew Gardens neighborhood in Queens. The association survived on money McLaughlin obtained from the state, and from membership fees and donations. Letters seeking Little League sponsors said, "A CHILD IN SPORTS STAYS OUT OF THE COURTS!"

From 1997 up to his arrest in 2006, McLaughlin took $95,000 from the Electchester Athletic Association.

One day in 2004, McLaughlin told an associate he needed $6,000 from the athletic association to pay the rent on his apartment in Albany. The associate—not named in McLaughlin's indictment—replied that another of McLaughlin's associates had used $2,800 of the athletic association's money "for softball and other expenses and was not willing to part with the remaining funds." In other words, this unnamed official of the

Electchester Athletic Association preferred to spend its money on children's sports programs.

That angered McLaughlin. "All that fucking money, he's fucking spending on other stuff, that ain't his money . . . that's mine," he said.

Sometimes, McLaughlin's campaign paid people identified on paperwork as "consultants." These consultants kicked back the bulk of their payments to McLaughlin. The campaign paid for a cleaning person who spent most of her time at McLaughlin's home. Campaign money also paid for McLaughlin and his family to join a country club on Long Island.

McLaughlin stole from the Central Labor Council, a labor group, by setting up a bogus consulting firm that billed the council thousands of dollars a month.

He stole from the state by hiring an associate into a no-show legislative job and then ordering him to kick back half of his salary.

He was so greedy he stole by cheating on his Assembly expense reports.

Legislators were reimbursed for expenses every day they spent in Albany at the IRS per diem rate—in 2005, the rate was $139 per day.

McLaughlin wanted that money even on days he wasn't in Albany. So he had associates drive from New York to Albany and back to New York.

McLaughlin's associates kept the receipts they got from New York State Thruway toll-booths. McLaughlin filed the receipts with his faked expense reports to show he'd been in Albany on legislative business on days when he was in fact elsewhere.

Later, when E-ZPass electronic badges became widely used to pay tolls, McLaughlin ordered his pals to drive back and forth to Albany with his personal E-ZPass in their cars.

Once, McLaughlin gave his E-ZPass badge to an associate to pay tolls for a drive to Albany. On the way back to New York City, the associate used his own E-

ZPass. The next day, the associate drove back to Albany with his personal E-ZPass. He returned to New York City by using McLaughlin's E-ZPass.

Thus McLaughlin's E-ZPass records showed he'd been in Albany for two days. "Bang them for two days' per diem," as he explained to his associate. Under the IRS rules, McLaughlin could net $278 from this little scheme.

"My tax dollars hard at work," the associate replied.

McLaughlin's indictment was unsealed in October 2006. After his arrest, McLaughlin became a government informant. In May 2009—when he was finally done helping the prosecutors—McLaughlin was sentenced to 10 years in prison. He caught a break five years later, in May 2014, when a federal judge decided McLaughlin's aid to the government's efforts to put his colleagues in jail warranted reducing his sentence to six years. He was released from prison that October.

One of the people McLaughlin helped investigate was Anthony Seminerio, a Democratic Assembly member from Queens. Seminerio was cynical about his job as Assembly member. "What the fuck does it mean that we are elected officials? It means shit," he told McLaughlin one day in 2007. Though the charges against Seminerio were by then public, McLaughlin had no trouble getting him to talk. Seminerio didn't know McLaughlin was helping FBI agents record their conversation.

Some of Seminerio's frustration mirrored his honest colleagues' complaints that they had little say in how Silver ran the Assembly. From a September 2008 FBI report: "While in Albany, Seminerio's work is routine. Many bills are passed. Seminerio stated that 'Eighty percent of the bills that I vote for, I don't know what the hell it is.'"

In Albany, Seminerio was another nose for the leadership to count. But at home in Queens, Seminerio saw himself as "the Godfather." He said he "did a million things for a million people." He was glad to help you out if you lived in Woodhaven or Glendale, adjoining middle-class neighborhoods that comprised most of his Assembly district. "I don't charge my constituents," he said.

Among the million things Seminerio said he did was helping people get jobs at the Long Island Rail Road. In April 2007, Seminerio used some of the state discretionary money Silver allotted him to fund a $250,000 Long Island Rail Road painting project. In February 2008, Seminerio called a railroad official to inquire about a job for a "dear friend of the family"— someone referred to him by his son. Seminerio explained to McLaughlin, "You know how many people I got jobs in the Rail Road? Any time that I would give them a $250,000 contribution, or $500,000, for repairs on the rail in there, I need two jobs."

Seminerio expected cash for some of the million things he did. He sought taxpayer funds for state programs that had the effect of helping hospital executives hold on to their jobs and helping business people make big money. Seminerio figured he too deserved big money—and that he could get it by supplementing his state paycheck with a side hustle. He explained his plan in one of the government's recorded conversations: "Screw you. From now on ... I'm a consultant."

Seminerio set up a consulting company as a vehicle for his non-legislative work. He figured he was paid for "advice" and to "get something done."

One of his consulting clients came to regret hiring him. Arlene Pedone, a longtime Seminerio supporter, ran a company called Neighborhood Marketing Services, which focused on marketing health-care services to low-income people. Among Pedone's clients was Jamaica Hospital Medical Center, a big hospital in Seminerio's district. In the mid-1990s, Jamaica Hospital hired Pedone's firm to recruit Medicaid patients to health insurance programs.

Seminerio went to work for Pedone in 1996. About two years later, as his relationship with Pedone faltered, Seminerio demanded half of her company's gross receipts. Pedone replied that the company's profit was, of course, a lot smaller than its gross. She refused. Seminerio persisted. He called Pedone's clients and asked them to stop paying her, and start paying him instead. Government investigators said Seminerio told Pedone's clients that "they really needed Seminerio, not Pedone, because Seminerio could do things that Pedone could not."

"As a result of Seminerio's actions, Pedone's company lost its client base. Pedone terminated her marketing business which had once generated between $300,000 and $400,000 per year," prosecutors said.

Seminerio's other schemes involved doing the same work as lobbyists—except that unlike lobbyists, Assemblyman Seminerio could act directly on behalf of his clients as an elected official. "Seminerio received hundreds of thousands of dollars from various entities with business before the State of New York—or from entities whose clients have business before the State of New York—in exchange for which Seminerio has taken official action," federal prosecutors said in court papers.

Seminerio had help from Bernard Gordon Ehrlich, an ex–major general in the New York National Guard. Ehrlich was convicted in 1988 of federal racketeering charges in the Wedtech scandal, which involved a Bronx company that prosecutors said illegally obtained no-bid Defense Department contracts.

Ehrlich and Seminerio worked together as consultants. In a wiretapped conversation, Seminerio explained the relationship: "We charge a consulting fee. He [Ehrlich] charges the consulting fee to the hospital, and I work for his consulting firm. . . . It's perfect, it works out nice. . . . And we don't have to do nothing . . . I mean I don't have to do nothing."

Seminerio helped Jamaica Hospital get state financing to expand. In return for this kind of help, from 2000 to 2008 the hospital paid Seminerio's consulting firm $310,000.

FBI agents asked David Rosen, the CEO of MediSys—Jamaica Hospital's corporate owner—what Seminerio did for the company. From a document filed in Seminerio's criminal case:

"Rosen explained that Seminerio does not do anything 'specific in nature,' but 'provides guidance on issues, tells [Rosen] about the political landscape, makes introductions to the New York State Assemblymen and the New York State Senators as well as others outside the legislative body.' When asked for examples of work Seminerio had done as a consultant in the previous six months, Rosen could only provide two: Seminerio introduced him to Gordon Ehrlich and a potential investor. In fact, both the potential investor and Ehrlich were separately paying Seminerio to be their consultant."[6]

Seminerio saw the basic flaw in his business plan: "The day I leave the Assembly ... I'll lose maybe 60 percent of my business."

Seminerio was sentenced to six years behind bars. He died in a federal prison in North Carolina in January 2011, after he served less than a year of his sentence.

Carl Kruger, a corrupt state senator, also tried to grab money from Jamaica Hospital and MediSys.

Kruger was first elected to the Senate in 1994. Though Kruger was a Democrat, Joseph Bruno—the Republican majority leader—decided in 2007 to name him chair of the Senate's Social Services Committee. Kruger was the only minority party senator to ever chair a committee. In 2009, during a period of Democratic control of the Senate, Kruger became chair of the Senate Finance Committee. "He exercised great influence over the budget for New York State," prosecutors noted. Kruger was consulted on matters large and small, and in Albany his gruff and abrupt manner helped make him more feared than loved.

Like Anthony Seminerio, Kruger expected to be paid for helping lobbyists.

The government identified four "bribe-payors" in Kruger's conspiracy. Richard Lipsky, a lobbyist, was one. Another was Rosen, MediSys's highly paid CEO. Rosen pulled in a $2.2 million salary in 2006, the government found. Two more were Robert Aquino, CEO of financially troubled Parkway Hospital in Forest Hills, Queens, and Solomon Kalish, a health-care consultant.

According to court papers, between 2006 and 2011, Lipsky, Rosen, Aquino, and Kalish forked over more than $1 million to Kruger via bank and investment accounts controlled by Michael Turano, a gynecologist. Turano was such a close friend of Kruger that the newspapers called him Kruger's "intimate associate." The relationship led gay activists to accuse Kruger of hypocrisy when he voted against a gay marriage bill in 2009.

Supposedly, Kruger shared a home with his sister and her husband in Brooklyn's Canarsie neighborhood. But neighbors said Kruger was rarely there. Prosecutors said Kruger really lived with the Turanos: Michael, Gerard— also a gynecologist—and their mother, Dorothy, a minor local government official. The Turanos lived in Brooklyn's Mill Basin neighborhood, in a waterfront home originally built for a boss of the Lucchese mafia family. It was big enough that some people called it a mansion. It was so gaudy the New York *Daily News* called it "Chez Tacky." Much of Kruger's illicit income was funneled to Michael Turano, the feds said—and it was enough that one of the family cars was a four-door Bentley worth $200,000. It was registered to Gerard Turano, the feds said.

The government developed plenty of evidence of Kruger's closeness to the Turano family. "Kruger typically began his day by calling the Turanos or having breakfast with them and typically ended his day by calling the Turanos or having dinner with them," prosecutors said in court papers. Kruger and the Turanos celebrated holidays together and vacationed together. Kruger helped run the Turano household. The feds said he directed the installation of security cameras at the

Turano home. He also set up the purchase or maintenance of the home's appurtenances, which included an elevator, a waterfall sculpture, and an in-home movie theater. Chez Tacky needed lots of upkeep.

Despite the Bentley and other signs of his wealth, during 2008 and 2009 Kruger "did not disclose any outside income in excess of $1,000—from consulting fees or otherwise—except for dividends from New York State Dormitory Authority Bonds," an FBI agent wrote in an affidavit.

Parkway Hospital had a long history of financial problems. Aquino, Parkway's CEO, sought Kruger's help keeping the hospital open. In 2008, Parkway hired Adex Management, a consulting firm run by Solomon Kalish, to lobby the state to save the hospital. Parkway paid $60,000 to Adex Management. In turn, Adex paid $26,000 to a company controlled by Kruger's friend Michael Turano. With this arrangement in place, Kruger went to work lobbying Governor David Paterson—Eliot Spitzer's successor—and other state officials to adopt a rescue plan. His effort failed, and Parkway was shut down.

Kruger's efforts to help these people led to a sort of circle of iniquity. It started with a company called Compassionate Care Hospice, which cared for terminally ill people.

Compassionate Care hired Kalish's consulting firm, Adex Management, in hope of generating business. Kruger had an interest in Adex Management via his friend Michael Turano. Rosen, as CEO of MediSys, persuaded MediSys-owned Brookdale Hospital—located in Brooklyn's Brownsville neighborhood—to give some business to Compassionate Care. This boosted Compassionate Care's fees to Adex Management.

In return for these management fees, Kruger sought state money for Jamaica and Brookdale hospitals. With Kruger's help, Brookdale got $325,000 in state grants in

November 2007. In 2008, Kruger got a $100,000 equipment grant for Jamaica Hospital.

Kruger also lobbied Governor Paterson and the state Department of Health to save two financially troubled hospitals in Queens, Mary Immaculate in Jamaica and St. John's Queens in East Elmhurst, by allotting them to a hospital consortium that included MediSys's hospitals.

As a politician, Kruger was probably obliged by his constituents to try to save Mary Immaculate and St. John's, which besides providing medical care employed 2,500 people, many of them no doubt his constituents. But the circle of iniquity closed in 2009, when the state decided that Mary Immaculate and St. John's weren't worth saving. They shut down.[7]

Nonetheless, Kalish and Adex Management paid Kruger nicely for his help, via Michael Turano. From November 2007 to March 2011, Adex paid $197,000 to one of Turano's companies.

Richard Lipsky's lobbying clients included several businesses affected by Albany machinations—including beer and wine distributors, real estate developers, mom-and-pop retail stores, and a supermarket company. From 2006 to 2011, Lipsky paid $252,000 to bank and investment accounts controlled by Michael Turano. In return for the money put in Turano's accounts, Kruger did all kinds of helpful deeds for Lipsky's clients.

Kruger's help to Lipsky illustrates a truth of state legislatures across America: the issues they deal with are often advanced by lobbyists whose influence has nothing to do with voters' desires.

One of Lipsky's causes was persuading the state to collect cigarette taxes on Native American reservations within its borders. The reservations sold cigarettes at less than half the price charged by the rest of the state's retailers. They argued that as sovereign nations, they were legally exempt from the cigarette tax. For years, New York officials held off collecting the tax from them.

That the state let this situation fester was a problem for the businesses Lipsky represented to the Legislature—they lost customers to the reservations' cheap smokes. "If taxes are increased again, there should be no doubt in anyone's mind where even more New York consumers are going to purchase their cigarettes," said a 2006 newspaper op-ed piece by John Catsimatidis, a supermarket owner who ran for New York City mayor seven years later.

Most of Kruger's constituents in southern Brooklyn could not possibly have cared whether the state got cigarette tax money from the reservations upstate and on Long Island. At the time, New York's cigarette tax was the country's highest. The smokers in Kruger's district might have been happier if he sought to lower the tax instead of improving how it was collected.

But the smokers were not as well represented in Albany as Lipsky and other lobbyists.

So cutting the state's cigarette taxes was not on anyone's agenda in Albany. But Lipsky's lobbying clients did care about ending the Native American reservations' ability to sell tax-free smokes. If Lipsky and his clients cared, Kruger cared too. On this issue, what Kruger's constituents wanted didn't count.

In November 2009, Kruger made sure reporters were present when he visited Governor Paterson's office to demand that the state treasury collect cigarette taxes from the reservations. *The New York Times* reported, "With a fleet of cameras following him, Mr. Kruger, the chairman of the Senate Finance Committee, marched up the steps to Mr. Paterson's second-floor office in the Capitol, clutching a white envelope that contained a letter making his demand to the governor. He handed it to one of Mr. Paterson's aides, who accepted it on the governor's behalf." Kruger insisted the reservations would provide the state $1.6 billion in tax revenue each year. Paterson and state tax experts said that figure was wildly inflated. Paterson's spokesman called Kruger's claim a "gimmick."

A few months later—on March 1, 2010—Kruger wrote another letter to Paterson demanding better state tax collection on the reservations, and issued subpoenas in a legislative investigation of the issue. Eventually the state won a federal court ruling saying it was within its rights to collect the tax from cigarettes sold on the reservations. Tax collectors decided the best way to get the money was to seek it from the companies that sold cigarettes wholesale to the reservations. But that idea flopped when the reservations set up their own cigarette manufacturing operations, which made it easier to avoid the state tax. Lots of New York smokers preferred the reservations' cheap cigarettes to pricier name brands sold off-reservation. Kruger's efforts on the issue didn't add up to much.

Kruger took up another cause of Lipsky's lobbying clients in 2009 when he opposed expanding the state bottle law to require retailers to collect a five-cent deposit on bottles and cans of water. The same year, Kruger also took up a cause of the supermarket industry by pushing for a law that would expand supermarket wine sales. Neither of Kruger's efforts fully succeeded. Against his wishes, the bottle law was expanded to include bottled water, and supermarket wine sales remained limited.

One day, Lipsky sent one of Kruger's staffers an email. Kruger responded in a conversation recorded by the government: "The emails to [the staffer] ... I mean ... No good. I thought we were anti-emails?"

"I thought it was innocuous," Lipsky answered. "I just didn't see—"

"All emails are never innocuous ... even the weather report," Kruger replied.

"All right, I got ya," said Lipsky.

Though Kruger wasn't formally connected to any of the shell companies through which he paid Michael Turano, the FBI was ready to show he benefited from them by his closeness to Turano, his brother, Gerard, and their mother, Dorothy. In a February 2011 phone call taped by FBI agents, Kruger said the money paid to Turano's consulting firm was the result of "my work." "This whole world was built around 'shared.' ... It was supposed to be that we were gonna all share in the benefits of it," Kruger said.

That phone conversation was evidently what the government needed to bring its case against Kruger. He was formally charged in March 2011. Kruger pleaded guilty and was sentenced to seven years in prison. Michael Turano was sentenced to two years, Kalish got two years, Aquino was sentenced to four months, Lipsky got three months, and Rosen got three years.

Another Brooklyn legislator escaped the prosecutorial net that snared Kruger, Turano, Seminerio, Lipsky, and Rosen—but that legislator didn't stay free for long.

Between 2003 and 2008, Medisys CEO Rosen and his company allegedly paid off Assemblyman William Boyland of Brooklyn with a $35,000-per-year no-show "consulting" job. Rosen told the FBI that paying Boyland was part of his effort to build complex relationships to advance his hospitals' interests. "You gotta push a lot of buttons," Rosen explained.

Boyland was charged on March 9, 2011—the same day as Kruger—with taking MediSys's money. A judge freed him on bail.

Despite being on bail on a federal corruption charge, Boyland continued to pursue illicit schemes. A bit more than two weeks after he was freed—on March 25— Boyland took a pair of undercover federal agents on a tour of his legislative district. "Everything we've seen here I'm in control of," he told the agents, who posed as businessmen. The agents gave him $7,000 in cash, and Boyland hinted that in return he could help get them state money for development projects.

Boyland had another larcenous idea for the agents. At a meeting in Atlantic City on April 29, 2011, he suggested they buy a hospital in New Jersey for $8 million, apply for grants to renovate its buildings, and resell it for $15 million to a nonprofit corporation he controlled.

One of the undercover agents posing as a businessman wanted to know, How much would it cost to get in on the scheme? "Don't be shy," the agent advised.

Boyland said they would have to pay him a $250,000 bribe to set up the deal.

Boyland was acquitted in November 2011 of taking money from MediSys via the no-show job. The feds weren't finished with him. Later that month, they charged him with soliciting bribes from the undercover agents. That case ended with a judge sentencing Boyland in September 2015 to 14 years in prison.

Like Plunkitt, all these corrupt politicians—McLaughlin, Seminerio, Kruger, and Boyland—saw their opportunities and took them. Plunkitt never spent a day in jail. But Plunkitt's crimes weren't covered by the mail fraud statute. McLaughlin, Seminerio, Kruger, and Boyland were all charged under the mail fraud statute's honest services clause.

Seminerio's indictment said his "duty of honest services arose, in part, from various provisions of New York State law, which prohibit public officials from accepting payments in connection with official acts, from laboring under conflicts of interest, and from using their offices to extort illegal payments."

McLaughlin's indictment charged him with failing to provide honest services to "union members whose interests he was supposed to serve with undivided loyalty." Kruger was charged with participating with Kalish, Rosen, Aquino, and Turano in "a scheme and artifice to defraud, and to deprive New York State and its citizens of their intangible right to Kruger's honest services." Boyland's second indictment said he deprived "citizens of the State of New York and the Assembly of their intangible right to ... honest services."

This legal concept brought trouble to Sheldon Silver.

Chapter 10 – Lies and secrets

Sheldon Silver presented himself to the public as honest. He seemed to have no idea why anyone would think otherwise.

He took umbrage when a reporter asked him about a May 5, 2008, editorial in the *New York Post* about efforts by New York State's chief judge, Judith Kaye, to raise judges' salaries. The editorial noted that Kaye's lawyer hoped to ask Silver and Senate Majority Leader Joseph Bruno about their nongovernment income.

"Now *this* could be interesting," the editorial said.

Silver "has long been reaping untold amounts from what may be the country's most prolific personal-injury law firm—untold, because neither he nor Weitz & Luxenberg has ever had the courage to disclose how much he's paid, or even precisely what he does for the firm," the editorial said. The *Post*—exaggerating a little—called Silver's Weitz & Luxenberg income "the most tightly guarded secret in New York state history."[1]

"I do disclose to the Ethics Commission in the most appropriate way, you know, but they don't bother to read it," Silver griped of the newspaper the next day. That disclosure, Silver said, was that he was engaged in the "practice of law, limited to personal injury actions, representing claimants."

"And then I put in an amount of money the way I'm supposed to disclose it, consistent with the law," Silver told his interviewer.

This was not exactly a lie. Silver did comply with the law, which required him to report information about his income to the state Commission on Public Integrity.

But Silver's complaint that the *Post*'s editorialists didn't bother to read his disclosures was utterly dishonest and misleading. The law Silver boasted of obeying—enacted by the Legislature and Governor Eliot Spitzer the year before, in 2007—did not require his income information to be disclosed to the public. Much of his disclosure to the Commission on Public Integrity was kept secret.

The *Post* was right to complain that Silver and Weitz & Luxenberg never said what Silver did for the firm, or how much he was paid to do it. The law did not require Silver or the law firm to disclose this information in detail. The law also forbade the Commission on Public Integrity from publishing what little Silver did report.

Here's what wasn't publicly disclosed about Silver's income in 2008—the year the *Post* complained:

Silver earned $764,630 from Weitz & Luxenberg. This included $218,742 from asbestos cases, $421,272 in fees from other cases he referred to the firm, and $124,616 in salary, a bit over his usual $120,000 base pay.[2] It was his best year ever at Weitz & Luxenberg. But this information was not made public for years. It wasn't even detailed on the secret ethics forms Silver boasted of filing. The form Silver filled out covering 2008 listed his $764,630 in Weitz & Luxenberg income as "Category F — $250,000 or over."[3]

Even that fact—that under "Category F" Silver earned more than $250,000 from Weitz & Luxenberg in 2008— was not public information under the law of the time. Even had the "Category F" classification been made public, it wouldn't have given anyone an idea of what was really going on: Silver's actual income from the firm was nearly three times the $250,000 sum suggested by "Category F."

Silver's complaint about the *Post* editorial was especially dishonest because, as Assembly speaker, he could have pushed to change state ethics laws to require him and his fellow politicians to disclose this information to the public. Sure, Silver filled out the forms in accord with the law. But the most telling information on the forms was secret. It was years before subpoenas and a criminal investigation ferreted out the information Silver boasted of writing down on the forms.

The *Post* was right: nobody except Silver and his Weitz & Luxenberg colleagues had any idea how much he made from the firm.

Even as he misled the reporters and their readers, Silver still claimed to be a paragon of transparency.

"I do more than most people, which is why they know what they know, you know, because I put it right there and I tell them exactly what it is ... I disclose in the way that everybody else discloses," Silver went on in his media interview. "There's no difference. It's a manufactured thing."

It's hard to parse this bit of blather. Silver seemed to be saying, How could anyone complain? He was boasting that he obeyed the 2007 law—as if obeying a law was something to boast about. He omitted from his boast that the law was so weak obeying it divulged very little useful information.

On top of that, Silver claimed lawyer ethics rules barred him from disclosing where his money came from.

"Now as an attorney you can't disclose your clients. ... You are prohibited from doing that," Silver said. That was a narrow reading of New York statutes on attorney-client privilege. State law protects "confidential communication made between the attorney or his or her employee and the client." It doesn't say lawyers could not disclose clients' names, which were routinely made public in court documents.[4]

State law and legal ethics aside, Silver offered another reason for keeping his clients' names secret. During the interview, he stated his clients might be harmed by his political prominence. Silver disliked New York's tabloid newspapers—the *Post* and the *Daily News*. He feared if he named his clients, *Post* and *News* reporters would hassle them.

"I know what would happen. They'd get hounded," Silver said. "I mean, my clients are you know, little people."

Silver also stated, "I don't represent any corporations. I don't represent any entities that are involved in the legislative process, except individuals who happen to be injured in a variety of ways, period."

That was only partly true.

The mesothelioma patients and accident victims Silver referred to Weitz & Luxenberg indeed had no direct interest in business before the Legislature. But Weitz & Luxenberg itself had a stake in Albany politics.

For one thing, Weitz & Luxenberg needed to bar passage of any law that might restrict the lawsuits it brought on behalf of its injured clients, or the fees it collected for handling their cases. The reporter didn't ask Silver about tort reform—a catchall term for proposals to rein in asbestos cases and other lawsuits seeking money for injury or harm. Democratic politicians oppose tort reform. Any other Democratic Assembly speaker probably would have quashed tort reform much as Silver did. But tort reform supporters were within reason to ask whether Silver's stance had something to do with Weitz & Luxenberg.

Silver also said nothing in this interview about the fees he collected from Glenwood Management and the Witkoff Group for bringing their property-tax-appeal business to his friend Jay Goldberg. Maybe that was because he was earning little from Goldberg at the time— he didn't get any fees from Goldberg's firm during 2007, and only $807 in 2008.[5] The state's income reporting form only required Silver to report sources from which he earned more than $1,000.

Though his property-tax-appeal earnings were low those years, his agreement with Goldberg was still in effect. But Silver did not mention Goldberg's firm on the portion of his 2008 ethics form that asked for a "general description of the principal subject areas" of his legal work. Perhaps Silver justified this omission by considering that he never represented Glenwood or the Witkoff Group in any court or tax proceeding. Jay

Goldberg or his partner, Dara Iryami, filed the paperwork and would represent the companies in court if needed. Silver never did any legal work for the companies. All he did was take their money, via Goldberg's sharing of fees.

Both Glenwood and the Witkoff Group had business before the Legislature. Glenwood was interested in laws regulating residential rents. Glenwood used state-backed loans for its projects. As Assembly speaker, Silver from time to time voted in favor of Glenwood's borrowing as a member of the state Public Authorities Control Board. Glenwood was one of the state's biggest political donors. State laws cutting property taxes on new housing projects were also important to Steve Witkoff. This was one reason Witkoff thought it wise to stay friendly with Silver. Witkoff said Silver could help with "anything from a regulatory perspective that might affect my business."

Silver never mentioned his relationships with Leonard Litwin of Glenwood or Steve Witkoff in any media interview. Nothing about his financial relationship with Goldberg's firm was publicly known.

Absent a government subpoena—or better ethics laws, which Silver had the power to thwart—it is hard to see how anyone would have found out about the fees he got from Goldberg and from Weitz & Luxenberg. The fees weren't mentioned on his ethics forms. Witkoff said he knew nothing of the arrangement. Litwin might have known something. The public record shows only three people certainly knew of the arrangement: Silver, Goldberg, and Iryami.

Silver's interviewer suggested that one reason he did not disclose more was to protect other Assembly members. If Silver disclosed more on his ethics forms, then other legislators would be obliged to follow suit, the reporter suggested.

"That's ridiculous," Silver replied.

"We all disclose pursuant to the law, all right? Some more than others. I do it to the full extent provided under the ethics law." He said he would disclose nothing about his clients, "other than to say they are individuals who have claims against other individuals, that's it, whether it's an auto accident, an asbestos case—"

That was the only time Silver ever said in public that he had anything to do with asbestos litigation.[6]

It's hard to keep your story straight when you lie. But judging by another media interview three weeks later, on May 27, Silver was either incredibly disciplined or genuinely believed his behavior was ethical. In this interview, he kept his story straight and made the same points he'd made earlier.

The reporter pointed out to Silver, "A lot of people make an issue about this in editorials, you know, about how you don't disclose—"

"It's right there," Silver interrupted. He wrote down, right there on the ethics disclosure forms, what kind of law he practiced.

"Well, about how much do you make?" the reporter asked.

"Uh, well, I disclose within the categories" outlined in the law. "But that part is not available to the public."

The reporter asked, Should legislators be required to disclose more about their income?

Silver didn't answer the question directly. "I will conform to whatever law is in effect, period," he said.

Omitted from this comment was the idea that Silver had a hand in approving the law he followed. The reporters did not ask him why he didn't seek an ethics law that would have required more openness.

"My clients are individual people who have nothing to do with the political life at all. They are just individuals who have heard—I have been a lawyer for 40 years, just about. And I've done pro bono work. And a lot of people have in some way or another ... recommended people to me. ...

"I don't represent anybody who in any way has an impact on anything we do legislatively."

Silver proceeded to plug Weitz & Luxenberg. He said his clients "are individuals who through some unfortunate circumstance are injured. And I am then called upon to represent them. And, you know, I do that with what I believe is the backing of a great firm."[7]

Everything Silver raked in beyond his legislative salary gave him more "extra money" to put to work.

A few weeks after these interviews—on June 20, 2008—Silver put another $225,000 into Counsel Financial, which was proving a lucrative investment. From June 2007 to April 2008, Silver had gradually put $325,000 into the company—and by June 2008, he'd earned $24,829 in interest. But the amount of his Counsel Financial investment was shielded from the public. In August 2008, a *New York Times* story put the amount of Silver's Counsel Financial investment at "at least $50,000." A company official declined to tell the *Times* the actual amount.[8]

The year 2008 was good for Silver, and not just because his earnings at Weitz & Luxenberg peaked. In July, Silver dodged a legal bullet when a judge ruled he wasn't personally liable for $480,000 of taxpayer money spent to settle allegations of sexual misconduct against Michael Boxley, a lawyer and a top Silver aide. Boxley was arrested in 2003, after a female colleague accused him of rape. Boxley eventually pleaded guilty to sexual misconduct, a misdemeanor, and kept his law license. The state settled the lawsuit that resulted from the accusation for $500,000. Of that sum, Boxley paid $20,000, and taxpayers paid the rest.

Back home in lower Manhattan that September, Silver turned back his first serious primary election challenge in years. His principal opponent, Paul Newell, cited Silver's failure to disclose his income and complained that he let too much Albany business be conducted behind closed doors.

In a radio interview just before the primary election, Silver said that how he conducted business in Albany was not his constituents' concern: "This is about representing lower Manhattan. ... I am here to talk about my record for delivering to the residents of lower Manhattan. They are the people that are voting ... not my colleagues in the Assembly who vote for speaker. ... When somebody runs for speaker and there is a race we will deal with those issues."[9]

Silver wasn't even fazed by Anthony Seminerio's arrest shortly after the September 2008 primary on charges of illicitly earning fees as a "consultant."

Seminerio had backed Michael Bragman's attempt to overthrow Silver in 2000. Slowly, Seminerio worked his way back toward the Assembly's centers of power—his seniority justified his appointment as chair of something called the Majority Program Committee, which brought him a stipend of several thousand dollars a year on top of his salary. Federal investigators said Seminerio told a hospital executive he could set up a meeting with an Assembly leader. Silver's staff had to admit it didn't know what leader Seminerio was talking about—they couldn't even rule out it was Silver himself. Happily for Silver, no other Assembly members were netted in Seminerio's case.

An odd scandal involving Silver emerged late in September 2008. Though it didn't involve big sums of taxpayer money, it did show Silver had a cavalier attitude about how money was spent on his perks.

The New York *Sun* found that for years, Silver regularly flew from New York to Albany on US Airways itineraries routed through Washington, DC. Not counting the hassle of airport security, these trips took three and a half hours or more. Traveling from New York to Albany by car or train took about two and a half hours. The flights were also expensive. An Amtrak ticket from New York to Albany cost $110 at the government rate, while Silver's airline tickets cost taxpayers $500 to $760.

His travel wasted government money. But by 2008—with help from his frequent Albany trips and jaunts around the country largely funded with campaign donations—Silver had become a "chairman's preferred" member of US Airways' Dividend Miles program.[10] That made it easy for him to snag first-class seats for the flights. It also gave him miles to spend on personal travel—more miles than he would have accumulated if he'd bought the tickets out of his own pocket.

It was embarrassing—but it wasn't enough to draw law enforcement attention, or to damage him politically either in his lower Manhattan district or in the state capitol.

Silver was also unscathed by the next big indictment. Joseph Bruno, the ex–Senate majority leader who'd retired in June 2008, was indicted in January 2009 on charges that, between 1993 and 2006, he illegally took $3.2 million in consulting fees from financial services firms that worked for labor unions. Federal prosecutors in Albany said the unions believed that in return for their payments, Bruno advanced their legislative agendas. Bruno was infuriated by the charges, which followed his feud with Governor Eliot Spitzer over the release of information about his use of state aircraft. "I've been the target of a 'Get Joe Bruno' campaign, whether by the former Governor Spitzer or a politicized U.S. Attorney," Bruno said.

The case did not stick. Over the next five years, trial court juries and appeals court judges cleared Bruno of all the charges.

The Seminerio and Bruno cases put more pressure on the Legislature to reform its ethics rules. In June 2009, the Assembly passed a bill sponsored by Silver that would have given voters more information about who legislators worked for. It was crafted in a way that wouldn't touch Silver himself.

Silver's proposal was complex—it involved reconstituting and renaming several agencies that dealt with government ethics. But like so many other bills in New York's Legislature, Silver's proposal got no serious public hearing. Records show it passed the Assembly just two days after it was referred to the Assembly's Governmental Operations Committee, and cleared three other committees the day of the Assembly vote.

Silver explained its provisions to reporters several months later, in October 2009. He was, as usual, worried about having to disclose the names of his legal clients— which, he claimed again, was against legal ethics rules. He said the Assembly got around that problem by requiring "any lobbyist or lobbying organization to disclose any contracts they have for relationships with individual legislators. So while I can't disclose the name of my client, the client can say, 'I hired Sheldon Silver as an attorney.' So if I'm XYZ insurance company, or ... a lobbying entity, I can avoid the legal ethics problem by ... having the affirmative requirement of saying, 'Yes, I have paid Sheldon Silver $10,000 to represent me in a lawsuit.'"[11]

Which, as Silver undoubtedly knew, would never happen.

The mesothelioma patients Silver referred from Robert Taub's clinic to Weitz & Luxenberg had no business before the Legislature, so they would never be required to disclose that they'd done business with him.

The Assembly's bill was also no threat to the money Silver earned from Jay Goldberg's real estate clients. Years after Goldberg took on the Witkoff Group and Glenwood Management as clients, he never formally told them that a cut of their fees ended up in Silver's bank and investment accounts. If Witkoff and Glenwood executives and lobbyists didn't know about these payments to Silver, how could they report them on any ethics forms?

The 2009 ethics proposal was also a wonderful propaganda opportunity. Silver could tout its passage in the Assembly as an advance in the fight against government corruption. Publicly, he could present himself as an ethics champion. Yet the bill—even if it passed the state Senate and was signed by the governor—wouldn't require him to disclose anything he wanted to hide. Silver's greed would still be a secret.

The bill died in the Senate. That let Silver knock Senate Republicans for failing to act on his idea. "They never passed the main bill that we had passed," Silver told the reporters, seemingly in lament.

Two months later, following news reports of Bruno's later-to-be-overturned conviction on federal fraud charges, Silver discussed his ethics bill again. "I passed one in June," he said. Well, that wasn't what he really meant: "The Assembly passed one," Silver corrected himself. "I was proud to sponsor it, because what I believe is, an ounce of prevention is better than a pound of cure."[12]

As Silver touted his ethics bill, Robert Taub had dried up as a source of new mesothelioma cases. The $218,742 in asbestos fees Silver earned in 2008 was from older cases. For 18 months, from March 2008 to September 2009, Taub didn't send any patients to Silver at all. During the last part of 2009, Taub sent Silver four cases.

Silver noticed Taub wasn't sending him cases as steadily as before.

When Silver asked why, Dr. Taub gave two reasons. One was that he was seeing more patients with peritoneal mesothelioma, in which the cancer afflicts the lining of the abdomen. Those patients usually saw surgeons before they showed up in Taub's clinic. Taub found that the surgeons had already referred those people to lawyers.

Another reason was that Taub was getting research money from a nonprofit foundation controlled by the law firm Simmons Hanly Conroy, which was Weitz & Luxenberg's main rival in the mesothelioma claim business.

Through the foundation, Simmons in January 2010 promised that it would give $3.15 million to Taub's research clinic. "That was the amount that he needed to do his research, and it was suggested by him," said

Simmons chief executive Gregg Kirkland. The money was to support Taub's research in "combined modality treatment" for mesothelioma. Combined modality treatment fights a disease with different combinations of treatment—such as radiation combined with chemotherapy. The Simmons Mesothelioma Foundation formally promised the money in a January 29, 2010, letter to Columbia University, Taub's employer.

Kirkland admitted that Simmons hoped Taub would reciprocate by recommending the firm to his patients. Asked if the firm expected Taub to hand it some of the names of his patients, Kirkland answered, "Probably from time to time we would receive referrals, yeah." [13] Asked if such referrals were valuable, Kirkland answered, "Sure." And Simmons maintained some leverage over the universities to which it gave money. In a letter promising money to Columbia, the Simmons foundation said, "The University understands that the Foundation will have the right to discontinue funding." If the referrals stopped, the money could stop, too.

Taub's first referral to Simmons, on March 11, 2010, was a dud—the patient declined to hire the firm. But the next referral worked out. Deanna Lane, a native of Tulsa, Oklahoma, signed up with Simmons, records show. Over time, Simmons did well with Taub's referrals. From 2010 to mid-2014, Taub gave Simmons the names of 29 patients, 16 of whom eventually hired the firm. [14]

The Simmons foundation made good on the bulk of its promise to Taub, the foundation's IRS filings show. From 2010 to 2015, when the foundation went out of business, it gave $2.62 million to Taub's research.

Taub's lab got the lion's share of the foundation's money. Records show that Columbia University got 47 percent of Simmons's giving to mesothelioma research. The foundation also donated to New York University, the University of Pennsylvania, the University of Chicago, the Pitt Cancer Institute and Cal State San Francisco. Simmons kept careful track of the patients it got from the university researchers. "We tracked all of our intakes, including all of the intakes from the medical programs," Kirkland said. [15] A lawyer was assigned to each university research program whose doctors steered cases to the firm. Simmons lawyer Christopher Guinn was assigned to handle Taub's cases.

Taub told Silver that the Simmons firm's generosity "might well impact the volume of referrals to Weitz & Luxenberg in the future." [16]

"I told him the Simmons firm was giving us a large donation," Taub said. "And I said I was referring cases to Simmons." [17] Taub thought telling Silver of Simmons's promised donations was a good idea, as it might persuade Weitz & Luxenberg to give as well.

Silver passed along to his Weitz & Luxenberg colleagues word of the Simmons donations to Taub's research, and told them Taub was accordingly cutting back the cases he gave to him. "He seemed unconcerned about the decrease. ... He was confident that Dr. Taub would resume sending cases," said Arthur Luxenberg. [18] But both Luxenberg and his partner, Perry Weitz, said Silver never discussed with them the idea of having their firm support Taub's research.

Silver was right not to worry.

"Since he is my friend, I will try to accommodate him," Taub told his former nurse, Mary Hesdorffer, in an email on May 25, 2010. Besides getting Taub $500,000 in state money, Silver had helped him in small ways. In January 2007, Silver wrote a letter to a Manhattan judge to suggest that he interview Taub's daughter for a clerkship. And early in 2008, Silver sent a $25,000 state grant to the Shalom Task Force, which helps women in New York's Jewish community who face domestic violence and was a favorite charity of Taub's wife.

At the time of the email exchange with her former boss, Hesdorffer was head of the Mesothelioma Applied Research Foundation, which raises money for mesothelioma research. She and Taub traded emails that day about the Simmons firm and its support of their cause.

Some universities won't take any money that is part of a quid pro quo, nor will they allow doctors or anyone else to give patient names to lawyers. In the email exchange, Hesdorffer mentioned that the University of Pennsylvania took money from the Simmons foundation at the same time it stipulated that it would give no patient referrals in return.

Taub doubted Penn was so honest. "U Penn may be lying to you—it's always better to pretend to be a holy man," he told Hesdorffer. "I feel sure that they will refer cases."

He knew how important his referrals were to the lawyers. "Of course they will all be nice to you for the cases, and hate you if they don't get them," he said.

In Taub's view, referring patients to Silver had only an upside. "I will keep giving cases to Shelly because I may need him in the future—he is the most powerful man in New York State," he wrote.

"As the Bible says, 'we need to get past the time when 'Each man does as is righteous in his own eyes,'" he wrote Hesdorffer. "No enterprise (excluding patient care) ever, ever grew or succeeded as a result of pure righteousness. Usually success is propelled by greed, envy, or both. I thought you knew that."[19]

Taub's Bible paraphrase seems to come from the Old Testament book of Judges: "In those days there was no king in Israel; every man did that which was right in his own eyes." Judges tells of a time of anarchy when Israelites followed a misguided sense of what was right instead of the rule of God.

Taub's interpretation of this passage was muddled. He appeared to be saying in the email that doing what he could to raise money from the law firms would bring the world closer to a mesothelioma cure than righteously declining their help.

But neither God nor his judges checked the mesothelioma lawyers' greed.

The following November, Taub referred a patient to the Simmons firm via an email to Joy Wheeler, who was director of the Simmons foundation. When he spoke to the patient, Taub told Wheeler, he "mentioned that your firm is interested in supporting meso research throughout the country, not just private jets"—a snarky reference to Weitz & Luxenberg's ownership of such an aircraft. Taub also mentioned that the day after the diagnosis, the patient's stepson got a call "out of the blue by someone from Weitz & Luxenberg."

That led Taub to comment on mesothelioma law firms' aggression seeking clients. "Boy, the environment for new cases in NY is canine-eat-canine," he wrote.[20]

Chapter 11 – Big spenders

Sometimes it was hard to tell who led the state Senate after Majority Leader Joseph Bruno's scandal-scarred career ended with his retirement in June 2008. But Bruno's immediate successor, Dean Skelos, was always involved in the maneuvering that roiled the Legislature's upper chamber in the following years.

Skelos, a Long Island Republican, was first elected to the Senate in 1985. He rose slowly through the ranks and became the majority leader upon Bruno's departure. Skelos' stint as majority leader ended after just six months, in January 2009, when Democrats took 32–30 control of the Senate—their first majority in 44 years.

Events proved the Democrats' two-vote majority was weak. Over time, Skelos worked that weakness to advantage.

One of the Democrats' problems after they took over the Senate in January 2009 was that the lieutenant governor, David Paterson, had automatically become governor when Eliot Spitzer resigned amid his sex scandal. The lieutenant governor's only real job was breaking tie votes among the 62 senators. To fill the vacancy caused by his promotion to governor, Paterson named Richard Ravitch as acting lieutenant governor. Ravitch was a veteran and respected public official. But Attorney General Andrew Cuomo and several lower-court judges believed the state constitution did not allow Ravitch's appointment. It wasn't until September 2009 that the courts decided the issue in favor of Ravitch and Paterson. In the meantime, it took only one Democratic defection on any bill to put the Senate in a 31–31 tie. Under the rules, such ties could not be broken.

Another problem for the Democrats was a Rochester billionaire, Thomas Golisano, who couldn't get himself elected governor in three tries.

Golisano had spent $5 million backing the 2008 campaign that put Democrats in charge of the Senate in 2009. He expected results. He didn't get them. Golisano was angry that the state budget the Democrats passed in mid-2009 with the backing of the Senate majority leader, Queens Democrat Malcolm Smith, raised spending and didn't cut taxes as much as he wanted.

Golisano decided he wanted the Republicans back in power.

Finally, the Democrats were undermined by a pair of corrupt and ambitious senators in their own party: Pedro Espada of the Bronx and Hiram Monserrate of Queens.

On his home turf in the Bronx, Espada operated a clinic called the Soundview Health Center that thrived on federal government money. Soundview Health Center was a big employer and served thousands of people. Soundview also put hundreds of thousands of dollars in Espada's pockets. Investigators found that Espada charged more than $100,000 on a Soundview American Express card to pay for restaurant meals, window treatments for his home, and tickets to Broadway shows and sporting events. He also was accused of diverting funds from Soundview to his own pockets through a shell company operated by his son.[1]

Espada had also been fined tens of thousands of dollars over the years for violating campaign finance rules. And for whatever it was worth, lots of people suspected Espada really lived in Mamaroneck, a well-off suburb in Westchester County—outside his Bronx legislative district. Eventually, in 2012, Espada's crimes landed him a five-year prison sentence.

The criminal case was well in Espada's future as he jockeyed in June 2009 to increase his influence in the state Legislature.

Monserrate, an ex-cop, was hotheaded and volatile. And as with Espada, his legal problems were already underway as he maneuvered for Senate leadership.

Hiram Monserrate was first elected to the Senate in the November 2008 election that gave Democrats Senate control. He hadn't even taken office when he was arrested December 19 on charges of assaulting his girlfriend. The court case that followed was still grinding on in mid-2009 when he and Espada joined Republican leader Dean Skelos in a Senate leadership coup.

With Espada and Monserrate on their side, the Republicans suddenly had 32–30 control of the Senate. That gave the Republicans the votes to formally take over. On June 8, 2009—after the state budget was finished, but before the Legislature was done with its annual term—the Republicans, led by Skelos and aided by Espada and Monserrate, made their move.

Through a series of Senate floor maneuvers that led to the shutting off of the Senate chamber's lights and internet, and to threats of locking the chamber's doors, the Republicans—joined by Espada and Monserrate— voted to install Dean Skelos as the majority leader, ousting Smith from the post. Espada's prize for backing this coup was the title of temporary president of the Senate—a post he could hold as long as there was no lieutenant governor.

Thomas Golisano was reported to have brokered the coup. He was not bothered that the coup was made possible by Espada and Monserrate, two of the Senate's most ethically challenged members.

"Don't talk to me about ethical backgrounds in Albany," Golisano said. "We have a governor who stood on a podium on national television and said he had extramarital affairs and used cocaine."[2] This was true. Governor Paterson said those things on TV the day after he was inaugurated. The new governor's personal ethics weren't nearly as problematic as Eliot Spitzer's. But Golisano had a point.

The turmoil was not over. Monserrate soon had second thoughts about the deal, and a few days later realigned himself with the Democratic caucus.

Monserrate's re-defection put the Senate in a 31–31 deadlock. But Skelos and Espada hung on to their leadership jobs. The setup was good for Skelos. If Espada stuck with him and the Republicans, they could force unbreakable tie votes on any Democratic bills. If the Democrats wanted anything to pass, they needed Espada's and Skelos's help.

Then Espada also defected back to the Democratic fold. On July 9—a month after the turmoil began—Espada rejoined Democrats after he was promised the title of Senate majority leader. Malcolm Smith was named temporary president of the Senate during a "transition period" after which another Democrat, John Sampson, would become president of the Senate and thus the Democratic leader. Now the Democrats were back in charge with a 32–30 majority.

The whole mess made New York's Senate a national laughingstock. It was also a problem for Albany lobbyists. Those lobbyists who worked for the real estate industry wanted the Senate back in Republican hands. "We needed a rational legislative climate," said Richard Runes, the Glenwood Management lobbyist and lawyer.[3]

And the real estate industry needed the Republicans back in power in time for the 2011 legislative session, when the rent regulation laws and the 421-a laws that gave housing developers tax breaks would be up for renewal.

That meant pushing Republican Senate candidates in the 2010 elections. It was a big, expensive job. Leonard Litwin, Glenwood Management's owner, did his part. During 2009—a nonelection year—Litwin and Glenwood spent $874,000 on campaign contributions for New York state and local offices. That was nearly twice the $473,000 Litwin and Glenwood donated to campaigns in 2007, the previous nonelection year, and more than seven times the $121,000 they spent in 2005, the previous nonelection year that preceded a renewal of the rent regulation and 421-a laws.[4]

As the real estate business prepared for the money battle, events drifted further in favor of Senate Republicans.

Monserrate's criminal assault case involving the alleged attack on his girlfriend rolled ahead in Queens in a way that turned to Republican advantage.

Security footage of the assault showed Monserrate forcing his girlfriend out of his apartment building. But Monserrate's girlfriend still testified on his behalf. In October 2009, the judge deciding the case tossed the felony charges against Monserrate, convicting him instead of misdemeanor assault. Monserrate's criminal defense lawyer, Joseph Tacopina, was "thrilled" with this outcome. "The senator was vindicated," he said.[5] Also, Monserrate escaped jail time. Several weeks later, on December 4, 2009, the judge sentenced him to three years' probation and a $1,000 fine.

Despite Tacopina's elation at the outcome—"There are no winners," Monserrate himself said—the conviction proved too much even for Senate Democrats. The Senate voted in February 2010 to remove Monserrate from office by a 53–8 vote.

With Monserrate out of the way, Democrats now held the Senate by a 31–30 majority. To the landlords and real estate lobbyists, this was a tiny improvement. But they still needed to expand their influence. They needed Skelos's help.

Skelos lunched with Glenwood lobbyists Charles Dorego and Richard Runes in March 2010 to discuss ways to boost donations to Republicans in that year's elections. Dorego, Runes, and their boss, Leonard Litwin, saw the situation as dire.

"I don't know how many people would have given the Senate Republicans a chance had they lost two elections in a row, so I think it was pretty clear that we really needed to win this one. ... I think there was optimism," Dorego said. The Republicans and their allies believed they had good candidates, and backing from big business groups. "But I do think there was something of an underlying desperation that this needed to be won."[6]

Litwin decided to spend big.

During the 2010 election year, Litwin and Glenwood spent $1.65 million on campaign contributions for New York state and local offices. That sum was 55 percent more than the $1.06 million they spent in 2008, the previous legislative election year, and 77 percent more than the $932,000 Litwin and Glenwood spent in 2006, the previous legislative election year that preceded a renewal of the rent and 421-a laws.

Landlords were shocked that election-year summer of 2010 by an event—little noticed by the public—that took place on the Senate floor.

Amid the turmoil in the Senate, two Democrats—Liz Krueger and Daniel Squadron, both of Manhattan—advanced a bill to repeal the Urstadt Law, which gave the Legislature and governor the power to set rules for New York City rents. If the Urstadt Law was wiped off the books, the real estate industry's rent fight would be utterly lost. Without the law, rent rules would be set by the New York City Council, overwhelmingly dominated by Democrats with little sympathy for landlords.

On August 3, Krueger and Squadron got their Urstadt repeal bill moved by a voice vote to the Senate Rules Committee, which would decide whether it was to reach the Senate floor. Even journalists who spend years trying to understand how Albany works might have missed the significance of this procedural vote. That Krueger and Squadron got their bill to the Senate floor and then moved it to the Rules Committee was cataclysmic news to the real estate lobbyists. It was the furthest they'd ever seen such a bill advance in the Senate. Nothing like it had happened before.

"All hell breaking loose," Dorego wrote in an email to fellow Glenwood lobbyist Runes. "Liz Krueger and squadron [sic] moving bad bills to the floor. ... [Democratic Senate majority leader John] Sampson fucking us." Apparently, Dorego and the other real estate lobbyists had reason to think Sampson was going to block this bill. It was a shock to see it move forward in the legislative process in any way.

The real estate lobbyists didn't think the bill would ever pass. "They don't have the votes," Dorego wrote of the floor maneuver. But seeing the bills move to the Rules Committee for further consideration was "terrible precedent giving those bills credibility," Dorego wrote.[7]

Maybe the real estate lobbyists were right not to trust Sampson, a lawyer. Federal prosecutors later determined that from 1998 to 2008, Sampson stole $400,000 in proceeds from home foreclosure sales he supervised. He eventually went to prison and was disbarred.

Ultimately, the Urstadt repeal bill went nowhere. But its slight progress further motivated the real estate lobbyists to seek more campaign money for Republicans. Here was another reason Runes and other lobbyists saw a need for the Senate to revert to being "rational."

The political careers of Monserrate and Espada also went nowhere.

Despite his humiliating ouster by his Senate colleagues, Monserrate didn't give up his dreams of political power. He ran in the September 2010 Democratic primary in a vain effort to get his Senate seat back. But Queens voters had had enough—Monserrate got just 35 percent of the vote.

Weeks after the primary, in October 2010, Monserrate again found himself in the criminal courts, this time on federal charges of misappropriating $100,000 in New York City taxpayer money a few years earlier, when he was a member of the City Council. The federal government said he used the money to finance a failed run for state Senate in 2006. Eventually, Monserrate spent 21 months in prison.

Espada—labeled by his Democratic primary opponent the "poster child of Albany dysfunction"—also came up a loser in the September 2010 primary election. One problem was that Democratic Party leaders angered by his treachery backed Espada's primary opponent. Another, perhaps, was that Espada's constituents in the Bronx were more concerned about his corruption than impressed by his position as an Albany power broker. Espada had to face headlines about the investigation of his medical clinics, which the FBI had raided. The controversy over whether he really lived in his district was also in the news.

A few months after his primary loss, in December 2010, Espada was indicted by a federal grand jury on embezzlement and theft charges that sent him to prison.

The real estate industry lobbyists' anxiety about the November 2010 election intensified late in the campaign season.

Runes sent Dorego an email on October 25, days before the November 2 vote: "Skelos needs money."[8] Between the time of that email and the general election, Glenwood put even more cash into the campaigns. Its LLCs donated $50,000 to the Rent Stabilization Association political action committee, or PAC, and $30,300 to the Real Estate Board of New York's PAC. In turn, those two PACS handed big contributions to the Republican State Committee. On October 29, the Republican committee got donations of $75,000 from the Real Estate Board of New York PAC, and $69,000 from the Rent Stabilization Association PAC.[9]

Litwin spent well. Republicans won 32 Senate seats in the 2010 general election, and Democrats won 30. The margin was just two votes—the same margin the Democrats could not hold after the election two years earlier. But the Republicans were a unified group. Glenwood-friendly Republicans no longer needed any Democrats' help. They were firmly in charge of the Senate—just in time for renewal of the rent and tax laws during the 2011 session.

The Senate was "rational" again. Again, the Republican senators would be led by Dean Skelos, the

Long Islander who was their majority leader after Joseph Bruno's retirement in 2008. But Glenwood's and Litwin's relationship with Skelos turned into a complication.

Litwin and his executives invited Skelos to a meeting in Glenwood's headquarters in New Hyde Park, Long Island, on December 20. Joseph Strasburg from the Rent Stabilization Association was also present, Dorego recalled. One purpose of the meeting was to slap each other's backs. "We had won the election, took the majority back. Everybody was in very high spirits," Dorego said.

They talked a bit about the upcoming 2011 legislative session. Strasburg floated the idea of extending the rent laws and 421-a law without any changes—"but I don't think anybody really focused too much on that," said Dorego. "I think everybody was talking about, really, sort of a postmortem on the election. Everyone was pretty upbeat."

Litwin was seated on one of the two sofas in his office. At the end of the meeting, Dorego helped the old man rise from his seat. As Litwin struggled to stand, Skelos came over to thank him for his help putting Republicans back in power.

"You know, my son is getting into the title [insurance] business," Skelos said. The senator directly asked Litwin to give some business to his son, Adam Skelos: "If you could see fit, Mr. Litwin, to throw some title work his way, it would be really appreciated."

Upon these words, Dorego and Litwin locked eyes. They didn't speak, Dorego said, but they knew each other's thoughts. "We both sort of registered a little bit of surprise," Dorego said.

Maybe Skelos's request for a job for his son was illegal. If it went badly, Litwin and his company might be found guilty under the federal bribery statute—which applies to "whoever directly or indirectly, corruptly gives, offers or promises anything of value to any public official." Not only that, if anyone found out about such a direct favor to one of the state's most powerful politicians, Glenwood might have a hard time getting its way in the upcoming real-estate-bill battle.

Litwin stood up and said goodbye. Runes, Skelos, and the other guests headed out of the office. Dorego arranged some of the office chairs until Runes returned.

Dorego said he was uncomfortable with the idea of finding a job for Adam Skelos.

"And Mr. Litwin decided—don't—let's not even go there."[10]

But they did go there. Dean Skelos was the only Republican in Albany with any real power. Glenwood Management needed a good relationship with him. Litwin and his executives could not ignore Skelos's requests for jobs and money for his son, however ethically and legally problematic those requests might be.

So Litwin made sure the younger Skelos got credit with a title insurance company for bringing it some of Glenwood's title insurance work. Glenwood persuaded the insurer to pay the younger Skelos $20,000 in commissions in a way Skelos and Glenwood officials believed wouldn't trace back to Glenwood, investigators later found.[11]

Glenwood also helped Adam Skelos get work with AbTech Industries, which sought a $12 million contract to clean storm water in Nassau County by installing sponge-like filters in drainage pipes. AbTech said these filters would absorb heavy metals and other pollutants. "Adam has sales experience," Dorego wrote to AbTech's president.

AbTech gave Adam Skelos a starting salary of $4,000 a month. His pay grew to $10,000 per month even though he was required to do little work.

As Litwin feared, these favors would in time cause problems for his company.

Chapter 12 – Rent

Rent is a big issue in New York. About 60 percent of New Yorkers rent their homes, and the proportion of renters is a bit higher in Manhattan, which included Sheldon Silver's political base. [1] Jimmy McMillan, an eccentric fringe candidate for governor in 2010, got 41,000 votes under the banner of his Rent is Too Damn High Party. He had a campaign rap: "Ain't nothin' else to talk about. Rent is too damn high." [2] Rents are set through a bramble of city and state laws and regulations. At city hearings on rent regulation, tenants' emotional pleas and demonstrations for lower rent increases go on for hours.

As leader of the Assembly Democrats, one of Silver's jobs in the 2011 legislative session was to look out for renters.

In the years after the passage of the 1997 rent law—which took effect around the start of Silver's financial relationship with Leonard Litwin and Glenwood Management—the Legislature renewed the rent regulation laws without fuss or significant alteration. Joseph Strasburg, the president of the Rent Stabilization Association, expected the same in 2011. Contrary to the idea conveyed by its name, the landlords belonging to the Rent Stabilization Association sought to end rent regulation. Everyone in New York knew that was politically impossible. Strasburg knew this well. The best he could hope for was to see the rent laws renewed every four years unchanged, or without changes that hurt members of his association.

"Our end game really was retention of the status quo," Strasburg said.

During Silver's time as Assembly speaker, the rent regulation laws were always renewed in the same bill as the 421-a tax break for real estate developers. That meant the developers had to go along with rent regulation if they wanted the Legislature to renew the 421-a law.

Rent Stabilization Association members didn't care much about 421-a. It was more of an issue for big developers like Leonard Litwin and Glenwood Management. Most Rent Stabilization Association members are landlords in Brooklyn, the Bronx, and Queens who are busy managing properties they already own. "They own it and they keep it," Strasburg said.[3] These landlords weren't as interested in growing their businesses as Leonard Litwin was in growing his. They mostly weren't involved in big new projects aided by the 421-a tax break.

The 421-a law greatly helped Glenwood Management build luxury rental apartments in Manhattan by easing new buildings slowly onto the property tax rolls. It's complicated, but in essence this is how it worked: Under 421-a, brand new buildings might pay zero property taxes. The buildings' taxes would increase gradually over the following decade until the exemption was gone.

This law—which the Legislature let expire in 2022 without any immediate plan to replace it—saved property developers millions of dollars a year. Developers like Glenwood—and the bankers who loaned them money—considered the lower initial property-tax costs as they developed new projects' financial plans.

Strasburg also expected the 421-a tax break would be extended by the 2011 Legislature. "There were just too many compelling reasons," he said. In his view, 421-a fueled construction jobs and a lot of other economic activity that boosted state and local tax revenue. Repealing the law would hurt too many people.

But Litwin—then 96 years old, a member of the Rent Stabilization Association's board, and a veteran of this periodic Albany battle—didn't buy Strasburg's confidence.

Litwin should have had reason to be confident the rent laws and the 421-a laws would be renewed in Glenwood's favor. He and his company worked hard and spent millions in 2009 and 2010 to make sure pro-developer and pro-landlord Republicans controlled the state Senate.

Perhaps he was still spooked by the turmoil in the Senate the previous two years. Maybe the complications of his relationship with Dean Skelos worried him. Also, there was a new wrinkle: The new governor, Andrew Cuomo, had served as U.S. Housing and Urban Development secretary under President Bill Clinton. Besides being a Democrat and thus presumably a supporter of New York's rent-stabilization and rent-control laws, Cuomo had experience with housing issues.

Strasburg recalled that at a strategy meeting at his Manhattan office in April 2011, Litwin said he was not fully confident in getting 421-a passed.

"We have to make some changes," Litwin told Strasburg.[4]

The needs of smaller landlords Strasburg represented didn't have to factor in Litwin's approach to that years' housing bills.

Litwin's $2.5 million in campaign contributions during 2009 and 2010—and his favors to Skelos—would let Glenwood go its own way on the rent and 421-a issues. Litwin had Skelos, and maybe Sheldon Silver, on his side. Glenwood's campaign contributions held out the possibility that Skelos, Silver, and maybe Cuomo would put Glenwood's interests ahead of those of the Rent Stabilization Association and the rest of the real estate industry.

The opening move in the 2011 rent and 421-a debate came in an Assembly bill. As Litwin feared, the Assembly's bill sought to end the 421-a property-tax exemption. Also, the bill would reregulate rents on vacant apartments. That change would cost landlords millions by keeping more of their stock under rent limits.

For the landlords, there was worse: the Assembly bill raised the threshold rent at which apartments would be removed from rent regulation from $2,000 per month to $3,000 per month. This was a big deal to members of Strasburg's group. Because rents on regulated apartments rose just a few percent per year, it might take another decade before a $2,000-per-month apartment in a small-time landlord's building hit the $3,000 deregulation threshold. The Assembly plan thus would have put many landlords' goal of moving their apartments from regulation to the open market further out of reach.

But the idea of a $3,000 rent threshold was not a big worry to Glenwood. Because many of its monthly rents already were near or over $3,000 per month, Glenwood would not be affected much by the $3,000 threshold. "Because the rents in Manhattan were so much higher... I don't think that Glenwood—and we were a very large Manhattan landlord—we felt that that was not a critical component," said Glenwood lawyer and lobbyist Charles Dorego. If the threshold went to $3,000, Dorego said, "we could live with that."

Similarly, the Assembly wanted to raise the incomes at which a renter's apartment could be deregulated. At the time, if a family's household income exceeded $175,000 per year, its rent could be deregulated. The Assembly's bill raised that figure to $300,000 per year—a good deal for high-income renters and a bad deal for landlords hoping to get more money from them. This also was not much of a problem to Glenwood. Many of its tenants were already high-income people.

Deeper in the bill, there was more for landlords to dislike.

Under the rules already in effect in 2011, a landlord who renovated an apartment could increase its monthly rent by one-fortieth of the renovation's cost. Thus a landlord who made $40,000 worth of improvements to an apartment could raise its monthly rent by $1,000. The Assembly bill would have slashed the amount of renovation expense landlords could charge to tenants each month to cover just one-sixtieth of the costs. Under this plan, the landlord who spent $40,000 on renovations would only be allowed to raise the rent by $666 per month—and that rent increase would have to be rolled back after 60 months, once the landlord recouped their costs.

Litwin and his executives understood the issues raised by the Assembly proposal. "We didn't think it was a very good bill," said Richard Runes, Dorego's colleague as a Glenwood lobbyist. One of Runes's jobs was pushing to make sure whatever bills Albany politicians passed were to Glenwood's advantage. He wasn't worried about the Assembly's rent rule ideas, or the Assembly plan to repeal 421-a. "That bill was never going to pass the Senate," Runes said. He viewed the bill as merely the Assembly's "statement of position for negotiating purposes. ... It would show me their wish list. It would be theoretically what the Assembly majority would like to see."

Runes's fellow Glenwood lobbyist Brian Meara also wasn't worried. Meara had long experience lobbying on the rent-control and 421-a issues. Over the years, he'd also remained close with Sheldon Silver. Meara saw it as "traditional" for the Assembly to pass a stringently pro-tenant bill that Senate Republicans would never approve. He said the Assembly's rent bill let its members show constituents and the news media "that they're pro tenants, and that the Republicans are not."[5]

What happened as the Legislature worked its way through the rent issue displayed the power Litwin had obtained from his smart lobbying staff, campaign contributions, and his sway with Silver and Skelos.

Because the Legislature had other work to do—and because legislatures everywhere make their most important decisions under tight deadlines—lobbying on the quadrennial rent-and-property-tax bill didn't begin in earnest until early in June 2011, as the existing law was about to expire.

Glenwood's and Litwin's influence over the process was shown by their presence on Cuomo's official schedule. On June 3, Litwin and two Glenwood executives— Dorego, the company's senior vice president and counsel, and Gary Jacob, an executive vice president—joined legislators and lobbyists for the Real Estate Board of New York and the Rent Stabilization Association for a meeting with Cuomo in the governor's Manhattan office. Glenwood was the only real estate developer with executives in the room. Every other developer in the state was represented by lobbyists for industry groups.

The timing was ironic. Just before he met with the real estate interests, Cuomo sat down with representatives of several good-government groups, including the New York Public Interest Research Group, Common Cause, and Citizens Union. All had complained about the campaign finance laws that let Glenwood Management become a big political donor.

Another critical meeting came June 6, when Runes and Meara met with Silver in his office in Albany.

"Both the Speaker and I stated our positions on certain issues in the rent laws," Runes recalled.

Runes told Silver that Glenwood could live with deregulating rents that rose to $2,500 a month—$500 less than the Assembly had proposed. He also said Glenwood could live with raising the income at which a renter's apartment would be deregulated to $200,000 a year—$100,000 less than the original Assembly plan.

Runes's proposal was certainly less generous to renters. It also didn't do much for many members of the Rent Stabilization Association. Sure, it was a better deal for the small-building landlords than the $3,000 rent threshold and $300,000 income threshold in the Assembly's original bill. But Runes understood that it would still hurt landlords who were far less wealthy than Leonard Litwin. "The Rent Stabilization Association represented a lot of outer-borough [non-Manhattan] landlords with smaller buildings who would have been adversely affected by the increase in those numbers," Runes admitted. From these landlords' perspective, a $2,500 rent threshold and $200,000 income threshold still pushed out of reach their desire to own more deregulated apartments.

Nonetheless, Runes's proposal was an easier pill for the real estate industry as a whole to swallow than the original Assembly bill. And by adopting Runes's idea, Silver could claim to be making a deal favorable to renters. If that was indeed to be the public perception of the negotiation, Runes was in a good position to ask, What could Silver give the real estate lobby in return?

The answer was obvious: Runes suggested to Silver that the final bill should restore the 421-a tax-break program.[6]

No doubt Silver expected Runes to make this suggestion. He undoubtedly knew that developers like Glenwood cared more about the 421-a tax breaks than they did about rent rules. Members of the Real Estate Board of New York also would have been pleased with the restoration of 421-a. But the members of Strasburg's Rent Stabilization Association would have cared little— this tax break wasn't for smaller landlords.

Real Estate Board and Rent Stabilization Association members didn't know the Glenwood lobbyists, Runes and Meara, were meeting Silver behind their backs to cut a deal. "It was not our public position—this was a confidential discussion," Runes said. He explained, "I was articulating the Glenwood position, not the industry position."

Silver made no promises to Meara and Runes.

"He didn't say yes, and he didn't say no," Meara recalled. "He probably said, 'I understand,' or 'I hear you,' or something like that. That would be typical. You didn't really know, when you left the meeting, whether he agreed or disagreed. He didn't say that. I guess that's the only way I could describe it."[7]

There was another meeting with Governor Cuomo that included Dorego, Runes, Strasburg, and Steven Spinola, president of the Real Estate Board of New York. Cuomo's office summoned the lobbyists on short notice on June 16. "We got into our cars ... and we drove up to Albany," Strasburg recalled.[8]

Again at this meeting, Glenwood was the only company represented by its own executives, in this case Dorego and Runes.

It was the first time Dorego had been in the state capitol while the final terms of the quadrennial rent bill were being discussed.

"It was sort of organized chaos. I mean, there were people everywhere," he said. Cuomo gave Dorego a brief tour of his office in the capitol's ornate Executive Chamber, pointed out a picture of his father, Mario Cuomo, and complained of some disparaging public comments Strasburg had made.[9] In a conference room outside Cuomo's office, Strasburg and Spinola got into a heated argument. Strasburg said he felt Spinola was letting Cuomo play the Real Estate Board against other real estate interests over the issues they faced. "There was always going to be an attempt to play each other off, because we had different interests," Strasburg said. "The only way we could ever succeed is that we all had to be in agreement not to be picked off by any entity."

Not much substantive happened at the meeting with Cuomo. The governor was ready to accept the $2,500 rent threshold Runes had secretly discussed with Silver. Runes and Meara's earlier meeting with Silver on June 6 evidently sealed the deal Glenwood wanted.

Like many important issues in Albany, the rent and tax-abatement bill was settled by the three men in a room—Silver, Skelos, and Cuomo. In line with Runes's suggestions to Silver, the final bill, approved by the Legislature on June 24, decontrolled apartments with rents over $2,500 as well as those where renters' incomes exceeded $200,000. It also tossed out a provision in the

Assembly bill that barred New York City's government from imposing more stringent rent regulations than those allowed by the law.

Glenwood's lobbying of the Legislature's most powerful leaders paid off. "It's always important to maintain good relationships with leadership," Runes said.

Though the bill could be seen as adverse to small landlords, the real estate industry in general considered it a win—because Silver, in the view of real estate industry lobbyists, could have done more for tenants.

Federal investigators learned the real estate industry's opinion of Silver's stance on the rent-regulation and 421-a issues from a document "prepared by an entity that represents real estate developers." In court papers, the investigators were not clear about exactly what pro-tenant ideas Silver opposed. But the court papers state: "Silver was considerably more favorable to the real estate industry than expected."

The papers quote the real estate developers' document: "Though he [Silver] may never be the owners['] advocate, given that the Governor wanted [certain proposals] off the table and wanted to restore his reputation with tenants, it would appear that he [Silver] could have successfully pushed for more."[10]

Yet Silver touted the bill as a win for renters. He claimed on his official website that in 2011, "rent regulations were strengthened for the first time in decades, increasing protections for over a million apartments in New York City."[11]

But the evidence does not support Silver's claim about strengthening rent rules.

The 2011 bill did not stem the loss of rent-regulated apartments in New York City, which had gone on for years and continued unabated after 2011. "Between 2005 and 2017, rising rents led to the disappearance of over 425,000 apartments renting for $900 or less (in 2017 dollars) from the City's housing inventory," said a 2018 report from the city comptroller. The study found a "substantial shift in the price distribution of rental apartments away from lower-priced units, to more middle- and high-rent units."[12]

After two decades of Silver's leadership in the state Assembly, many New Yorkers still found the rent too damn high. The 2011 rent bill failed them. Glenwood and its campaign contributions won the day. And Glenwood's financial relationship with Silver—via its hiring of Jay Goldberg's law firm, which shared with Silver 25 percent of the fees Glenwood paid—can not be overlooked as a factor in the company's lobbying win.

The link between Glenwood, Goldberg and Silver was about to cause a headache.

For a couple of years Goldberg's law partner, Dara Iryami, had worried over a new ethics rule from New York legal regulators. The rule, which Iryami learned of in 2009, required lawyers to tell clients when they shared fees with other lawyers. Because of this rule, Goldberg disclosed his firm's fee sharing to new clients. But the firm handled tax appeals for around 2,000 buildings, many of which it had represented for years. It wasn't easy for Goldberg and Iryami to reach out to their longtime clients affected by the new disclosure rule. "It got put on the back burner," Iryami explained. So Goldberg put off telling Glenwood Management and the Witkoff Group that Silver was getting a cut of their fees.

Six months after the 2011 rent bill was enacted—in December 2011—Iryami suggested to Goldberg that the issue be resolved. Thus Goldberg sent new retainer agreements to the Witkoff Group and Glenwood Management.

The Witkoff manager who oversaw the property-tax appeals filed the new retainer away without telling the company's boss, Steve Witkoff. The retainer sat unnoticed in the company's files for the next few years. Witkoff usually didn't bother signing such agreements anyhow.

The first anyone at Glenwood heard of the new retainer was a phone call from Silver to Brian Meara on December 21, while Meara was vacationing in Palm Beach, Florida.

"He told me there were certain disclosure records, the process of which for filing had been changed. And he had to file a new kind of disclosure form indicating he had received certain fees from certain people," Meara recounted.

To Meara, Silver seemed worried about a technical aspect of the fee Goldberg had shared with him for so many years. "What he said was, 'Do you represent Glenwood Management, or its LLCs [limited liability companies]?'" Silver apparently thought taking fees from the limited liability companies through which Glenwood owned apartment buildings was legally proper, so long as Meara was not lobbying him on the LLCs' behalf.

"I said, 'No. I only represent Glenwood. I don't represent its LLCs.'"

"That's not a problem," Silver replied. "Because I'm only getting fees from its LLCs."

But Meara knew it was, in fact, potentially a big problem—maybe legally, and certainly politically.

"I was surprised and concerned," he said. "I was primarily concerned about the fact that politically in his district, I didn't know how popular it would be if it became disclosed he was representing a large real estate company. I also thought it would be politically a problem for his conference [his fellow Assembly Democrats] in Albany."

Meara didn't see why it mattered to Silver whether he got fees from Glenwood's LLCs or from Glenwood itself. [13] The executives at Meara's client, Glenwood Management, also didn't see the difference. Either way, the situation posed problems for Glenwood. Was it illegal to lobby a legislator who was also taking money from that lobbyist's client? If they tried to fix the situation by ending their business relationship with Goldberg, would Silver be angry?

"It was a shock and a surprise. I was not happy," said Runes.

"I was concerned because Mr. Silver was the speaker. So it was complicated. It's really good to have a good relationship with the speaker," he said. "I didn't know how this was going to play out. I didn't know whether this was in fact legal. There were too many complications for me to be happy about it."[14]

Leonard Litwin was unhappy too. Runes did not believe Litwin knew anything about Silver's fees until then. "He was upset—he was, in a sense, angry," Runes said. In his view, Litwin feared there would be "repercussions legislatively." [15]

Goldberg sent Glenwood a new retainer agreement that disclosed Silver was getting a share of the fees it paid whenever Goldberg won a property-tax appeal. Litwin wasn't sure whether to sign it. "He wanted to know whether it was legal under the lobbying and ethics laws in New York for Mr. Silver to be participating in legal fees on the buildings," Runes recounted.

Also, Runes recalled, Litwin did not want to "make an enemy out of Mr. Silver. We had no desire to do that."[16]

It was a big, ugly mess.

"If you hold a tiger by the tail, you have a difficult choice to make: Do you let go, or not?" Runes asked.[17]

Glenwood looked for a way to hold on.

Runes consulted a lawyer who specialized in lobbying law. He gave the lawyer a hypothetical question: "If a real estate management company manages apartment houses and properties, and the properties are owned by LLCs, and the real estate management company hires lobbyists but the LLCs don't, may a New York state legislator do business with the LLC's?"

"His response was, 'Yes,'" Runes recalled.

Runes didn't tell the lawyer that the LLCs were getting state benefits—tax breaks, and state-backed loans that Silver had to approve. He also didn't tell the lawyer that the LLCs were donating campaign money to Silver and other legislators. Also, the question posed to the ethics lawyer did not make clear whether the real estate management company owned the LLCs.

But the lawyer's "yes" was good enough.

And Litwin had an idea.

He asked Goldberg to redo the retainer agreement Goldberg & Iryami had sent Glenwood so Silver's name was omitted. He also asked Goldberg to separately send Glenwood a letter—a side agreement—that disclosed Silver was getting a cut of the fees.

Dorego would sign the side agreement and return it to Goldberg, and Goldberg would keep the side agreement in his files.

That appeared to meet Dara Iryami's concern that Glenwood be informed that Silver was being paid fees for having brought Glenwood's business to Goldberg about 15 years earlier.

Goldberg was fine with this arrangement. "It didn't matter to me as long as I conformed to the ethics rules," he said. [18]

Early in the New Year—January 18, 2012—Runes went to Albany to see Silver in his state capitol office. He described the new arrangement for the company's retainer agreement with Goldberg, and the side letter. Runes was asked how Silver responded when told of this new arrangement. "He said, 'Fine.'"

Runes called Litwin and Dorego and told them Silver would go along with the plan.

But Runes remained unhappy. "I was uncomfortable with the arrangement," he said.

One problem was that the side letter was secret. Glenwood's retainer agreement with Goldberg was "filed someplace" and "available to be viewed," Runes said. "Whereas, the side letter would not be."

And Glenwood still had that tiger by the tail.

For Litwin's plan to work, Goldberg needed Silver's signature on the side letter. "This was a technical compliance I wanted to perform," he said.

So Goldberg arranged to meet Silver at the three-way intersection of Lewis Street and Grand Street on the Lower East Side, nearly in the shadow of the Williamsburg Bridge and a few blocks from Silver's home.

Both men drove to the corner in a mixed business and residential area on an unseasonably warm late-January day—the temperatures that week were in the 40s and 50s. The meetup went smoothly. "Double-parked, no tickets," said Goldberg. There Silver signed the side letter.

Despite the anger and upset in Glenwood's offices over the fee-sharing arrangement between Silver and Goldberg, everyone carried on business as usual.

On December 19, days before Goldberg informed Glenwood that he was sharing fees with Silver, Goldberg sent Silver a check for $114,567, the fruit of successful property-tax appeals on Glenwood buildings. Also, Silver worked for Glenwood on another front, by fighting plans for a methadone clinic that was to open near Glenwood's building at 10 Liberty Street in Manhattan's Financial District. And at the end of January 2012, soon after Goldberg had Silver sign the side letter, Glenwood assigned Goldberg tax-appeal work on six more properties.

Litwin made sure Silver and his fellow Assembly members got a generous share of his campaign contributions.

One day in June 2012, Silver called Runes seeking money for the Democratic Assembly Campaign Committee. "We exchanged pleasantries. He said he was calling to raise money for DACC and, would we consider a contribution to DACC?" Runes recalled.

Runes said he wasn't authorized to make such a decision—he would have to ask Litwin. But he thought he knew roughly what Litwin would contribute. "I was pretty confident I could suggest to Mr. Silver a $25,000 contribution," Runes said.

Silver replied, "How about $125,000?"

"I'll get back to you on that," Runes answered.

"I spoke to Mr. Litwin about it, and he made the decision to make the contribution," Runes said.

Glenwood sent the money on July 11 in five separate $25,000 checks. Each was drawn on the bank accounts of LLCs representing different Glenwood buildings in Manhattan. One was again drawn on the LLC that owned the Barclay at 1755 York Avenue. The others were drawn on the 210-unit Pavilion at 500 East Seventy-Seventh Street, the 58-unit Marlowe at 145 East Eighty-First Street, the 233-unit Cambridge at 500 East Eighty-Fifth Street, and at the 282-unit building marketed as Liberty Plaza at 10 Liberty Street in the Financial District.

A $125,000 gift to Assembly Democrats "was not a lot of money compared to how much we gave the other house [the Republican Senate]," Runes said. But it was worthwhile nonetheless—"it was good for our relationship" with Silver. And the contribution didn't much change the balance of Glenwood's giving—the company still gave far more to Senate Republicans.[19]

Glenwood couldn't afford any hard feelings. It won big from the Assembly in the 2011 rent and 421-a debate. And Leonard Litwin found a way to let Silver's money-grabbing continue.

Chapter 13 – Do for me

Soon after Andrew Cuomo became governor in January 2011, he embarked on an exercise in futility—trying to persuade the Legislature to ignore "special interests," political and media shorthand for the lobbyists who shower legislators with campaign money and crowded the state capitol on days the Assembly and Senate are in session.

Cuomo made his point in that month's State of the State address, an annual event held in Albany before a crowd made up mostly of lobbyists, state officials, and politicians—"significant people in state government," said Richard Runes, the Glenwood Management lobbyist. He made a point of attending every year and standing by Sheldon Silver's office, "as all those people would come by."[1] Attending the speech let Runes see and be seen, which helped maintain his presence in legislators' lives.

Cuomo had some words about the special interests represented that day by Runes and many others. The new governor was aided by an animated cartoon that showed the Assembly, Senate, and himself as three ships "passing in the night."

"Hold on a second. Bring those ships back—I think I recognized someone," Cuomo said.

"Is that—zoom in on that man on that battleship—yes, it is! Senate Majority Leader Dean Skelos. And look, it's Commander Sheldon Silver!

"Oh, and there I am. And here are the special interest groups." The special interest groups fired at Cuomo's ship. "You notice, Dean, how all of the missiles from the special interest groups went into my battleship? I would humbly suggest as the new governor that maybe, just maybe, we try doing it a different way this year. What do you say?"[2]

As Cuomo gave the battleship speech, former state comptroller Alan Hevesi awaited sentencing on charges

that he took $1 million in what prosecutors called
"benefits" from California businessman Elliot Broidy.
Unusually, Hevesi was prosecuted in New York state
courts by lawyers who worked for Cuomo when he was
attorney general. Usually, the federal government
pursued such cases.

Hevesi got the "benefits" from Broidy in return for
steering $250 million of state pension money to Broidy's
investment firm. The "benefits" Hevesi received included
$500,000 in donations to his campaign fund and $380,000
in fees steered to one of his friends. Broidy also funded
some of Hevesi's vacation travel. Hevesi pleaded guilty
and got a prison term of one to four years, of which he
served about 20 months.

Hevesi's woes did not scare Silver from seeking more
money from Robert Taub's mesothelioma patients.
Though his clinic no longer got state funds, Taub still
sent patients to Silver and Weitz & Luxenberg. In April
2011—around when Hevesi was sentenced—a Taub
patient named Setenay Itez showed up in Weitz &
Luxenberg records. Days after Taub first saw her, she
died at age 60. Hers was a good case for Weitz &
Luxenberg, and for Silver. Over the next four years, the
case brought in settlements of $814,453 from asbestos
trusts. Of that sum, Weitz & Luxenberg netted fees of
$178,910, and Silver netted fees of $89,455.

The month after the Itez referral, Silver took his
corrupt scheme to the Assembly floor—stealthily. On
May 10, 2011, at Silver's behest, the Assembly approved
a proclamation honoring Taub, who was about to get an
award from the American Cancer Society. The Assembly
routinely approves big batches of such proclamations on
voice votes. No one took any note of the Taub
proclamation, which Silver packaged with proclamations
for two other Cancer Society honorees.

That day, Silver ordered the Legislature's staff to
create artful, framed versions of the three proclamations.
It was a rush job. "We did it in an afternoon," said a

legislative employee. Top Silver aide Judy Rapfogel wanted to bring the proclamations from Albany to New York that night.

Silver presented the framed resolution to Taub at an American Cancer Society fundraising dinner two days later, on May 12. Taub paid for Silver's ticket and seated him at his table. "I thought Mr. Silver would lend prestige to the event, and perhaps help in fundraising by his presence," Taub said. An irony: Simmons Hanly Conroy, Weitz & Luxenberg's rival in the mesothelioma litigation business, gave the Cancer Society $6,500 to be named sponsor of Taub's table. Silver's appearance at the event was partly supported by a Weitz & Luxenberg competitor.

Taub was pleased with the framed Assembly resolution, which he hung in his office. It was "very nice," he said.

Meanwhile, Cuomo pushed ahead with his ethics plans. "I want people to pass a reform package," he said in a speech that spring. "If they don't, there are other options that I can consider."[3] One of those options was a state commission to investigate government corruption.

An element of Cuomo's plan for more ethics rules was public disclosure of legislators' assets and outside income. Under existing law, this information was kept in secret state files. This was the information Silver boasted of detailing in May 2008—without mentioning that the forms on which he detailed the information were kept from public view. Cuomo's proposal finally would have made details of legislators' assets and income public.

Under the law of the time, Silver was required to report—on the secret forms—the value of his wife's "notes and accounts receivable" in her Counsel Financial investment. The couple's Counsel Financial investments were in the form of a loan or note to the company, which paid interest. If the public had access to his disclosure form covering 2010, it would have seen that Sheldon Silver held a Counsel Financial note worth "$250,000 or over," and Rosa Silver held a Counsel Financial note with a value of "$100,000 to under $250,000."[4]

Silver did not want to make public the couple's entire Counsel Financial investment under Cuomo's new ethics law.

To keep details of the investment secret under Cuomo's proposal, Silver needed to take two steps. The first was to make sure his wife's share of the Counsel Financial notes was formally separated from his share. The second was to make sure Cuomo's final ethics law exempted from disclosure any "notes and accounts receivable" belonging to Rosa Silver.

Silver took the first step in May 2011 by asking Jordan Levy, who set up the Counsel Financial investment, to break apart his and Rosa's notes with the company. "It was $600,000 split equally, $300,000 in Rosa's name and $300,000 remaining in his name," Levy said. According to Levy, this was how Silver explained why he wanted to divide the investment: "It would allow him to not have to disclose in his annual statements, his documents, his filings, that particular piece of his investment that he had been previously disclosing."

How Silver's second step was accomplished—getting the law written so that Rosa Silver's notes would be exempt from disclosure—was known only to him, and perhaps to Cuomo and the Senate majority leader, Dean Skelos. They were the three men in a room who agreed upon the ethics bill's exact terms.

The Legislature passed Cuomo's ethics bill over three days in June 2011, weeks after Levy and Silver shifted the money in the Silvers' Counsel Financial account.

Cuomo touted the Clean Up Albany Act of 2011 as "the tough and aggressive approach we need." He called it "historic" reform that created "unprecedented transparency."[5]

No one ever publicly discussed the loophole that served Silver's aim of hiding the Counsel Financial investment Levy set up in Rosa Silver's name. The new law required Silver and other legislators to report "all notes and accounts receivable ... *held by the reporting individual.*" (Emphasis added.) In other words, Silver had to report the value of his share of the Counsel Financial investment. But he did not have to report his wife's share, which Levy had placed in a separate note. [6]

Silver reported on his ethics form for 2011—which covered a period before the Cuomo ethics law took effect—that his and Rosa's separate notes with Counsel Financial were each worth "$250,000 or over." These separate investments were the result of Silver's mid-2011 request to split the couple's $600,000 investment. The form, filed in May 2012, also reported that Silver earned between $60,000 and $100,000 from his note, and his wife earned between $20,000 and $60,000 from her note.[7] But this form was not required to be made public. It was not disclosed until years later.

Silver's ethics form covering 2012—which he filed in May 2013—was the first made public under the Cuomo ethics law passed in 2011.

The form reported that a Counsel Financial note held by "the reporting individual"—Sheldon Silver—was worth between $350,000 and $400,000.[8] But it did not give information about Rosa Silver's Counsel Financial note, or her other assets.

Yet the law did require disclosure of the couple's income. Thus the form said Rosa Silver earned between $50,000 and $75,000 in interest from Counsel Financial. Sheldon Silver reported earning a similar amount.[9]

Considering his effort to hide his wife's Counsel Financial notes, Silver's statement in June 2011 touting the ethics law's passage reeks of hypocrisy. It said, "Transparency and accountability are the pillars of good government, and today's action will strengthen our citizens' faith in their elected leaders and hold accountable those who betray the public trust."[10]

In 2012, Silver found another way to help Taub.

Ohel Children's Home and Family Services, a nonprofit Jewish organization, learned in March 2012 that thanks to Silver, it would get a $2 million state grant to help build a summer camp for troubled children in the Catskills. Around the same time, Taub's son approached Silver seeking help in finding work with a Jewish social services organization. Jonathan Taub had a master's degree in special education but was having a hard time making the connections he needed to land a job in the field.

Silver gave Jonathan Taub's name to Ohel leadership. It took several months, but Ohel eventually hired him.

"Did you believe that sending patients to Silver might help in getting him to provide assistance to your son?" a lawyer later asked Taub in court.

"It could," Taub answered.[11]

While Ohel was deciding whether to hire Jonathan Taub during May and June 2012, Taub referred two more patients to Silver and Weitz & Luxenberg. One was Joseph Goldman, who was a month shy of his 91st birthday when he first saw Robert Taub in April 2012. Goldman's name was entered in Weitz & Luxenberg records in May 2012, and his case—pursued against several asbestos defendants—brought $1.7 million in awards. Of that, Weitz & Luxenberg netted $373,344 in fees, and Silver netted $186,672, the law firm's records show. Goldman died in September 2013. Weitz & Luxenberg pursued his case for 18 months more, until April 2015.[12]

Soon, yet another scandal surfaced in the Assembly. In August 2012, *The New York Times* and other media reported that the state spent more than $100,000 to settle allegations that Vito Lopez, a Democratic Assembly member and Brooklyn political boss, sexually harassed and abused women on his staff. State investigators found Lopez "engaged in an escalating course of conduct with respect to multiple female staff members." Lopez started with "demeaning comments about appearance and dress as well as demands for fawning text and email messages." He then escalated to "requirements for companionship outside the office, and culminated in attempted and forced intimate contact." The women who tolerated Lopez's creepy behavior or acceded to his demands were rewarded with "cash gifts, promotions, salary increases, and plum assignments."[13]

Lopez got angry at female employees who spurned his sexual advances, the investigators found.

"He's just weird," one of these women remarked in a recorded conversation. She added, "I'm OK. Sick of this shit, but aren't we all."

Another employee took sick with pink eye after Lopez insisted she put medicine drops in his infected eyes. The employee traded texts with a coworker. "Vito man. It's not a problem when he is gross everywhere and infects others. Just when people do it to him," she wrote.

"Blargh!" her colleague replied. "He made you put drops in his eyes. Fing sadness!!! I'm so sorry."[14]

Silver was implicated in the Legislature's cover-up of Lopez's repulsive behavior. When the women complained of Lopez's piggishness, Silver looked the other way. He backed his staff's decision not to report Lopez to the Assembly Ethics Committee. The investigators also found that Silver's staff did not investigate the women's complaints or do anything to protect them from more harassment.

Dean Skelos, the Senate majority leader, carried on with his corrupt ways by getting another no-show job for his son, Adam. Early in 2013, Skelos used his influence to get Adam on the payroll of Physicians' Reciprocal Insurers, a medical malpractice insurer with business before the state Legislature. It was a sales job that came with a $78,000-per-year salary.

State insurance regulators believed Physicians' Reciprocal Insurers was underfunded to the point where it might have difficulty paying claims. Anthony Bonomo, the company's principal owner and CEO, needed the

Legislature to pass laws exempting it from the regulators' scrutiny. Senator Skelos had always supported the special legislation, and Bonomo felt he needed to stay in Skelos's good graces. Bonomo hired Adam Skelos because he thought it might help the situation.

One of Bonomo's lobbyists warned him that hiring Adam Skelos was a bad idea. Bonomo would have gained by heeding this advice.

Soon after Adam Skelos started work in January 2013, his supervisor asked him to show up at the office now and then. The two began feuding, and Adam Skelos complained to his father about how he was being treated at work.

So on January 10, 2013—it took less than 10 days for Adam Skelos to prove himself a lousy coworker—Dean Skelos called Bonomo. "I have never received a call from a parent" of an employee, Bonomo said years later.

Bonomo was worried. "I didn't want to have the senator upset that something might have been going on with Adam," he said. He feared firing Adam Skelos would lead to "a reprisal, or something not happening properly in Albany."

In two phone calls that day, Bonomo discussed with Senator Skelos the problems he had with his son. "Adam was not coming in, he was going and coming as he pleases, that he was saying some things to the supervisor that were not proper and ... he was just not being a good employee," Bonomo said.

Skelos listened to Bonomo's complaint. He seemed "upset about the whole thing and he just told me to 'work it out.'... He was upset about what was going on," Bonomo said.

The situation festered, and Bonomo and executives at Physicians' Reciprocal Insurers got desperate enough that they contacted former U.S. Senator Al D'Amato's lobbying firm, to which they paid a retainer as part of the company's efforts to keep an eye on things in Albany. It was one of D'Amato's associates who'd advised Bonomo not to hire Adam Skelos in the first place.

D'Amato set up a meeting with Dean Skelos for April 12 at Skelos's district office in Rockville Centre, on Long Island.

"I told the senator that his son was not coming in when he should, there are days when he wasn't at work, and that there were a number of occasions where he was very disruptive in the office," D'Amato said.

"It appeared to me that he was going to be let go unless something was done—or he would be fired," D'Amato said. He said he spoke to Skelos "as a friend, because I wanted to warn him about what was taking place."

Skelos told D'Amato that his son needed the health insurance from the Physicians' Reciprocal Insurers job, as his wife was pregnant.[15]

The meeting did not resolve the problems.

The following August, Adam Skelos got into an especially ugly argument over the phone with his supervisor, Chris Curcio, who had asked Skelos to show up at a meeting at the office. Curcio recounted Skelos's words: "Hey, Chris. It's Adam," Skelos said. "Let's stop pretending. You and I don't get along. Guys like you couldn't shine my shoes. Guys like you will never amount to anything, and if you talk to me like that again, I'll smash your fucking head in."[16]

Anthony Bonomo and his brother—who was also a Physicians' Reciprocal executive—decided to put Adam Skelos in a lower-paying job that didn't require him to show up in the office as much. The position required Skelos to generate 100 sales leads every week. Bonomo said he didn't believe Skelos ever met that goal.[17]

Dean Skelos should have known better than to use his political position to help his son. All state senators were required to attend a three-hour ethics-training seminar in February 2011. Skelos signed in to the event.[18]

In April 2013 came the arrest of Malcolm Smith, the Queens Democrat who had spent several months in 2009 as Senate majority leader. Smith somehow felt qualified for even higher office. He was charged with trying to pay $40,000 in bribes to a pair of Republican Party leaders to put him on their primary ballot as a candidate for mayor. Smith fantasized that running as a Republican was a better play than competing for the job in a primary election against his fellow Democrats. It was a dumb idea. Smith's constituents voted him out of the Senate in a Democratic primary, and he ended up with a seven-year federal prison sentence.

Then came the August 2013 arrest of Assemblyman Eric Stevenson of the Bronx, who was accused of seeking $20,000 in bribes in return for introducing a bill that imposed a temporary moratorium on the opening of new adult-day-care centers in New York City. The bill, which would have taken effect in February 2013, was meant to ensure a monopoly for the owners of the existing adult-day-care centers in his district.

"If half of the people up here in Albany was ever caught for what they do . . . they . . . would probably be in [jail] . . . so who are they bullshitting?" Stevenson said on December 27, 2012, in a recorded conversation. A few days later, on January 1, 2013, he talked about needing to be "careful" about "the recorders and all those things" worn by government informants in order to not "put yourself in jail."[19]

Stevenson had no idea how careful he needed to be. The person recording him was fellow Assembly member Nelson Castro, who was helping the feds in hope of easing his sentence on a perjury charge. Stevenson was sentenced to three years in prison.

"It becomes more and more difficult to avoid the sad conclusion that political corruption in New York is indeed rampant," Manhattan U.S. Attorney Preet Bharara told reporters after the arrests of Stevenson and Smith. "A show-me-the-money culture in Albany is alive and well." Voters agreed. Pollsters found in April 2013 that 9 out of 10 New York voters believed corruption was a serious problem, and 1 in 3 believed their own legislators might be arrested.[20]

Silver wasn't as worried. At a celebration of a department-store expansion in the Financial District, a *New York Post* reporter asked Silver about Eric Stevenson's arrest. "In any group there are rotten apples. It's unfortunate that it happened," he answered. Silver also—in the *Post*'s word—"deflected" responsibility for the corruption taking place under his leadership. "I don't feel any responsibility. I don't interview people [when they run for office]," he said.[21]

All the corruption—and the Legislature's lack of interest in doing anything about it—seemed to frustrate Cuomo. When the Legislature met in 2013, he again proposed a system of public financing for state political campaigns. He also proposed a further round of ethics reforms. One of his ideas was to increase penalties for corruption crimes. Another was to stop local political bosses from granting candidates ballot access in primary elections. If the Legislature didn't act on his ideas, Cuomo said, he would establish a commission to investigate its corruption.

The Legislature did nothing with his ideas. So two days after the Legislature adjourned for the summer—on July 2, 2013—Cuomo established a commission to investigate legislative corruption.

The commission—called a Moreland Commission under the state law that allowed its establishment—had the power to interview witnesses under oath and "subpoena any necessary records," Cuomo said in a news release. The attorney general, Eric Schneiderman, helped by designating the commission members as deputy attorneys general.

Soon the media buzzed with headlines about Albany corruption—and about Silver's income. The same ethics form Silver filed in May 2013 that disclosed for the first time he had invested between $350,000 and $400,000 in

Counsel Financial also made public for the first time information about his outside earnings.

The form omitted the value of the Silvers' apartment in Manhattan and his vacation home upstate in the Catskills, as well as the amount of Rosa's Counsel Financial investment and whatever other investments she may have owned. But it did show that, counting their retirement accounts and a slew of stock holdings, the Silvers had assets of between $2.15 million and $3.7 million.

The form also said that in 2012, Silver was paid between $350,000 and $450,000 for what he described as "General practice of law with emphasis on representation of individual clients and personal injury actions and 'of counsel' to law firm." This was entirely Weitz & Luxenberg money. As in 2008, Jay Goldberg's firm wasn't mentioned on the form, but Weitz & Luxenberg was.

Additionally—besides the $50,000 to $75,000 in interest Silver and his wife each reported earning from the Counsel Financial notes—the ethics form disclosed the $20,000 Silver earned from the Clover Communities fund investment Jordan Levy set up for him.

In all, counting Silver's legal fees, investment income, and $122,000 legislative salary, the couple reported 2012 income between $764,000 and $1,117,000.[22]

The disclosure gave only a partial picture. It didn't give exact amounts for his earnings, or exact values for his investments. But the forms clearly showed Silver was no mere public servant. He may have started out in his government career as a humble courthouse lawyer and underpaid state legislator. But now, after more than three decades in the Legislature, Sheldon Silver was wealthy.

Silver added little to the media reports about his assets and income. "The speaker invests in blue-chip stocks as do millions of Americans in their retirement accounts," said his spokesman.[23] Well, yes. That much was clearly true. But it was yet another statement from

Silver's office that didn't come close to telling the whole story.

Cuomo's Moreland Commission got to work in the summer of 2013. It subpoenaed records from several big real estate developers about their lobbying for the 421-a residential real estate tax abatement program, which they considered vital to their businesses. The commission also subpoenaed several Albany lobbying firms. Late that summer—on August 27—the commission asked Silver and other legislators for data about their earnings beyond their legislative salaries. They had until September 13 to respond.

This was an affront to how Albany and its lobbyists did business—in secret, with few public hearings, lubricated by public and private favors, presided over by the three men in a room—the governor, Assembly speaker and Senate majority leader—who alone decided what important bills became law. Cuomo's commission and its subpoenas were not conducive to the status quo so comforting and lucrative to Albany's establishment.

Silver and the establishment pushed back. Within two days, Silver alerted other Assembly members that he'd hired an outside law firm, Kasowitz, Benson, Torres & Freedman, to "represent in the Assembly in connection with ... matters which may be the subject of the Commission's work." Assemblywoman Amy Paulin, the Westchester County Democrat, took Silver's announcement as meaning the Kasowitz firm would be available to "any member who has been called before the Moreland Commission."[24]

Unsaid in Silver's announcement to his colleagues was the idea that the commission might have been interested in Silver's outside income—or the idea that the Kasowitz firm, hired with taxpayer money, might help Silver hide his illicit schemes.

Silver would have been right to worry about the Moreland probe. In October, the commission subpoenaed Weitz & Luxenberg's documents about Silver's income, his clients, and anything related to the firm's lobbying in Albany.

The Moreland investigators aimed to be thorough. They sought "invoices, billable hour reports, timesheets, expense reports and reimbursement forms" related to Silver's side job. They demanded "Documents and Communications relating to the solicitation and engagement of any and all Weitz & Luxenberg clients ... by Assembly Speaker Sheldon Silver." They requested whatever marketing materials and retainer agreements Silver might have had. They wanted Silver's client list and "a general description of the services provided by Assembly Speaker Sheldon Silver to such clients." The subpoena also sought information about Weitz & Luxenberg's donations to New York politicians.

If Weitz & Luxenberg complied with this request, the Moreland Commission would reach the heart of Silver's effort to earn money from Taub's patients.

Gary Klein, Weitz & Luxenberg's managing attorney, asked Arthur Luxenberg what to do. Luxenberg advised him to contact the Kasowitz firm. The firm's lawyers provided Weitz & Luxenberg with language it could use to file what Klein called a "me too" affidavit—a legal motion to oppose the subpoena for the same reasons the Legislature was fighting its subpoenas.

The Moreland Commission issued a preliminary public report in December. "One out of every eleven legislators to leave office since 1999 has done so under the cloud of ethical or criminal violations, and multiple sitting officials are facing indictments on public corruption charges," the report said.

The commission said it had issued "200 subpoenas and requests for information," and that it was conducting "undercover operations, including surveillance, recorded calls, and meets." It was using data analysis "to focus in on and uncover connections and relationships that otherwise would have been difficult or impossible to discern." It was investigating "pay to play" arrangements, "in which wealthy interests allegedly exchange targeted campaign contributions for targeted pieces of legislative action." Among those was "a tax abatement program benefiting certain real estate interests"—undoubtedly a veiled reference to the 421-a program.[25]

Silver had reason to be nervous. He had plenty to hide. But publicly, he argued that the Legislature had to fight the Moreland subpoenas to ensure its independence from Cuomo and the rest of state government. Silver said the commission's queries showed it was "engaged in a fishing expedition to intimidate legislators."[26]

In his January 2014 State of the State address, Cuomo praised the commission and the idea of further reforming ethics laws. "There is a disagreement about the need for more ethics reform. I understand that," the governor said.

He said many in the Legislature believed the Clean Up Albany Act of 2011 went far enough by creating a new state ethics commission and requiring more disclosure about the personal finances of Silver and other legislators. No doubt Silver and his colleagues would balk at disclosing more about their finances. But Cuomo wanted to reveal more. "There has been a string of bad acts, almost on a daily basis," he said. "Open up the newspaper, even today, and you see more and more stories of individual legislators who have done bad acts."

Cuomo pushed a new plan he called the Public Trust Act—"public financing of elections, independent enforcements at the Board of Elections, and disclosure of outside clients with business before the state." The act would also make bribery charges easier to prove by aligning state law with federal law, which did not require prosecutors to prove a direct quid pro quo between bribe takers and bribe payers. This concept is important in Sheldon Silver's case. Silver never directly asked Robert Taub to provide him with names of mesothelioma patients in return for the $500,000 in state grants, or the various other favors Silver performed. But the quid pro quo was hinted at in Taub's dealings with Silver. Taub felt obligated to help Silver, in return for the state money and other favors. As in federal law, that informal quid pro quo would have been enough to satisfy the proposed state law.

As Cuomo pressed publicly for more reform, his commission poked around the Legislature. Silver pushed back. Federal investigators later said that by his challenge of the commission's subpoenas and other efforts, "Silver sought to prevent, and in fact prevented, the disclosure of information about his outside income."

Assemblywoman Amy Paulin learned firsthand that the commission had no impact on the Legislature's status quo.

Paulin, long interested in education issues and in combating child sex trafficking, spoke out in early 2014 against actions of the New York Board of Regents, which sets state education policy. Paulin said the Regents were moving in a "terrible direction." She wanted the board to scale back what she deemed its excessive academic testing of schoolchildren, and planned to question candidates for the Board of Regents on the topic.

This was a direct challenge to Silver's power. Members of the Board of Regents were selected by a joint vote of the Assembly and Senate. Given the overwhelming size of the Democratic Assembly majority, this effectively meant Silver, as the Assembly Democrats' leader, decided who served on the board.

"He was not happy with my activity with the Regents," Paulin said.

At the same time Paulin argued for the Board of Regents to change its testing policies, she moved with 80 or 90 of her Democratic Assembly colleagues to add $3 million to the state budget for an anti-sex-trafficking program. That many Democratic votes should have been enough to get the money added to the Assembly's budget proposal. But the original Assembly budget plan published early in March 2014 omitted the money Paulin and her colleagues wanted.

Paulin caught up with Silver in a state capitol hallway and asked him why.

His answer was curt: "You do for me, I do for you."

Paulin realized she wouldn't get the money unless she changed her tune on the Regents.[27] So she relented, and did for him. "I did stop being as vocal about the Regents as I had been." And Silver did for her: Paulin's anti-sex-trafficking program was funded in the state budget.

Cuomo relented too. He agreed with Silver and Skelos to put the Moreland Commission out of business. It was a classic Albany three-men-in-a-room deal, which federal prosecutors later determined was part of the annual state budget agreement between Cuomo, Skelos, and Silver.

It appeared Cuomo got something in return for calling off his investigators: Silver and Skelos agreed to include much of his proposed Public Trust Act, including the rewrite of the state's bribery law, in that year's state budget bill.

Cuomo never publicly admitted shutting down the commission was part of the deal. He said only that disbanding the commission was his right.

"The Moreland Commission was my commission. It's my commission. My subpoena power, my Moreland Commission. I can appoint it, I can disband it. I appoint you, I can unappoint you tomorrow," he told some media interviewers.

Preet Bharara, the Manhattan U.S. attorney, said he and his staff would look carefully at whether Cuomo interfered with the commission's operations. Cuomo responded skeptically. "So, interference? It's my commission," he said. "I can't 'interfere' with it, because it is mine. It is controlled by me."[28] Besides, Cuomo said, the commission had persuaded the Legislature to finally pass the ethics law he wanted.

But Cuomo must have been at least a little nervous about the possibility Bharara would investigate his decision.

Sometime in April 2014—around the time the Moreland Commission was shutting down and Bharara asked it to preserve its documents and records—Cuomo called the White House to complain about Bharara. He spoke with Valerie Jarrett, a top aide to President Barack Obama. Skeptical, Jarrett quickly ended the call and consulted a White House ethics officer. An August 2021 article in *The New Yorker* quotes Cuomo's words to Jarrett as recalled by a member of the White House legal team: "This guy's out of control," Cuomo said of Bharara. "He's your guy."

Cuomo's call came to naught. Jarrett and others in the White House saw it as an improper attempt to influence a possible investigation. Justice Department officials had no intention of stopping Bharara's investigation—but they did tell him about the phone call. Bharara told *The New Yorker*'s Ronan Farrow, "Andrew Cuomo has no qualms, while he's under investigation by the sitting U.S. Attorney for the Southern District of New York [Bharara's formal title], trying to call the White House to call me off."

"[Future President Donald] Trump did that," Bharara said. "That's an extraordinary thing, from my perspective." [29]

Bharara's investigation of the commission's demise found no crime. But Bharara—without naming Cuomo—said in a January 2015 speech that he had been "very confused" about the decision to shut down the commission, and that he had stopped trying to analyze Cuomo's motives. "Various people have, I think, over time ... given maybe 18 or 19 different explanations depending on the time as to what its powers were, what its level of independence was or should be, as a practical matter or as a legal matter." [30]

Bharara didn't tell the whole story. All along, the Legislature's stonewalling of the commission was probably futile.

In June 2013—the month before Cuomo established the commission—a federal grand jury began investigating Sheldon Silver. The federal investigation was based on "prior investigations of corruption by members of the Legislature, cooperating witnesses related to those investigations, and a review of public disclosures and statements" by Silver.[31]

Silver and his Senate counterpart, Dean Skelos, were in more trouble than they knew.

Chapter 14 – Visitations

Aided by new leads in the Moreland Commission's documents, Preet Bharara's FBI agents, investigators, and prosecutors pressed ahead. Sheldon Silver had this in common with the Department of Justice people who pursued him: they said little. Bharara and his team said nothing in public about the Silver investigation. But Silver and those around him learned soon enough.

Silver's friend Jay Goldberg telephoned one of his biggest clients, the Witkoff Group, in mid-2014, barely two months after Governor Cuomo, Silver, and Dean Skelos reached the budget deal that shut down the Moreland Commission. Goldberg wanted to tell the company that his relationship with Silver was under federal investigation.

On June 3, Goldberg left a message for Scott Alper, a Witkoff associate. "Pretty important," a Witkoff employee wrote in an email to Alper alerting him to the call.

Alper got on the phone with Goldberg. After the call, he relayed what he learned to Steve Witkoff, the company's lead owner.

"Scott came into my office and said to me that there was some sort of investigation with regard to Goldberg & Iryami's tax certiorari work for us and that there had been apparently fee splitting between Goldberg & Iryami and Mr. Silver," Witkoff said.

"And of course I didn't know about it. It's not anything I was aware of. And I was pretty incensed."

"So I said to Scott, 'Let's get Mr. Goldberg on the phone,' and that's what we did." [1]

When Witkoff called, Goldberg was with his wife in his car, driving upstate. He'd never met Witkoff before and didn't recognize his voice. He said of Witkoff's call, "I can best characterize [it] as a tirade. He kept going on and on and on about how terrible I am, about how unethical I am, how nasty I was. He kept going on and on and on. It was a rant."

Witkoff owned up to his fury—he described his tone in the call as "angry and belligerent."

During the call, Goldberg told Witkoff that for years he and Silver shared the fees the Witkoff Group paid Goldberg & Iryami to pursue property-tax appeals.

Witkoff replied that he didn't know. He recalled telling Goldberg, "You never told me about that. ... You should have made me aware of it."

Goldberg replied, "What, you don't remember? You didn't know that Mr. Silver was getting part of this fee? I sent you a retainer in 2012 wherein it stated that Mr. Silver was getting part of the fee."[2]

Which was true. Goldberg had sent Witkoff a new retainer mentioning Silver two and a half years earlier, in January 2012—the one a Witkoff aide filed away without seeking Witkoff's signature. Silver was still getting 15 percent of whatever Witkoff paid Goldberg's firm.

Witkoff—a lawyer by training—didn't know what to do. He feared Goldberg's fee-sharing setup with Silver put him and his company in trouble with the law. "It certainly didn't feel right to me. It certainly didn't feel right that he didn't disclose it to me, and it just felt unseemly."

"I wasn't sure what the legality and what the ethical issues were," Witkoff said. He decided to call his lawyer.

And as soon as he could, he did something Glenwood's lawyers dared not do—he fired Goldberg & Iryami.

The media also turned up the heat on Silver. On July 2, 2014—weeks after Goldberg called Witkoff—Silver's ethics filing for 2013 became public.

Silver reported his "Law Practice" in 2013—"Including of Counsel W&L [Weitz & Luxenberg]" paid him a sum in category "N" of the ethics form, between $650,000 and $750,000. News reporters assumed this meant only his Weitz & Luxenberg money. The form said nothing about

Goldberg & Iryami. Thus, despite Silver's use of the word "including"—which implied he got some legal fees elsewhere—journalists wrote their copy as if Weitz & Luxenberg was the only source of Silver's law-firm income.[3]

The New York *Daily News* noted in a story about the disclosure that Silver's law-practice earnings in 2013 were "at least $200,000 more than the earnings of $350,000 to $450,000 he reported for 2012."

It took federal investigators' subpoenas to dig out the truth about Silver's earnings in 2013. Silver reported honestly the amounts in the form—investigators found his law-firm income that year was $709,573.13, near the middle of the ethics form's category "N."

That total included $670,477.46 from Weitz & Luxenberg that year—of which $340,901.22 came from Taub's mesothelioma patients, $145,955.06 came from non-mesothelioma personal injury cases he referred to the firm, and $115,384.75 was salary. The total also included $35,317.32 in fees from Goldberg's firm.

Reporters knew about Silver's Weitz & Luxenberg affiliation, but they had never heard of Jay Goldberg. "The details of Silver's work for Weitz & Luxenberg—a firm that specializes in personal injury cases, especially involving asbestos exposure—have been one of the statehouse's enduring mysteries," the *News*'s story said. It quoted Silver's spokesman, Michael Whyland: "The speaker's salary fluctuates from year to year depending on the disposition of his cases."[4] Whyland said nothing about the Goldberg & Iryami fees, and the reporters didn't write about them—because they didn't know.

The *News* kept asking about Silver's earnings, and in a follow-up story it quoted Whyland saying that Silver worked only a few hours a week for all that money.

So how did he get all those case referrals anyway? "He's been a lawyer for more than 40 years," Whyland explained. Yes—but that statement didn't go one inch toward explaining how Silver got the names of mesothelioma patients from Robert Taub. "People know him," Whyland told the newspaper. "It's not unlike any other attorney in this state, anywhere."[5]

The *News*'s July 3 story mentioned that Silver previously said he spent hours evaluating clients' cases. That was a lie as far as the mesothelioma cases went, according to Weitz & Luxenberg lawyer Charles Ferguson—who said all Silver did was write down the patients' names when Robert Taub gave them to him over the telephone.

Whyland was worried enough about stories reporters might write about Silver's ethics form that he gave Jason Fink, a subordinate, a script to use when reporters asked about Silver's income. He headlined his email to Fink on the subject "off topic." That term is political public relations speak for questions asked by reporters that are off the topic of the main subject of a press conference or public appearance. Politicians and their publicists often don't like off-topic questions. They shift attention away from a politician's message, and on top of that they can nudge the politician into unrehearsed, potentially damaging answers.

Under the heading "Weitz income," Whyland gave Fink this explanation that he or Silver should use if asked about Silver's Weitz & Luxenberg earnings:

"My salary fluctuates from year to year depending on the disposition of my cases." It was the same line Whyland used with the *Daily News* and other media.

Whyland offered another line about the Weitz & Luxenberg income reported on Silver's ethics form: "I disclose everything that is required. These are clients who have no business before the state."

This line didn't mention that Silver had a say in writing the reporting requirements that let him hide assets he held with his wife—in particular, the rule that hid his wife's Counsel Financial investment from public disclosure.[6]

The line also lied when it said Silver's clients had no business with state government. Glenwood Management and the Witkoff Group relied on state laws providing property-tax breaks, as well as state financing for some of their projects. They needed laws that favored their businesses. Glenwood needed favorable rent-control and property-tax laws. Steve Witkoff had for years talked with Silver about the need to improve real estate development prospects in lower Manhattan.

Poor Whyland was stuck feeding journalists these half-truths and lies. He simply didn't know the real story about his boss's income. What about the Goldberg fees? "I had no knowledge of that," he said. And who, exactly, were the clients Silver took to Weitz & Luxenberg? "I didn't know the nature of the cases. ... I always understood it as personal injury cases," he said. [7] Whyland didn't know anything about Robert Taub.

Taub knew something was up with Silver.

Taub was vaguely aware that the Legislature was under "scrutiny," but he wasn't sure he'd ever heard of the Moreland Commission. As the Moreland Commission and the Manhattan U.S. Attorney's Office investigations proceeded in 2013, Taub referred just two patients to Silver. It's unclear from the public record whether the first case made money for Silver and Weitz & Luxenberg. The second case, entered in the law firm's records in November, was a dud—the patient's family apparently didn't want to go ahead with the matter.

Sometime in mid-July 2014—shortly after Sheldon Silver's 2013 ethics forms became public and the publication of the *Daily News* stories—Taub got a visit at his Upper East Side apartment from Daniel Chill, the mutual friend who'd introduced him to Silver. Chill suffered from a series of cluster headaches, Taub recalled. The headaches were getting worse. Maybe Taub, his old friend, could help.

As Chill was leaving, he offered a bit of news about their mutual friend.

"They're after Shelly," Chill said.

Taub's wife asked whether her husband needed a lawyer.

Three weeks or so later, Taub learned firsthand of a service provided by attentive Manhattan doormen: they alert you when law enforcement is headed to your apartment.

At 6 a.m. on August 8, 2014, Taub's doorman called to say that two Federal Bureau of Investigation agents were on their way to his home. It was all the notice he got before the agents were at his doorstep. He greeted them in his pajamas. "I was terrified and confused," said Taub.

They talked in Taub's living room.

"First, they told me that they were going to—that they were investigating me at my home at 6 a.m. because they didn't want to come publicly to my office. So I had a premonition that this was going to be—I had a feeling I was going to be escorted, in public, out of my office." His nurse Mary Hesdorffer—whose ethical sense Taub ridiculed as that of a "schoolteacher" or "nun"—had been right to admonish him that referring patients to law firms put him at risk of being taken from his office in handcuffs.

"It was quite intimidating," Taub said of the agents' visit. The agents didn't physically threaten him. "But they are imposing-looking and they were investigating me in their large investigation, which I had previously not thought I was going to be involved in."

Taub panicked. "I felt threatened and terrified. ... It was a primal response."[8]

The agents wanted to know if Taub had sent any of his mesothelioma patients to Sheldon Silver. Taub lied. "I told them that I did not refer any cases to Mr. Silver," he said.

After the agents left, Taub got in touch with Silver by phone. "I used a Hebrew term—I told him I had had a visitation from investigators," Taub said.

The Hebrew term he used was *bikur cholim*, which refers to visiting and aiding the sick. Taub said that by using the phrase, he meant to get across the idea that "I had been rendered ill or rendered sick by a visitation."

Silver asked if Taub had told the agents anything.

"I said I didn't think so," Taub recalled.

But Taub was troubled by his dishonesty to the agents.

"I realized that what I had said was a lie and that this would compound an already terrible situation, and I needed to act to try and reverse it," Taub said.

He talked it over with his wife, and he lost sleep. He called his daughter, a lawyer, for advice. Taub didn't say in court testimony exactly what she told him—but he came to realize his lie to the agents was likely a felony. "I knew it was an error that subsequently needed to be corrected. ... It was big trouble," he said.[9] His daughter put Taub in touch with a criminal defense lawyer.

Taub came clean. "It took a while for me to tell the truth—a few days."[10] He signed an agreement in which he promised to "cooperate fully" with the prosecutors.

Investigators grew their knowledge of Silver by demanding information from Weitz & Luxenberg. In September, Gary Klein, the firm's managing attorney, was interviewed by the U.S. Attorney's Office in Manhattan. Weitz & Luxenberg employees began appearing before the grand jury weighing Silver's case. The firm also began producing documents for the prosecutors, including one in late November that listed all of Silver's clients.

A story in *The New York Times* on December 8, 2014, mentioned in passing that prosecutors found Silver "failed to disclose some of the income he earned in the private sector. While he has disclosed earnings from a major personal-injury law firm for years, prosecutors found other law-firm income that he did not detail as required." [11] That wasn't quite true—Silver was never charged with lying on his disclosure forms. But it was now public knowledge that Silver might be in some kind of trouble.

The heat was on—and Silver slipped up.

On December 10, Victor Franco, a staffer on the Assembly's Ways and Means Committee, got an email from his boss asking him for information about money disbursed under the Health Care Reform Act—the law that let Silver appropriate $500,000 in taxpayer money for Taub's clinic. "Initially, I did not know where the request was coming from," Franco said. "But ultimately, I learned it was coming from the Speaker's office."[12]

Prosecutors took this incident as a sign of Silver's guilty conscience.

"Silver knew what he had done," Assistant U.S. Attorney Carrie Cohen said. "Silver knew that he had directed these state grants to Dr. Taub. No one else knew that. He knew that.

"And so, when the government was starting to put Weitz & Luxenberg witnesses into the grand jury to seek an indictment, the defendant [Silver] knew exactly what he had done and he wanted to get and see whatever documents existed. ... He knew exactly what grants to pull."

Silver asked for the documents "on an expedited basis," Cohen said. Silver didn't give his subordinates a reason for the request—"he knew what he had done, and wanted the documents."[13]

Franco produced a document that listed all the money allocated under the Health Care Reform Act from 2002 to 2014. It included Taub's grants—but it didn't mention Taub by name. It listed the grants as having gone to the "Trustees of Columbia University" and "New York and Presbyterian Hospital."

The day after Franco was asked to pull the records, a pair of Albany reporters encountered Silver at the state capitol. They interviewed him as he walked to an event at the Egg, an auditorium and convention venue next to the capitol, so named because it's shaped like a giant egg on a pedestal.

Despite the *Times* story on December 8—a few days before—that hinted that prosecutors had looked into Silver's income, the reporters still didn't know much more than they knew in July, when Silver's 2013 ethics form was released.

"Mr. Speaker, your ethics form for 2013 disclosed at least $650,000 in outside income," asked one reporter.

"Yeah."

"What percentage of that came through Weitz & Luxenberg? And what was the rest of it from?"

"I can't, I can't tell, all I can tell you is I, I disclose everything. Uh, all my income, otherwise I wouldn't be disclosing everything income-wise. ..."

"In addition to what you've already reported. No additional sources of any kind?" asked a second reporter.

"No, no."

"Well, you, you said from the practice of law," said the first reporter.

"Right."

"Uh, my understanding is, do you have clients who are coming to you outside of Weitz & Luxenberg?" the first reporter asked.

"Yes. Absolutely."

"Would you say who some of those clients are?"

"No. I don't think it's required. I follow the law."

"And, what, what kinds of clients are those? Because they are..."

"A variety." Which was sort of true, if you think a pair of real estate development companies constitute "a variety" of clients.

"All right, thanks, guys," said Michael Whyland. The encounter was unplanned, and the reporters' questions were off-topic. But the walking interview continued—Silver's and the reporters' footsteps can be heard on the recording.

"They are a variety," Silver answered. "A variety. I—that's all I can elaborate on at this point."

The second reporter asked, "Can you say the clients are not involved in any kind of state work?"

"They are not involved in any kind of state work. Yes, I can say that." Which was sort of true, if Silver and the reporters meant the non–Weitz & Luxenberg clients—Glenwood Management and the Witkoff Group—had no state contracts.

"How did they seek you out?" asked the first reporter.

"Well, people like you give me a lot of publicity."

The reporters chuckled at this gag line—which Silver had used before—but it was a lie too. Media publicity had nothing to do with how he got mesothelioma clients, or Goldberg's real-estate-tax-appeal work.

"And what, what percentage was through the firm and what percentage was otherwise?"

"I would say, a majority—more than a majority—was through the firm"—apparently a reference to Weitz & Luxenberg. "More than a majority was through the firm. More, much more than the majority."

"Is there anything you want to add from your thinking about this or any other issue on this?"

"Nope."[14]

Dean Skelos also carried on business as usual.

After the 2010 Census, the state Senate was expanded by one seat so that it had 63 members. Because there was now an odd number of senators, tie votes were less likely.

But the new seat didn't end the Senate's leadership turmoil. In the November 2012 election, Democrats won a 33–30 majority—which again proved too thin to hold. Weeks after the election, Senate Republicans cut a power-sharing deal with four Democratic senators who became known as the Independent Democratic Conference. Skelos shared the title of Senate majority leader with Jeffrey Klein, a Democratic senator from the Bronx.

It got better for Republicans in November 2014, when the party again won an outright Senate majority. No longer did Republicans have to share power with Democrats. So Skelos was able to push away Senator Jeffrey Klein of the Bronx, the leader of the Independent Democratic Conference.

Skelos explained to his son what the 2014 Senate victory meant.

"I'm going to be president of the Senate. I'm going to be majority leader. I'm going to control everything," he told Adam Skelos in a December 22 phone call recorded by federal investigators. "I'm going to control what gets— who gets on what committees, who—what legislation goes to the floor, what legislation comes through committees, the, the budget, everything."

Klein's breakaway group still existed—but Skelos didn't plan to cut it many breaks.

Skelos told his son he'd let Klein take credit for a bill passed now and then, if it suited Republicans. "But I mean, that's it. I told him, 'You lost, I won.'" He hoped shutting out Klein would increase the discord among Democratic senators. "You got to keep them separated, and that's what this is going to do, keep them separated and fighting and hating each other," Skelos explained to his son. "And that's what's worked for us for the last six years, is keeping them at each other's throats, and that's what this will do."[15]

Word leaked late in December to *The New York Times* that Bharara was investigating Jay Goldberg's law firm. Aside from that, the *Times* reporters had few details. They wrote about Goldberg's work on behalf of the Lower East Side co-op apartment building where Silver lived, and other properties in Silver's neighborhood. But the December 29 story didn't say anything about Glenwood.[16] A few days later, Goldberg was photographed outside his Staten Island home wearing a Russian-style fur hat with a Soviet hammer-and-sickle enamel pin. "There was absolutely nothing illicit going on," he told a *New York Post* reporter.[17]

That wasn't how Bharara and his prosecutors and investigators saw it. They were preparing to file their criminal case.

Silver's imminent arrest was leaked to *The New York Times*, which put the story online early in the morning of January 22, 2015. A few hours later, Silver turned himself in at the federal court complex in lower Manhattan. A magistrate judge set his bail at $200,000, and Silver was released. "I am confident that after a full hearing and due process, I will be vindicated of these charges," he told reporters in a courthouse hallway. The *Daily News* said Silver appeared "relaxed."

Bharara had a warning for the public and for Silver's colleagues: "Stay tuned." His investigation wasn't over.

Whatever the status of the federal case, Silver's arrest brought a rapid end to his speakership.

Newly elected Assembly member Todd Kaminsky, a former federal prosecutor, had a dark view of the charges against Silver. Kaminsky won his Long Island–based Assembly seat in 2014 with Silver's support. Silver campaigned for Kaminsky in the Five Towns area of southern Nassau County, which has a large Orthodox Jewish community. Kaminsky appreciated Silver's help, but it was also something he expected. "When you are running to be part of the Assembly majority, the speaker helps," he said.

But having worked on political corruption cases for the Brooklyn U.S. Attorney's Office, Kaminsky was under no illusions about the crookedness he would encounter in the Legislature. "My first day in Albany, I shook hands with seven people I had investigated," he said. "Some of it was smoke and not fire and some of it didn't go anywhere." Kaminsky said of the Legislature's corrupt ways: "I came there to change that."

So he was conflicted on January 22 when news broke of Silver's arrest. "It was very difficult to have that news land on your lap," he said. "None of this was pleasant when it happened. But I also couldn't ignore the evidence that was piled up in front of me."

Some in the Legislature did ignore the evidence. A few Assembly members stood up for Silver at a news conference the day of his arrest. "Even though it's a serious charge and it probably hampers his ability somewhat to be speaker, he still has the confidence of his members," said one, Brooklyn Assemblyman Joseph Lentol, a Democrat.[18]

Kaminsky was not buying any of that. "I knew none of them had read the [criminal] complaint," he said. "I read the whole complaint, and I was obviously stunned at how incriminating it was."

Kaminsky wasn't the only Assembly member shocked by the charges. "A number of us got together a day or two later at an Applebee's outside of Albany and decided we were not going to stand with Silver," Kaminsky said. He and his colleagues decided to disclose their views at a private meeting of Assembly Democrats the next day.

The next morning, Kaminsky met Silver on his way into the state capitol. "He asked me, 'Are you going to support me today?' I told him I couldn't. It was a very tough moment." [19]

At a five-hour meeting, Kaminsky and others among Silver's Democratic colleagues made clear they'd lost confidence in him and wanted him out of the speaker's chair. He was innocent until proven guilty—but still the allegations cost him the trust of the caucus he led. "It changed the way we looked at all of the negotiations when we heard that accusation," said Assembly member Amy Paulin, who'd been forced to abide Silver's "You do for me, I do for you" maxim.[20] No longer could anyone see Silver as an honest broker of Democrats' interests.

Silver had no choice. He resigned as Assembly speaker 11 days after his arrest, on February 2. His staff and his power vanished in an instant.

Just as Silver did to Michael Bragman nearly 15 years earlier, the Assembly's new leadership moved Silver to a seat in the back row of the Assembly chamber. Sometimes a reporter sat nearby, listening to Silver's analysis of what was happening on the Assembly floor— whose interests were at stake, why this or that legislator voted one way or another.

Silver's indictment made it obvious to the Skeloses that they were also in Bharara's sights. Glenwood Management's involvement in the Silver case became public knowledge upon Silver's arrest. Skelos and his son were in deep with Glenwood. But all Dean and Adam Skelos could do was wait tensely for whatever would happen.

It was more than Adam Skelos could bear. He called his father on March 28.

"I'm kind of freaking out," Adam Skelos said.

Not to worry, said Dean Skelos. "Dad is here to help. ... Don't freak out. It'll work out. It always does," he said.

Father and son talked. "I can't even have a conversation with you, because you're in fucking politics, about everything, you know," Adam said. "It's just frustrating."

"It is," said Dean.

Adam went on. "I'm going through a rough time. I want to have a conversation, just, you know—you could give me real advice rather than, 'Oh, everything'll work out.' It sucks."

"No, I can give you advice," Dean said. "Talk to me."

"No, no, no, you can't, because you can't talk normally," said Adam. "Because it's like fucking Preet Bharara's listening to every fucking phone call. It's just fucking frustrating."

Adam Skelos was almost right. Bharara wasn't listening to the call—but the FBI was. Its transcript eventually was entered in the Skeloses' case as Government Exhibit 1533-T.

Chapter 15 – Sentences

On his first sentencing day, Sheldon Silver showed up at Manhattan federal court in a politician's uniform: a blue shirt and a red tie, worn inside a business suit garnished with an American flag lapel pin.

"Good luck, Mr. Silver," called out a well-dressed woman on the security line.

After a five-week trial, a jury on November 30, 2015, found him guilty of crimes of greed and of selling out his high office. He betrayed his constituents and his fellow Assembly members to real estate developers who paid him thousands in illicit fees. He used taxpayer money to leverage a scheme that filled his bank and investment accounts with millions of dollars from the sick and dying. His conviction brought his automatic expulsion from the Assembly, to which he had been elected 39 years earlier, in 1976.

Still, Sheldon Silver had supporters. And still, he dressed like a politician.

Silver did not respond to the woman's encouragement. He removed his belt and emptied his pockets into an X-ray machine tray. Then he stepped through the metal detector, which rang an alarm. He had a pen, which he handed to a security guard. He tried the metal detector again—and the alarm went off again. The guard pulled him aside and patted him down.

"You're good now," the guard said.

Now, on May 3, 2016, at the Pearl Street entrance to the Thurgood Marshall Federal Courthouse, Silver was just someone else trying to clear security.

He was 72 years old, and he sat for sentencing before a federal judge, convicted by a jury on all seven counts of his indictment.

Silver was guilty of four counts of honest services mail and wire fraud. Two counts were related to the money he got from Weitz & Luxenberg, and two more related to the money he got from real estate developers via Jay Goldberg's law firm. The indictment said Silver cheated New York citizens and voters by carrying out "a scheme and artifice to defraud, and to deprive the public of its intangible right to Silver's honest services as an elected legislator and as the Speaker of the Assembly."

The fifth and sixth counts in Silver's indictment were labeled "extortion under cover of official right," and involved a federal law called the Hobbs Act. Extortion under the Hobbs Act means "the obtaining of property from another ... induced by wrongful use of actual or threatened force, violence, or fear, or under color of official right." The Supreme Court said in a 1992 case, *Evans v. United States*, that the words "under color of official right" means the law applies to someone who uses public office to take "money that was not due to him for the performance of his official duties."[1] One Hobbs Act count was for the Weitz & Luxenberg payments, and the other was for the Goldberg payments.

The seventh count was labeled "monetary transactions involving crime proceeds," which charged Silver with breaking the law by moving around the money he gained from his schemes. This is commonly called money laundering.

Silver's family and many of his friends wrote letters to the court asking for leniency or describing his good works. Silver wrote a letter of his own.

"I failed the people of New York. There is no question about it. ... What I have done has hurt the Assembly, and New York, and my constituents terribly, and I regret that more than I can possibly express. Because of my actions, New York's ethics rules were and continue to be analyzed, evaluated and criticized, everywhere. I worked hard for many years to make sure the Assembly and its members were respected as a vital legislative body. Because of me, the government has been ridiculed. I let my peers down, I let the people of the state down, and I let down my constituents—the people of lower

Manhattan that I live among and fought for. They deserve better."

But letting down his constituents was not a violation of the law. Silver's letter did not deal directly with the legal issues raised by his case, including the charge that he deprived his constituents of his honest service and that he profited by an extortion scheme. Silver said this was at his lawyers' request, "given the motions they filed and my possible appeal."[2]

Silver's letter didn't mention the legal fees federal investigators said he illicitly took in the case—$3.1 million from Weitz & Luxenberg's sick and dying clients, and $835,000 from the real estate tax savings Jay Goldberg's firm won for Glenwood Management and the Witkoff Group. Silver's total take was more than $3.9 million.

The letter also said nothing about the $500,000 in state taxpayer money he sent to Robert Taub's lab, or about the rent laws Silver twisted to the favor of Glenwood and its lobbyists. Nothing in the letter discussed how he twisted state ethics laws so his greed might go undetected. And he wrote nothing about the idea that he put his financial interests ahead of the interests of the public, or that his money-grabbing schemes deprived New Yorkers of his honest services.

Silver "could have admitted that he betrayed the people he served," Assistant U.S. Attorney Howard Master said at the hearing. "He corrupted the people's house"—a reference to Assembly members' belief that their chamber is more representative of New Yorkers than the supposedly more elite Senate, whose fewer members represent larger districts.

"He betrayed his fellow Assembly members, and he betrayed his staff when he used all the power and all the money that came with being a leader of the people's house, the power to grant or withhold benefits, legislation, the public's money, to advance not the people's interests but his own personal financial interests in violation of his duty of honest services, his duty to carry out his responsibilities as the speaker faithfully," Master said.

Silver's lawyers argued in court papers that the government's investigation—and everything it revealed—obscured Silver's "good conduct, his good character, and the acts he has taken to benefit his constituents and the people of the State. ... Whatever the Government has chosen to make public should not detract from that side of Mr. Silver's life and career."

Master took the defense argument that the government ignored Silver's good works as a claim that the government was "trying to harm him [Silver] and his reputation."

"He could have admitted that he himself is to blame for the investigation and the prosecution that revealed the truth and resulted in his downfall," Master told Manhattan U.S. District Court Judge Valerie Caproni, who heard Silver's trial. "Really, what did he think would happen when he made all of those millions of dollars, more than any other member of the state Legislature, when he did it corruptly, and when he covered it up with secrets and with lies?" Master asked.

Master mentioned Silver's colleagues who went to prison. "What did he think would happen when all of those state legislators ... were getting convicted for similar conduct, even while he persisted with his corrupt scheme and his lies?"

And he mentioned Silver's propensity for lying and secrecy. "Your Honor, even today, after a long trial and with months to gather letters in support, and to write his own letter, he hasn't produced a single person who knew the truth, who knew what was going on here. Why? Because he lied. Because he covered it up. How did the defendant think this would all end up?"

Master's words got to a truth of the case: Silver hid his crimes well. Those caught up in his crimes—the mesothelioma patients, the lawyers at Weitz &

Luxenberg, the real estate developers—had little idea of how he used his public office to profit from them. The people around Silver in the Legislature—his colleagues and his staff—knew even less. Even those who made sure Robert Taub got his $500,000 in grant money, or drafted the fine print of the Legislature's rent-control bills, didn't know the reasons behind Silver's instructions to them.

And his constituents—the people Silver professed to serve—had only suspicions that there was something dishonest about him. Probably he went up to the line—but did he go over it?

Throughout the case, prosecutors held back details of Silver's cheating on his wife. They finally laid them out in a sentencing motion "concerning certain character evidence." It was initially submitted under seal. When the document became public, the women's names and details of their relationships with Silver were blacked out.

One of the women was reportedly an Albany lobbyist and Silver's former chief of staff, Patricia Lynch. Though her name didn't appear in the government's motion, it was revealed in numerous press accounts. Lynch "lobbied the defendant on a regular basis on behalf of clients who had business before the State," the motion said.[3] During Silver's last years as speaker, Lynch had a diverse list of lobbying clients. They included the Legal Aid Society—which provides legal help to low-income New Yorkers—as well as the company that owned Madison Square Garden. She also represented real estate investor Vornado Realty Trust, and real estate developer Related Companies.

Silver and Lynch were caught on government surveillance recordings talking about legislation she was handling for her clients. Silver warned Lynch it was "not safe" for them to be seen together.

Lynch also complained that a member of Silver's staff was not treating her well in regard to an issue before the Assembly. "I don't talk to anybody about the issue except you," she said. Silver replied that the matter—its substance was not revealed—was "a difficult issue" for Assembly Democrats.

Silver's relationship with Lynch at the same time she lobbied him on behalf of clients was "highly probative of the defendant's [Silver's] integrity, ethics, honesty and truthfulness," federal prosecutors argued. "In particular, such conduct demonstrates Silver's willingness to further his personal interests while concealing his personal involvement from the staff and public."[4]

Silver's lawyers had a ready answer for this issue. "Mr. Silver is not charged with concealing his personal affairs—he is charged with performing official acts *in exchange for* private gain," they wrote. Prosecutors had no proof that Silver "'use[d] his official powers' to help [Lynch] in exchange for a purported sexual relationship, or even that he treated her lobbying proposals any differently than any other person's."[5] The defense argued that because Silver did nothing in exchange for the affair, the relationship did not deny "honest service" to his constituents or to the state.

Among Lynch's lobbying clients from 2011 to 2016 was the state Catholic Conference, which represents New York's Catholic bishops. John Aretakis, who as a lawyer worked with people abused by clergy—and whose zealous advocacy on behalf of his clients factored in the suspension of his law license—wished the government had presented evidence of how Silver's relationship with Lynch affected the Assembly's consideration of issues important to the Catholic Conference.

Clergy sex abuse victims pushed for years for a law that would let them sue the Catholic Church and other religious organizations. Aretakis believed Lynch worked with Silver to keep the bill from passing the Assembly. "Because Patricia Lynch was being paid a lot of money from the Catholic Conference, the bill from the Shelly side was dead," Aretakis said.[6]

The name of another woman who had an affair with Silver was also redacted from publicly available court papers. She was identified in the media and by government colleagues as Janele Hyer-Spencer, a former Assembly member the New York *Daily News* described as a former model. After Hyer-Spencer lost her bid for reelection in 2010 in her Staten Island–based district, Silver allegedly got her a job at the state Department of Education. Federal investigators asked around the department about Hyer-Spencer's hiring, the *Daily News* said.[7]

Evidently the investigators didn't get anywhere. Neither Silver nor Hyer-Spencer were ever charged with anything related to their relationship.

But Silver's affairs did figure in his sentence—particularly his relationship with Lynch, which Judge Caproni brought up at his sentencing hearing. "Did a lobbyist have preferred access because she was a better lobbyist than her competitors, or was it payback for a personal relationship? Did that result in a thumb on the scale for her clients rather than decisions being made on the merits?" Caproni asked. "Those sorts of doubts end up corroding trust in government, and that, Mr. Silver, is discernible harm to the people of New York."[8]

And Silver was not a fundamentally honest man, the judge said.

"Nothing that happened in the world of criminal prosecutions of Albany politicians seemed to have an iota of an impact on you beyond leading you to amend slightly what you disclosed on your financial disclosure form," Caproni admonished.

"One would think that the image of Mr. Silver's colleagues being arrested and led off to jail would have caused someone who was basically honest to reappraise what was going on. Instead, in the face of arrests and prosecutions, Silver stopped nothing. He lied to his own press officer and he lied to the press, holding himself as a paragon of virtue who had no business involvement with companies that had business with the state, a statement he knew full well to be absolutely false."

Caproni also recalled that Silver sought to counter investigations of his activities—including his hiring at state expense of a law firm to fight Cuomo's Moreland Commission. "He threw up every roadblock he could to thwart the investigation, portraying his actions—which, by the way, used taxpayer funds—as motivated by institutional concerns for the Assembly when, as we know now all too well, they were actually the desperate actions of a politician who was trying to ensure that the corruption in Albany could continue unchecked," the judge said. "Those are not the actions of a basically honest person." [9]

Caproni sentenced Silver to 12 years in prison and 3 years of supervised release—which is what the federal government calls parole. She also imposed a $1.75 million fine and ordered Silver to forfeit $5.4 million to the government—the $3.9 million he took, plus interest.

But Silver's first trial and sentencing—both of which were over within 15 months of his arrest—were the opening acts in a drama that played out for nearly five more years.

The first undoing of the prosecution case came not in Caproni's courtroom but several weeks after Silver's sentencing, in the U.S. Supreme Court.

Robert McDonnell, the governor of Virginia, was convicted of honest services fraud and Hobbs Act extortion—the same laws a jury found Silver violated. McDonnell was charged with taking $175,000 in loans, gifts, and other benefits from Jonnie Williams, a Virginia businessman who wanted the state's medical schools to study Anatabloc, a tobacco-based nutritional supplement.

Politicians routinely field business peoples' requests for favors that might boost their companies—think of AbTech, the company that sought Dean Skelos's help selling storm water cleaning devices to Nassau County on

Long Island, or anything Glenwood and other real estate developers asked of Skelos and Silver. Some businesspeople think coddling politicians can help clear their path to profit and success.

Williams bought McDonnell's wife, Maureen, $20,000 worth of designer clothing and gave the couple $15,000 to help pay for one daughter's wedding, as well as a $10,000 wedding gift to another daughter. He also loaned the McDonnells $120,000. He gave McDonnell's wife, Maureen, a Rolex watch which she presented to her husband as a Christmas present. Williams also paid for several rounds of golf with McDonnell and took the couple on a weekend trip.

In return for the loans, gifts, and other favors, McDonnell arranged meetings between Williams and various Virginia officials, hosted events for Williams's company at the governor's mansion, and contacted other government officials about the research studies Williams wanted.

The problem with the prosecution case was that McDonnell failed to persuade the state university system to study Williams's product. "I have limited decision-making power in this area," the governor explained to Williams. McDonnell's meetings, cajoling, and phone calls to university officials came to naught. He also failed to persuade other officials to pay for Anatabloc under the Virginia state-employee health plan.

McDonnell admitted setting up meetings to discuss Anatabloc but said he had set up similar meetings "literally thousands of times" as governor. He also said he expected his staff to do nothing but meet with Williams. He didn't demand they study Williams's product.

McDonnell's actions were "tawdry," said Supreme Court Chief Justice John Roberts. But they weren't illegal, the court found. A few weeks after Silver's conviction, the justices voted 7–0 to overturn the verdict against McDonnell. In the June 27, 2016, ruling, the justices said that "setting up a meeting, calling another public official, or hosting an event does not, standing alone, qualify as an 'official act'" under laws aimed at thwarting government corruption. An official act, the court ruled, "is a decision or action on a 'question, matter, cause, suit, proceeding or controversy'" involving "a formal exercise of governmental power."

The facts in McDonnell's case differed from Silver's case. McDonnell got his gifts in return for setting up meetings that came to nothing. Silver did carry out "a formal exercise of governmental power" in favor of the people who gave him money—he backed their views in deciding rent regulation and renewal of the 421-a tax break; he sent state money to Robert Taub's clinic in return for the names of his patients.

The problem, Silver's lawyers argued on appeal, was the jury in his first trial wasn't correctly asked to determine whether the favors Silver performed for the real estate companies and for Taub were official acts under federal law as defined by the McDonnell opinion.

The government and Judge Caproni gave Silver's jury a broad definition of an "official act"—they said it was, in prosecutors' words, "any action taken or to be taken under color of official authority."[10]

Silver's appeals judges decided Caproni's definition of an "official act" was more wide-ranging than the McDonnell decision allowed. There was plenty of evidence against Silver, the judges said. But the jury's understanding of an "official act" needed to be more specific. The appellate judges ordered a new trial and gave Caproni a road map for how to comply with the McDonnell ruling.

Near the close of Silver's second trial, Caproni gave the jurors a specific definition of what constitutes an official act. Her instructions echoed the appeals judges' ruling.

"An 'official act' or 'official action' is a decision or action on a specific matter that may be pending or may by law be brought before a public official," Caproni told Silver's second jury. "An official act must involve a decision, an action, or an agreement to make a decision or to take action. ...

"The decision or action must be made on a question or matter that involves a formal exercise of governmental power. That means that the question or matter must be specific, focused, and concrete—for example, the kind of thing that could be put on an agenda and then checked off as complete. It must be something that may by law be brought before a public official or may, at some time, be pending before a public official. In order to be 'official action,' the decision or action must be more than just setting up a meeting, consulting with a lobbyist or official, organizing an event, or expressing support for an idea." Setting up meetings and consulting with lobbyists was all McDonnell claimed to have done.

"Without more, those activities do not constitute 'official action,'" [11] Caproni explained.

Another key, the judge said, was whether there was a quid pro quo—in other words, whether Silver performed an official act in return for something else. "'Quid pro quo' is Latin, and it means 'this for that' or 'these for those,'" Caproni instructed the jurors. "The government must prove that a bribe was sought or received by Mr. Silver, directly or indirectly, in exchange for the promise or performance of official action."[12]

Because Silver's alleged crimes stretched over nearly two decades, many of the official acts he performed in exchange for legal fees from Jay Goldberg's law firm and for the names of mesothelioma patients he sent to Weitz & Luxenberg were outside the five-year statute of limitations. Under the statute of limitations, Silver could only be charged with crimes that fully or partly occurred within five years of the day he was indicted. That meant if Silver had carried out and completed his crimes before February 19, 2010, prosecutors would have had no case against him.

Under the law, official acts Silver undertook after February 19, 2010—inside the statute of limitations—could be seen as evidence of a continuing crime. Prosecutors argued that the proclamation praising Taub, which Silver got the Assembly to pass on May 10, 2011, was an official act that was part of the quid pro quo between Silver and Taub, and thus part of a continuing crime. Prosecutors said the same concept applied when Silver met with Glenwood lobbyists to ensure they were satisfied with the 2011 rent regulation and 421-a bill—and when Silver later voted in favor of it.

It must have seemed clear to the jurors at Silver's second trial. They deliberated for 40 minutes on the day Judge Caproni instructed them on the definition of "official acts" and other aspects of the case. The next day—May 11, 2018—they deliberated all day before they delivered their verdict. Like the jury at Silver's first trial two and a half years earlier, they found Silver guilty on all seven counts—including money laundering, bribery, and depriving the public of his honest services as a government official.

Again, Silver faced Judge Caproni at a sentencing hearing. This time—July 27, 2018—he was 74 years old, two years older than at his first sentencing hearing, and three years older than when he was indicted in 2015. Silver slouched in his courtroom chair next to the jury box, where news reporters covering the hearing were allowed to sit.

Some of Silver's friends sat in the spectator benches. Some in his neighborhood's tight-knit Jewish community spoke up for him in letters to the judge. "Sheldon has always been a truly observant individual, with faith in Hashem [a Hebrew term for God] and great concern for all types of people, especially those in need," said his longtime rabbi, Sherman Siff of the Young Israel Synagogue of Manhattan, who had known Silver since he was about 20 years old.

"However, this entire ordeal has shattered him, as could be expected," Siff wrote. "Your Honor, these past few years have been a nightmare for him and his entire family. He has experienced the depths of what might be called a personal and communal tragedy."[13]

Silver's words to Caproni were typically laconic.

"I just want to say that the last three years have been enormously difficult for me," he said. "The events that are outlined in these trials have brought a great distrust in New York's government. And I am extremely, extremely remorseful for that. I am—I spent my life believing in government and its ability to help the citizens of New York.

"Going forward, I fear that I will continue to be ridiculed, shamed by the stain that is upon me. I will not be able to share and participate in the life-cycle events of my grandchildren, my great grandchildren, the graduations, the bar mitzvahs, bat mitzvahs, their weddings. This will be off limits to me. And this is something that really, really affects me as a result of what I look to the future as. I ask you to please take this into consideration and show your mercy."[14]

Judge Caproni felt at least a bit sorry for him. "I feel like visually he's aged more than the three years chronologically that have gone by since he was first charged," she said.

But Caproni still doubted Silver felt any remorse. "His inability to publicly admit that which 24 New Yorkers [two juries] have now found proven beyond a reasonable doubt may suggest that Mr. Silver has not entirely come to terms with the fact that he is exactly what too many people think all politicians are, and that is deeply corrupt," she said.

"Many excellent public employees toil for many years, for pay that is less than what they are worth in the open market, because they want to make the world a little better for everyone. They recognize that there are tradeoffs. They get the psychic satisfaction of serving their fellow man, for they earn less than what they might otherwise have earned if they were in the private sector.

"Mr. Silver wanted it both ways. He wanted to be the elected politician that delivered for his constituents, but he did not want to live on the salary we pay members of the Assembly and did not want to actually work when the Assembly was not in session, to build for himself and his family the wealth he wanted. So he cheated." [15]

This time, Caproni knocked several years off Silver's sentence—she imposed a term of seven years, five years less than the 12-year term she imposed at his first sentencing hearing in 2016. "I do not think he deserves what would be the equivalent of a life sentence, which 12 years is," the judge said. [16]

Caproni also fined Silver $1.75 million—the same fine she ordered in 2016.

Silver was ordered to report to prison on October 5, 2018, the day after the end of the Jewish holiday of Sukkot. But the reporting date was moot: Silver appealed again. He was allowed to delay his prison term while the appeal was argued and decided.

This time, Silver's lawyers asked, Were there really quid pro quos between Silver and the real estate companies, or between Silver and Robert Taub?

The answer came in January 2020—nearly 17 months after Silver's second sentencing hearing. It hinged on the five-year statute of limitations for federal crimes.

A three-judge panel of the Second Circuit Court of Appeals wrote that there was plenty of evidence to convict Silver of all his crimes. But a problem with Silver's conviction, in the judges' view, was the five-year statute of limitations on federal crimes. The judges said that meant Silver could only be punished for events in his case that occurred before February 19, 2010, five years before he was indicted.

Citing the McDonnell case, the judges said that for the conviction to stand on the mesothelioma charges, anything Silver did for Taub after February 2010 had to relate to a "properly defined" "question, matter, cause, suit, proceeding or controversy."

"The Government presented no evidence that Silver made any promises to Taub, after 2007, regarding any action on any identified, or even identifiable, question or matter—much less a focused or concrete question or matter involving the exercise of governmental power," the judges wrote.[17]

Silver refused to send Taub's laboratory any state grants after 2007. But Taub referred patients to Silver and Weitz & Luxenberg after 2007, and he continued to do so after February 2010, inside the five-year statute of limitations period. But in the appeals judges' view, the referrals after 2010 had no strings attached—because Taub wanted nothing specific in return for them.

"Taub himself testified that the post-2010 referrals were, instead, intended to curry generalized goodwill," their opinion noted. They cited Taub's May 25, 2010, email to his former nurse Mary Hesdorffer, in which he wrote that he'd keep sending referrals to Silver "because I may need him in the future—he is the most powerful man in New York State."

To the judges, this was evidence that in the eyes of federal criminal law, whatever quid pro quo existed between Taub and Silver ended in 2007. By continuing to send patients to Silver, Taub was planning ahead. He had no idea what he might get out of the arrangement. He only told Hesdorffer that he "may" need Silver in the future. That wasn't enough to convict Silver of a bribery scheme involving Taub, the judges found.

The judges also noted that the prosecutors never contended that Taub's continued referrals to Silver were some kind of "back pay" for the state money Silver procured for Taub's lab before 2007. [18] The judges found the May 2011 Assembly proclamation and other favors Silver procured for Taub weren't part of their pre–February 2010 arrangement, and thus couldn't be considered as part of the criminal case.

In the absence of a claim that Taub's post-February 2010 referrals were "back pay," his admission that he continued to give Silver lucrative referrals in hope the favor would be returned in the future was irrelevant, the appeals judges found. As a result, they tossed Silver's convictions relating to Silver's relationship with Taub.

But the charges against Silver in the real estate scheme stood, the judges said, because Silver acted on behalf of Glenwood Management and the Witkoff Group after February 2010. Among other things, the appeals judges noted, Silver signed off on state financing for Glenwood projects as a member of a state board that approved loans for real estate development, and he pursued Glenwood's interests in changing the rent laws in 2011. He took those actions as he continued to collect fees from Goldberg & Iryami.

The charges of money laundering also stood, and the appeals judges made clear that Silver was properly convicted of laundering money he obtained before 2010 through Taub's patient referrals.

"This is a classic example of bribery, and, but for the statute of limitations, Silver's conviction for the Mesothelioma Scheme would stand," the appeals judges wrote.[19] You can be convicted of money laundering if the money you're laundering is obtained from an illegal scheme. The illegal scheme doesn't have to occur within the five-year statute of limitations. Because Silver's investment deals with Jordan Levy extended to 2011, the money laundering itself happened inside the five-year statute of limitations, the judges said.

It was a partial win for Silver. The appeals judges dismissed three of the seven charges against him and gave him a new sentencing hearing.

Chapter 16 – The wall

Perhaps because he was a man of few words, Sheldon Silver continued to have a difficult time showing contrition for his crimes.

His third sentencing hearing was July 20, 2020, in a large, stately wood-paneled ceremonial courtroom on the first floor of the Thurgood Marshall United States Courthouse in lower Manhattan—in what was once Silver's legislative district. COVID-19 pandemic social distancing was in effect. Seating was barred in every other row of benches in the gallery. On benches where seating was allowed, people were spaced six feet apart.

Silver was 76 years old, heavier than at his last sentencing two years earlier, a bit more stooped. He wore a blue suit with narrow light stripes laid out in a square pattern. His shirt was light blue with a white collar; his tie had a red-and-white pattern.

Gone was the politician's American flag lapel pin. Silver was out of politics now.

His successful appeal of his convictions of using state money to leverage his lucrative arrangement with Robert Taub gave Silver's lawyers a chance to persuade Judge Valerie Caproni to significantly cut his prison time. And there was still a possibility he could appeal to the U.S. Supreme Court.

Prosecutors didn't push hard in their sentencing argument. In a two-page letter to Caproni, they said they were satisfied with the seven-year sentence she had imposed in 2018. "The Government accordingly respectfully requests that the Court reimpose that sentence or a substantially similar one, and also reorder a substantial fine," the letter concluded.

Silver's lawyers contended he should not go to prison at all. They cited his good works as a legislator—that he had backed more school seats for his district, supported universal prekindergarten, and championed laws against gender discrimination. They also argued that given the coronavirus pandemic, any prison time for a man as elderly and infirm as Silver would be a death sentence. "Mr. Silver is 76-years old with multiple health conditions that significantly predispose him to the worst outcomes if infected with COVID-19, including death," they wrote in court papers. They hoped Judge Caproni would impose no more than "a substantial term of home confinement."

"I know that a lot of people have lost faith in their government," Silver told the judge when his turn came to speak. "There are a lot of reasons for this, and I know that my actions contributed to that loss of faith and, certainly, did not help the situation. It's very painful for me, and I'm sorry.

"It's painful because I know first-hand how elected officials can help people in deeply meaningful ways every day. I thought I was pretty good at it, and I think I helped a lot of people, but I destroyed that legacy that I've built over 35 years of work, day in and day out.

"I was so angry with myself, and still am, but now that anger has mainly turned to sadness," Silver said. "This is my third time before you, your Honor, for sentencing, and I say, without hesitation, that regardless of how complicated and nuanced legal questions are ultimately answered, which are, frankly, beyond me, my use of my office for personal gain was improper, selfish, and ethically indefensible, and it undermined the trust of the people of the State of New York.

"I want to be clear: What I did was wrong. I've given this a lot of thought ... I believe my actions were the result of a misplaced sense of entitlement and a loss of perspective that I developed as I spent time in office. Let me just say, I am very sorry."

This statement of contrition with its admission that his "ethically indefensible" conduct was based on a "misplaced sense of entitlement" went further than the statements Silver offered at earlier sentencing hearings.

"He has finally acknowledged to himself and to the public the wrongfulness of his conduct. It has been a long time coming," Judge Caproni said.

But the judge caught on to something still missing from this mea culpa.

"It's not entirely clear to me that Mr. Silver really gets it," the judge said.

Addressing Silver directly, she explained, "It's not just ethically challenged—your conduct was illegal."

Caproni's remark recalled the day decades earlier when Jay Goldberg asked Silver if it was appropriate for him, as Assembly speaker, to take legal fees from Glenwood Management. "Of course ... I'm a lawyer," Silver answered. Did Silver still believe it was legal for him, as Assembly speaker, to have taken fees from Glenwood?

Caproni had another question Silver never answered.

"If you really thought you were doing good for New York with the actions that were corruptly bought and paid for, why did you hide what you were doing? When it was going to be public which member directed HCRA [Health Care Reform Act] grants to what recipient, why shut down the grant pipeline to Dr. Taub if you really thought what you were doing was right for New York and for your constituents? Why hide your relationship with Goldberg & Iryami? Why impede the work of the Moreland Commission?"

"This was corruption, pure and simple."

The judge refused a request by Silver and his lawyers to put off his prison reporting date because of the COVID-19 pandemic. She reasoned that the pandemic wasn't affecting federal prisons better or worse than anyplace else.

"I understand Mr. Silver's desire not to die in prison. I do not want Mr. Silver to die in prison either. But my job is to impose an appropriate sentence under all the circumstances."

"I think Mr. Silver—his time has come. He needs to go to jail," the judge said.

She sentenced Silver to six and a half years in prison, just six months less than the term she imposed in 2018. She ordered two years of supervision after his release from prison and $1 million in fines—$750,000 less than the fines she imposed two years earlier.

Silver reported on time on August 25, 2020, to the federal prison in Otisville, New York, in the Catskills not far from his vacation home.

Dean Skelos was released to home confinement from the same prison four months earlier. Like Silver, Skelos was also tried and convicted twice. His second, 2018 conviction of using his position as Senate majority leader to obtain $300,000 in bribes and extortion payments to his son, Adam, stood on appeal. Dean Skelos was sentenced to four years and three months in prison. Partly because of the COVID-19 pandemic, Skelos went home in April 2020. His son, Adam, who was convicted at the same trials as his father, was released in June 2021.

Caproni noted that if Silver hadn't stayed out on bail while his case was on appeal, he might have been out of prison by the time of his hearing in July 2020. "Had Mr. Silver acknowledged the reality of his guilt, which was obvious to 24 New Yorkers—that is, two separate 12-person juries—who returned guilty verdicts in this case, and accepted the verdict, and surrendered to prison while his appeal was pending, there is a good possibility that he would have been released at about the same time Dean Skelos was," she said.

Nearly five months after Silver arrived at Otisville—as President Donald Trump was leaving office in January 2021—there was talk Trump might grant him a pardon. It was not clear where the impetus for this came from. A longtime Silver aide, Judy Rapfogel, had once been a property manager for Charles Kushner, whose son Jared is married to Trump's daughter Ivanka. Maybe that connection was strong enough to get Trump's ear.

Andrew Cuomo offered another guess—maybe the push for the pardon came from New York's Jewish community, which has many links to Republican politicians.

Trump seriously considered granting Silver a pardon.[1] But some Republicans in New York opposed the idea, as did the *New York Post,* a newspaper Trump read and respected.[2] In the end, Silver was not on the list of 74 pardons and 70 sentence commutations Trump issued on January 20, 2021, his last day in office.

Silver's final hope was a U.S. Supreme Court appeal, which the justices considered at a conference the week of Trump's departure and rejected on January 25, five days after Trump left office. If Silver didn't know for sure, now he was told by seven of the nine highest judges in the land: his conduct was illegal.

The rejection came with a brief dissent from Justice Neil Gorsuch, which was joined by Justice Clarence Thomas—two members of the Supreme Court's conservative wing. They had a question about Silver's conviction.

"Normally, extortion and bribery are treated as distinct crimes," Gorsuch wrote. This picked up on a theme pushed by Silver's lawyers, who in their brief to the court complained that in upholding Silver's conviction for taking money from Jay Goldberg's law firm, the Second Circuit Court of Appeals "conflated extortion and bribery, an approach Justices of this Court have long questioned."[3]

Before the case got to the Supreme Court, Silver's appeals judges said his getting of fees from Glenwood Management and the Witkoff Group "closely resembled classic bribery-based crimes," and the fees he got from Weitz & Luxenberg came from "a classic example of bribery." They were interpreting the Hobbs Act, which applies to politicians like Silver who extort money or property "under color of official right" by leveraging their public office.[4]

Judges disagree on how to determine when Hobbs Act extortion is carried out "under color of official right." Silver's lawyers hoped to persuade the Supreme Court to find a new definition for bribery and extortion that excluded Silver's scheme. They wondered whether the Hobbs Act required a more explicit quid pro quo to justify a bribery conviction. If there was no clarity in the quid pro quo between Silver and Robert Taub and the real estate developers Silver steered to Goldberg's firm, maybe Silver wasn't guilty of bribery, or extortion. And if he wasn't guilty of bribery or extortion, maybe he also wasn't guilty of honest services fraud.

Gorsuch and Thomas seemed to believe that as interpreted by lower courts, the Hobbs Act does a poor job of defining Silver's crime. Maybe what Silver did wasn't a crime at all. The two justices evidently thought Silver's case might have been a good vehicle to sort this ambiguity. But a majority of Supreme Court justices for whatever reason did not wish to take on Silver's case. They didn't have to explain their positions. The questions Gorsuch and Thomas raised would have to wait for another case.

Silver got a curious reprieve in May 2021, when he was briefly sent from Otisville to his Manhattan home as the federal Bureau of Prisons weighed letting him serve his time in home confinement. Silver's transfer was part of an effort by the bureau to move ailing and elderly prisoners out of prisons during the coronavirus pandemic. But two days after he was freed, Silver was back in federal custody. Soon he was sent to the federal prison in Devens, Massachusetts, which has a hospital facility. His scheduled release date was March 2026.

Silver's prison term was what he, his lawyers, and Judge Caproni feared—a death sentence. He died in custody on January 24, 2022, at age 77.

Albany changed in the years after Silver left.

Reform-minded Democrats took full power in the state Legislature in the 2018 election and kept it in the 2020 and 2022 elections. Democrats had unassailable majorities in the Assembly and the Senate. Republican senators—the legislators the real estate industry once deemed vital to stopping rent regulation—seem destined for a long period of powerlessness. In one sign of the real estate industry's diminished influence, the 401-a tax break that for decades was a focus of the industry's lobbying was allowed to lapse in 2022. Whether it is restored or replaced remains to be seen.

Silver's replacement as Assembly speaker, Assembly member Carl Heastie of the Bronx, recognized what had been wrought by the real estate interests, the Republicans, and Silver, even if he didn't call them out by name. "There's 20-something years' worth of history with rent regulations that I think has to be spoken about and talked about and fixed," Heastie said in April 2019. "It's going to be a huge, major focus of ours."[5] Those "20-something years" stretched back to Sheldon Silver's lunches with Leonard Litwin, and the day Silver excitedly brought business from Glenwood Management to his friend Jay Goldberg's law firm.

Maybe the Legislature runs more openly under Heastie's leadership than in Silver's time. Sandy Galef—one of a handful of legislators still around in 2022 from the days after Michael Bragman's failed 2000 coup—said Heastie allowed more transparency and member involvement than Silver did. With Silver, "I think everything was programmed to go a certain way," Galef said. "I don't have that feeling with Carl Heastie. He really does listen. ... I think that's a very good quality. He really does entertain all of our suggestions."[6]

But some things didn't change.

Big policies are still lumped into the annual budget bill—such as plans to toll motorists driving in lower Manhattan, requirements that more employers offer paid sick leave, legalization of sports betting via mobile apps, and a requirement that internet broadband providers provide discounted service to low-income people.

Andrew Cuomo—who as governor killed an investigation into the Legislature's ethics failings and, knowingly or unknowingly, agreed with Sheldon Silver to enact ethics laws written to Silver's advantage—found himself the object of a series of scandals that led to his resignation in August 2021. They included allegations that he skewed reporting of the number of COVID-19 deaths in the state, that he improperly had state employees' help in writing a book that landed him a $5 million advance, and that he sexually harassed female staffers.

Cuomo once positioned himself as an anticorruption crusader. He sought to maintain this reputation even as, right under his nose, Silver twisted state ethics rules to his own ends. Cuomo shut down his Moreland Commission when it got too close to the Legislature's corruption. Time will tell how the scandals harm Cuomo's long-term legacy, which for New Yorkers includes new bridges, a rebuilt LaGuardia Airport, and a new subway line.

Cuomo's case shows how feckless legislators and governors long failed to get New York any closer to fixing the ethics problems in the state capitol. A new state ethics commission established in mid-2022 promised reform by giving the state's comptroller and attorney general a say in the commission's membership. But the ethics rules themselves have changed little since Silver's decades-long scheme was finally uncovered by smart and aggressive federal investigators who worked outside state government.

Upon Cuomo's resignation, two of the three men in a room became women. One is Governor Kathy Hochul, a former Buffalo-area member of Congress, who as lieutenant governor ascended to the top job upon Cuomo's departure. The other is Democratic Senate Majority Leader Andrea Stewart Cousins of Yonkers.

But that was the only big change. The three people in a room still decide most issues, and the Legislature's work is no more transparent under Hochul's leadership. Hochul in 2022 pushed a new stadium for the Buffalo Bills football team and a new redevelopment plan for the Penn Station area in Manhattan without adequate public input and debate.

In Silver's era, Galef and others criticized legislative leaders for deciding too many issues without hearings. In Heastie's era, legislators show signs they simply don't care to be deeply involved in issues. A November 2021 hearing on the fraught finances of the Metropolitan Transportation Authority, which runs New York City's subways, buses, commuter trains, and toll bridges, drew just 2 of 26 members of the Assembly's Committee on Corporations, Authorities and Commissions. At least one Assembly member felt it was more important to attend a Thanksgiving turkey giveaway in her district than to attend a hearing that delved into the transit agency's money woes.[7]

"Let me show you something," a New York legislator said at the end of an interview in one of his offices one day in 2017, during the period between Silver's two trials.

He stood before photographs hanging on the pale-painted wall of his pleasant and sparsely furnished space. He wanted to make a point about his colleagues and the milieu in which he built a political career.

The photographs showed him in the state capitol in Albany with other members of New York's Legislature.

The legislator pointed to faces in the photos on his wall.

"This one went to jail. ... This one is in prison as of last week. ... This one is under indictment. ..."

Sheldon Silver was one of the faces in the legislator's photos. He was the Assembly's speaker for 21 years and 10 days—from January 24, 1994, to February 2, 2015. In New York's history, only one Assembly speaker served longer.

During his speakership, a dozen of Silver's fellow Assembly members were convicted of corruption crimes.

Two were sentenced to probation. Ten who went to prison got average terms of about 5 years. One was sentenced to 14 years.

Nothing the Legislature has done since Sheldon Silver's departure will stop another of its members from matching his record of cheating the public and raking in millions in corrupt money. It might be happening already.

"I never thought I would know so many people who went to jail," said the legislator as he looked at the pictures on his wall.

He seems like an honest person. Many of his colleagues seem honest too. But given the history of the New York Legislature's corruption, how can anyone be sure?

Sources and acknowledgements

Much of this book is based on testimony and evidence presented at the trials of Sheldon Silver and Dean and Adam Skelos.

Readers who want to see the filings in both cases will find trial transcripts and other documents on the federal court system's PACER website at www.pacer.gov. To find anything related to the Skelos case, look on PACER under the Southern District of New York under docket number 1:15-cr-00317. Silver's case can be found on PACER under the Southern District of New York under docket number 1:15-cr-00093. You can also search on their names. PACER contains many documents cited in this book's text and endnotes. PACER isn't cheap—you'll need a credit card, and you'll pay according to the quantity of documents you download.

Looking at the documents filed in Silver's appeal to the U.S. Supreme Court is free. Search on the Supreme Court's website at www.supremecourt.gov. Silver's case there is under docket number 20-60.

The public record in the Silver and Skelos cases includes many documents not in PACER. They are identified in the endnotes as government exhibits. I obtained these from the public information office of the U.S. attorney for the Southern District of New York. The numbering of these exhibits was the same for both of Silver's trials.

Sheldon Silver, Weitz & Luxenberg, Glenwood Management, and many other people and organizations discussed in this book chose not to help my research.

The endnotes name many of my sources—but not all of them. Some are anonymous. I thank everyone who spoke to me anonymously and publicly, and I am grateful for their patience over the years it has taken to get this book written. Any mistakes are my own.

Notes

Chapter 1

[1] Author notes of Jay Goldberg testimony at Silver's second trial, May 8, 2018, and transcript of Silver's second trial presented with appellate papers, United States v. Sheldon Silver, 2nd Circuit U.S. Court of Appeals, No. 18-2380 Joint Appendix Volume 2, filed Oct. 26, 2018, 306–7.

[2] Ed Litvak, "A Conversation with Sheldon Silver," *The Lo-Down*, April 18, 2011. After Silver's first trial, his lawyers submitted this interview with a Lower East Side news publication as part of a motion to reduce his prison sentence.

[3] Linda Greenhouse, "Zeferetti Is Apparent Nominee to Seek Carey Seat," *The New York Times*, September 17, 1974, 33.

[4] Document 262-9 in Silver's case file, Case 1:15-CR-00093-VEC in the Southern District of New York, 5, www.pacer.gov.

[5] Judges working on Silver's appeals noted that Litwin gave more business to Goldberg when rent regulations and other laws critical to Litwin's business were before the Legislature. See for example *United States v. Silver*, No. 16-1615, slip op. at 12 (2d. Cir. Nov. 30, 2016).

[6] Michael McKee, interview by author, November 14, 2018.

[7] New York City Rent Guidelines Board, "1997 Income & Expense Study," 3, accessed April 9, 2019, https://rentguidelinesboard.cityofnewyork.us/wp-content/uploads/2019/08/1997-IE.pdf .

[8] Tenant Net newsletter of September 8, 1997, http://tenant.net/nytenants-announce/nytenants-announce.9709.html.

[9] Judy Rapfogel letter to Judge Valerie Caproni, March 23, 2016, document 235 in U.S. v. Sheldon Silver, Case 1:15-CR-00093-VEC in the Southern District of New York on PACER.

Chapter 2

[1] Alfred E. Smith, *The Citizen and His Government* (New York: Harper & Brothers, 1935), 54.

[2] Joseph L. Bruno, *Keep Swinging: A Memoir of Politics and Justice* (New York: Post Hill Press, 2016), 91–92.

[3] Sheldon Silver, "Drafting a Budget outside the Back Room," *Newsday* (Melville, NY), April 21, 1998, A39.

[4] Richard Brodsky, interview by author, April 28, 2017.

[5] Sandy Galef, interview by author, August 24, 2021.

[6] Author notes of Arthur Luxenberg testimony at Silver's second trial, U.S. v. Sheldon Silver, May 2, 2018.

[7] Smith, *The Citizen and His Government*, 55–56.

[8] Richard Pérez-Peña, "Hint of Top Aide's Rebellion Weakens Image of Assembly Speaker," *The New York Times*, November 22, 1997.

[9] Galef, interview by author.

[10] Bragman's letters and other materials about the coup attempt are in the Assemblyman Eric N. Vitaliano Papers, Archives & Special Collections, Department of the Library, College of Staten Island, CUNY, Staten Island, New York, Box 6, folder 4.

[11] This chapter's account of the May 22, 2000, Assembly debate on Silver's speakership is based on a transcript provided by the Assembly Public Information Office.

[12] Edward Sullivan, interview by author, May 8, 2017.

[13] Paulin testimony at Silver's first trial, U.S. v. Sheldon Silver, November 3, 2015, 156.

[14] Jeremy M. Creelan and Laura M. Moulton, *The New York State Legislative Process: An Evaluation and Blueprint for Reform* (New York: Brennan Center for Justice at NYU School of Law, 2004), 6.

[15] Author notes of Meara testimony at Silver's second trial, May 3, 2018.

[16] Creelan and Moulton, *New York State Legislative Process*, xi.

[17] Richard Pérez-Peña, "Political Memo; A Major Health Measure, Passed without a Second Thought," *The New York Times*, January 17, 2002.

Chapter 3

[1] Edward Frost, "Top P.I. Lawyer Convicted; Prosecutors Charged 12 Cases Tainted by Fraud in Rare Racketeering Enterprise," *ABA Journal*, May 1991, 28.

[2] Transcript of Silver's first trial, November 3, 2015, 167.

[3] The indictment, brought in U.S. District Court in Brooklyn, NY, is captioned *United States of America vs. Morris J. Eisen, Joseph P. Napoli, Harold M. Fishman, Alan Weinstein, Dennis Rella, Marty Gave, Leonard Kagel and Geraldine G. Morganti*, Cr. No. 90-018, filed in June 1990. It is a source for many of this chapter's details about the Eisen firm's activities.

[4] *McKinney's Session Laws of New York 1986* (St. Paul, MN: West, date), 287–89.

[5] Transcript of Silver's first trial, 169.

[6] Juan Carlos Rodriguez, "Titan of the Plaintiffs Bar: Perry Weitz," *Law360*, November 10, 2014, accessed June 6, 2017, https://www.law360.com/articles/594503/titanoftheplaintiffsbarperryweitz.

[7] Somini Sengupta, "A Bitter Solace; $11.6 Million Awarded to LI Widow in Asbestos Case," *Newsday*, June 25, 1995, A03.

[8] Kenneth Lovett, "Silver Treasure—Tort-Reform Foe's Firm Won $280M in Suits," *New York Post*, April 14, 2003, 15.

[9] John Dearie, interview by author, September 20, 2017.

[10] Transcript of Silver's first trial, 178.

[11] Sealed Complaint, United States v. Sheldon Silver, Case 15 MAG 0170, filed in U.S. District Court for the Southern District of New York on January 21, 2015, 30.

[12] "Perry Weitz and Arthur Luxenberg Engineered Their Sophisticated Operation with Specialized Departments, a National Feeder Network, and an Appetite for Risk," Lawfuel.com, March 5, 2006, https://www.lawfuel.com/blog/perry-weitz-and-arthur-luxenberg-engineered-their-sophisticated-operation-with-specialized-departments-a-national-feeder-network-and-an-appetite-for-risk/.

[13] Author notes of Luxenberg testimony at Sheldon Silver's second trial, May 2, 2018.

[14] Transcript of Silver's first trial, 186.

Chapter 4

[1] Roger Worthington, "A Candid Interview with Barbara McQueen," posted October 31, 2006, accessed July 13, 2017, www.worthingtoncaron.com. Worthington is a lawyer who represents people sickened by asbestos.

[2] Raya Bodnarchuk, interview by author, May 16, 2017.

[3] Pliiny the Elder, *The Natural History*, http://data.perseus.org/citations/urn:cts:latinLit:phi0978.phi0 01.perseus-eng1:19.4.

[4] See for example In re Joint E. & S. Dist. Asbestos Litig., 129 B.R. 710, 735 (E. D. N. Y. 1991).

[5] Irving J. Selikoff, "Historical Developments and Perspectives in Inorganic Fiber Toxicity in Man," *Environmental Health Perspectives,* Vol. 88, (August 1990): 269–76. This is a publication of the U.S. National Institute of Environmental Health Sciences.

[6] Barry I. Castelman, *Asbestos: Medical and Legal Aspects,* 5th ed. (New York: Wolters Kluwer, 2005), 153.

[7] Bill Richards, "New Data on Asbestos Indicate Cover-Up of Effects on Workers," *Washington Post*, November 12, 1978, accessed on February 17, 2019, https://www.washingtonpost.com/archive/politics/1978/11/12/n ew-data-on-asbestos-indicate-cover-up-of-effects-on-workers/028209a4-fac9-4e8b-a24c-50a93985a35d/. This is a good contemporaneous rundown of the documents' content.

[8] Joseph Hooper, "The Asbestos Mess," *The New York Times Magazine*, November 29, 1990.

[9] See the U.S. Geological Survey 2018 fact sheet on asbestos: https://prd-wret.s3.us-west-2.amazonaws.com/assets/palladium/production/atoms/files/my b1-2018-asbes.pdf. This was published in August 2021. Data for earlier years is at https://www.usgs.gov/centers/nmic/asbestos-statistics-and-information.

[10] "Asbestos Litigation: 2016 Year in Review," KCIC management consultants, early 2017, http://www.kcic.com/asset/pdf/KCIC-2016-AsbestosReport.pdf.

[11] Stephen J. Carroll, et al., *Asbestos Litigation*, RAND Corp., 2005, Kindle location 936. This paper is also available online at https://www.rand.org/content/dam/rand/pubs/monographs/2005/RAND_MG162.pdf.

[12] Peggy L. Ableman, Peter R. Kelso, and Marc C. Scarcella, "The Consolidation Effect: New York City Asbestos Verdicts, Due Process and Judicial Efficiency," *Mealey's Litigation Report: Asbestos, Vol. 30, No. 7,* (May 2015), 1.

[13] Marianna S. Smith, Resolving Asbestos Claims: The Manville Personal Injury Settlement Trust, 53 *Law and Contemporary Problems* 27-36 (Fall 1990): 29 Available at: https://scholarship.law.duke.edu/lcp/vol53/iss4/5.

[14] *Asbestos Litigation*, Kindle location 1517. This report, written around the time Sheldon Silver began collecting fees from asbestos cases, found that lawyer fees and other costs ate about 39 percent of payouts to asbestos victims.

[15] "How Fraud and Abuse in the Asbestos Compensation System Affect Victims, Jobs, the Economy, and the Legal System," Hearing Before the Subcommittee on the Constitution of the Committee on the Judiciary House of Representatives, Serial No. 112-51, September 9, 2011, 114. Available at https://www.govinfo.gov/content/pkg/CHRG-112hhrg68187/html/CHRG-112hhrg68187.htm.

[16] Gregg Kirkland testimony at Sheldon Silver's first trial, November 10, 2015, 1207–8.

[17] Government Exhibit 529 at Silver's trials.

[18] Transcript of Silver's first trial, November 10, 2015, 1225.

[19] Chris Lake, "The Most Expensive 100 Google Adwords Keywords in the U.S.," *Search Engine Watch*, May 31, 2016, accessed July 19, 2018, https://searchenginewatch.com/2016/05/31/the-most-expensive-100-google-adwords-keywords-in-the-us/.

[20] Pew Research Center, "Local TV News Fact Sheet," July 13, 2017, accessed August 7, 2017, http://www.journalism.org/fact-sheet/local-tv-news/.

[21] Author notes of May 3, 2018, Kirkland testimony at Silver's second trial.

[22] Transcript of Silver's first trial, November 10, 2015, 1250.

Chapter 5

[1] Many of the Taub quotes in this chapter come from transcripts in his lawsuit, Robert N. Taub v. Columbia University it the City of New York, Trustees of Columbia University, etc., filed in 2015 in New York County Civil Court under Index No. 155657-2015. Columbia fired Taub after Silver's arrest, and Taub filed this suit in hope of keeping his job.

[2] Robert Taub testimony on November 4, 2015, at Silver's first trial, 2015, 250. Taub's testimony at Silver's two trials is also a source for quotes in this chapter. [Assuming this is the date of the testimony rather than the day the trial began.]

[3] Robert Taub, interview by author, November 8, 2021.

[4] Robert Taub testimony at Silver's first trial, November 4, 2015, 424.

[5] Taub , November 4, 2015, 254.

[6] Taub , November 4, 2015, 253–54.

[7] Author notes of Robert Taub testimony at Silver's second trial, May 1, 2018.

[8] All of Mary Hesdorffer's quotes in this chapter are from the author's notes of her testimony on May 2, 2018, at Silver's second trial.

[9] Taub, interview by author.

[10] Email from Robert Taub to Joy Wheeler, November 18, 2010, Government Exhibit 525-9 at both of Silver's trials.

[11] Author notes of Taub testimony at Silver's second trial, April 30, 2018.

[12] Author notes of Taub testimony, April 30, 2018.

[13] John Dearie, interview by author, September 20, 2017.

[14] Author notes of Taub testimony, April 30, 2018.

[15] Charles Ferguson testimony at Silver's second trial, November 11, 2015, 1149–50.

[16] One explanation of the money Silver controlled under the Health Care Reform Act is in the original criminal complaint against him, filed in U.S. District Court/Southern District of New York under docket number 15 MAG 0170 on January 21, 2015, 27–28.

[17] Dennis Whalen testimony at Silver's first trial, November 9, 2015, 936.

Chapter 6

[1] Jordan Levy testimony at Silver's first trial, November 18, 2015, 2402.

[2] Steven Witkoff testimony at Silver's first trial, November 17, 2015, 2022–25.

[3] Author notes of Goldberg testimony at Silver's second trial, May 5, 2018. Asked if his business was "struggling" at the time Silver sought work on his behalf, Goldberg answered, "No."

[4] Witkoff testimony at Silver's first trial, November 17, 2015, 2025.

[5] Author notes of Witkoff testimony at Silver's second trial, May 7, 2018.

[6] Witkoff testimony at Silver's first trial, November 17, 2015, 2022–25.

[7] Silver's earnings from Walter Bernabe's case are disclosed in Government Exhibit 1509 presented at both of Silver's trials. An investigator's report of a phone call with Bernabe's daughter was filed in *United States v. Silver* in July 2018, as part of Document No. 438.

[8] Sealed Complaint, *United States v. Sheldon Silver,* Case 15 MAG 0170, filed in U.S. District Court for the Southern District of New York on January 21, 2015, 15.

[9] Today the company is known as Crown Holdings, Inc.

[10] Government Exhibit 514-001, presented at both of Silver's trials. The summary of these payments is on page 5.

[11] A relative of Vincenza Lala contacted by the author remembered nothing about her case.

[12] Government exhibit 950 at both of Silver's trials.

[13] Government exhibit 953 at both of Silver's trials.

[14] Cody testimony at Silver's first trial, November 18, 2015, 2314.

[15] Government exhibit 1012 at both of Silver's trials.

[16] Levy testimony at Silver's first trial, November 18, 2015, 2394–467.

Chapter 7

1 Emma Maniere and Hayley Raetz, "Comparing the Current 421-a Exemption to Governor Hochul's Proposed Reforms," March 7, 2022, *The Stoop*, NYU Furman Center Blog, accessed May 16, 2022 at https://furmancenter.org/thestoop/entry/comparing-the-current-421-a-exemption-to-governor-hochuls-proposed-reforms.

² Alfred E. Smith, *The Citizen and His Government* (New York: Harper & Brothers, 1935), 149–50.

³ Dorego testimony at trial of *United States v. Skelos*, June 21, 2018, 375.

⁴ If you really want more detail on this, visit https://www.elections.ny.gov/CFContributionLimits.html, which the author viewed on May 17, 2022. This is a New York state government web page.

⁵ The contribution limits vary by year. See https://www.elections.ny.gov/CFContributionLimits.html to find the manuals stating each year's limits.

⁶ This conclusion is based on the author's analysis of New York State Board of Election records downloaded from data.gov at https://catalog.data.gov/dataset/campaign-finance-filings-submitted-to-the-new-york-state-board-of-elections-beginning-1999. The site is run by the U.S. General Services Administration.

⁷ "Testimony of the New York Public Interest Research Group before the Joint Legislative Budget Hearing on Higher Education," February 10, 2015, 14, https://nyassembly.gov/write/upload/publichearing/001183/002839.pdf.

⁸ Halstead Property, "Manhattan Rental Market Report," Second Quarter 2009, accessed March 21, 2018, http://media.halstead.com/pdf/Halstead_RentalReport_2Q09.pdf.

Chapter 8

¹ Jacob Gershman, "Spitzer Sends Tough Signal to Silver on Disclosing Outside Income," *New York Sun*, October 20, 2006, 1.

2 These examples come from 2006–2007 legislative initiative data published on the New York State Assembly's website, https://nyassembly.gov/comm/WAM/20061127d/2006_07legini t.pdf.

3 Michele Morgan Bolton, "Secret 'Pork' Data Targeted in Lawsuit; Times Union Seeks Access to How Tax Dollars Are Being Spent," *Times Union* (Albany, NY), June 23, 2006, 1.

4 Author notes of Richard L. Rodgers testimony at Silver's second trial, May 9, 2018. Rodgers was one of the assistant attorneys general assigned to the team.

5 Fredric U. Dicker, "Eliot Spits Fire – Blows Up at GOP Critic," *New York Post*, January 31, 2007, 5.

6 Joseph L. Bruno, *Keep Swinging: A Memoir of Politics and Justice* (New York: Post Hill Press, 2016), 52.

7 James M. Odato, "Probe Centers on Thoroughbreds; 'Good deal' on Two Mares from Politically Connected Manhattan Millionaire at Issue," *Times Union* (Albany, NY), June 3, 2007, A6.

8 Peter Elkind, *Rough Justice: The Rise and Fall of Eliot Spitzer* (New York: Portfolio, 2010), 133. The author has heard this story from other sources. Preet Bharara, the U.S. attorney in Manhattan, mentioned this admonition in a January 2015 speech discussed in Chapter 13.

9 State of New York Office of the Attorney General, "Report of Investigation into the Alleged Misuse of New York State Aircraft and the Resources of the New York State Police," July 23, 2007, 10. The *Times Union* sought information about the official schedules of Gov. Spitzer and Lt. Gov. Paterson, but not of Bruno. Probably the newspaper figured Spitzer's office wouldn't have schedule information about Bruno, who served in a different branch of state government.

10 James M. Odato, "State Flies Bruno to Fundraisers; Taxpayers Finance Trips of Senate Majority Leader to New York City Political Events," *Times Union* (Albany, NY), July 1, 2007, 1.

11 Fredric U. Dicker, "Gov's Trooper Snoop Job on Bruno— Ordered Police to Track GOP Foe's Movements," *New York Post*, July 5, 2007, 7.

[12] Danny Hakim and Nicholas Confessore, "The Feuding by Bruno and Spitzer Turns Bitter," *The New York Times,* July 6, 2007, B1.

[13] "Report of Investigation into the Alleged Misuse of New York State Aircraft," 2–3.

[14] Robert Taub, interview by author, November 8, 2021.

[15] Robert Taub testimony at Silver's first trial, November 4, 2015, 336–40.

Chapter 9

[1] William L. Riordon, *Plunkitt of Tammany Hall: A Series of Very Plain Talks on Very Practical Politics,* (New York: Penguin / Signet Classics, 2015), 3. This book was first published in 1905.

[2] McNally v. United States, 483 U.S. 350, 356 (1987). From the footnotes: "Representative Farnsworth proceeded to describe a scheme whereby the mail was used to solicit the purchase by greedy and unwary persons of counterfeit bills, which were never delivered."

[3] Shushan v. United States, 117 F.2d 110, 115 (5th Cir. 1941). For more on this case, see Zephyr Teachout, *Corruption in America: From Benjamin Franklin's Snuff Box to Citizens United* (Boston: Harvard University Press, 2014), 195–99.

[4] *Shushan,* 117 F.2d at 120.

[5] *McNally,* 483 U.S. at 356.

[6] Sentencing Submission of the United States of America, filed in *United States v. Seminerio,* Case 1:08-cr-01238-NRB in the Southern District of New York, Oct. 20, 2009, 9–10.

[7] Another hospital known as St. John's is still open in Queens. That hospital, St. John's Episcopal Hospital, is in the Rockaways neighborhood.

Chapter 10

[1] "Please Let It Go to Trial," *New York Post*, May 5, 2008, 26, https://nypost.com/2008/05/05/please-let-it-go-to-trial/.

[2] Government Exhibit 1507, presented at both of Silver's trials.

[3] Government Exhibit 919, presented at both of Silver's trials.

[4] See New York Consolidated Laws, Civil Practice Law and Rules - CVP § 4503, https://codes.findlaw.com/ny/civil-practice-law-and-rules/cvp-sect-4503.html.

[5] Government Exhibit 1507, presented at both of Silver's trials.

[6] Government Exhibit 1A-T, presented at both of Silver's trials.

[7] Government Exhibit 2-T, presented at both of Silver's trials.

[8] Danny Hakim, "Loans from Assembly Speaker Aid Firm That Finances Trial Lawyers," *The New York Times*, August 5, 2008, https://www.nytimes.com/2008/08/06/nyregion/06silver.html.

[9] Silver interview on The Brian Lehrer Show on WNYC-FM. This quote is from a portion of the interview played in a documentary about Paul Newell's campaign, "Excuse Me, Mr. Speaker," which was published April 20, 2016, https://www.youtube.com/watch?v=jf2YibIw8PA. The interview is at about the 57-minute mark.

[10] Jacob Gershman, "Silver Racks Up Miles at Taxpayer Expense," *New York Sun*, September 28, 2008, 1. The *Sun* published its last print issue September 29.

[11] Exhibit 3 in a defense document filed in Silver's first trial, "Defense Motion in Limine to Exclude Evidence of Unrelated Public Corruption Cases," filed September 11, 2015.

[12] Exhibit 4 in "Defense Motion in Limine to Exclude Evidence of Unrelated Public Corruption Cases."

[13] Transcript of Silver's first trial, November 10, 2015, 1250.

[14] Government exhibits 525 and 535 presented at both of Silver's trials.

[15] The Simmons firm document is Government Exhibit 529 at both of Silver's trials. Kirkland's comment is in the transcript of Silver's first trial, November 10, 2015, 1226.

[16] Author notes of Taub testimony at Silver's second trial, May 1, 2018.

[17] Transcript of Silver's first trial, November 5, 2015, 621.

[18] Author notes of Luxenberg testimony at Silver's second trial, May 2, 2018.

[19] This email exchange is contained in Government Exhibit 595-1, presented at both of Silver's trials.

[20] Government Exhibit 525-9, presented at both of Silver's trials.

Chapter 11

[1] U.S. Attorney's Office Eastern District of New York news release, "Former New York State Senate Majority Leader Pedro Espada, Jr. Sentenced to Five Years' Imprisonment," June 14, 2013.

[2] Kenneth Lovett, Glenn Blain, and Elizabeth Benjamin, "Dems Batten Down Hatches, Lock Doors: Ousted Malcolm and Senate Allies in Desperate Bid to Keep Albany Power," *Daily News* (New York, NY), June 10, 2009, 5.

[3] Runes testimony at Silver's first trial, November 16, 2015, 1901.

[4] All the data about Litwin's and Glenwood's campaign contributions in this chapter are based on the author's analysis of New York State campaign finance records.

[5] Tim Minton and Michael Clancy, "Monserrate Walks on Felonies; Guilty of Misdemeanor Assault," WNBC New York, October 16, 2009, accessed September 24, 2021, https://www.nbcnewyork.com/news/local/judge-returns-not-guilty-verdict-on-felony-charges/1903184/. Monserrate opted to have his case tried before a judge instead of a jury.

[6] Dorego testimony at Skelos's second trial, June 21, 2018, 380.

[7] Government exhibit 1118 at Skelos's trials.

[8] Government exhibit 1122 at Skelos's trials.

[9] Author's analysis of New York campaign finance records.

[10] The account of this meeting is based on Charles Dorego's testimony from the transcript of Skelos's second trial, June 21, 2018, 402–6.

[11] United States v. Skelos, Case 1:15-CR-s317-KMW, Document 18, filed in U.S. District Court for the Southern District of New York, July 21, 2015, 11.

Chapter 12

[1] New York City Department of Housing Preservation and Development, "Selected Initial Findings of the 2017 New York City Housing and Vacancy Survey," accessed September 25, 2018, https://www1.nyc.gov/assets/hpd/downloads/pdf/about/2017-hvs-initial-findings.pdf.

[2] See http://www.rentistoodamnhigh.org/index.html, among other places.

[3] Author notes of Silver's second trial, May 8, 2018.

[4] Author notes of Silver's second trial, May 8, 2018.

[5] Meara testimony of November 13, 2015, 1691.

[6] Runes testimony of November 13, 2015, 1741–45.

[7] Meara testimony of November 13, 2015, 1600.

[8] Strasburg testimony at Skelos trial, June 26, 2018, 874.

[9] Dorego testimony at Skelos trial, June 22, 2018, 490.

[10] U.S. Attorney's Office initial complaint against Silver, filed in U.S. District Court for the Southern District of New York, January 2015. According to the complaint, this document was dug up by the Moreland Commission set up by Andrew Cuomo in 2013 to probe legislative corruption.

[11] Silver official Assembly web page as of October 2015, archived at https://web.archive.org/web/20151010164456/http://assembly.state.ny.us/mem/Sheldon-Silver/bio/.

[12] New York City Comptroller's Office, "The Gap is Still Growing: New York's Continuing Housing Affordability Challenge," September 26, 2018, 1, accessed October 16, 2018, https://comptroller.nyc.gov/wp-content/uploads/documents/Growing_Gap_Update_2018_REVISED_180926.pdf.

[13] Meara testimony at first Silver trial, November 13, 2015, 1606–9.

[14] Runes testimony at first Silver trial, November 16, 2015, 1787–88.

[15] Author notes of Rune's testimony at Silver's second trial, May 7, 2018.

[16] Runes testimony of November 16, 2015, 1802.

[17] Runes testimony of November 16, 2015, 1898.

[18] Author notes of Goldberg testimony at Silver's second trial, May 8, 2018.

[19] Runes testimony of November 13, 2015, 1725–26.

Chapter 13

[1] Richard Runes testimony at Silver's first trial, November 13, 2015, 1746.

[2] Transcript of 2011 State of the State Speech, accessed May 9, 2017, https://www.governor.ny.gov/news/2011statestatetranscript.

[3] Jimmy Vielkind, "Cuomo: Moreland Commission an Option If Legislators Don't Act," Capitol Confidential, May 8, 2013, accessed December 4, 2018, https://blog.timesunion.com/capitol/archives/186713/cuomo-moreland-commission-an-option-if-legislators-dont-act/.

[4] See page 7-A of Government Exhibit 921 from both of Silver's trials. This is the form Silver filed with the Legislative Ethics Commission on May 16, 2011, containing his disclosures for 2010.

[5] News release, "Governor Cuomo, Majority Leader Skelos & Speaker Silver Announce Agreement on Historic Ethics Reform," issued by Gov. Andrew M. Cuomo on June 3, 2011, accessed December 6, 2018, https://www.governor.ny.gov/news/governor-cuomo-majority-leader-skelos-speaker-silver-announce-agreement-historic-ethics-reform.

[6] Italics are the author's. This was Assembly Bill A08301 and Senate Bill S05679 of the 2011-2012 legislative session. It passed both houses of the Legislature on June 13, 2011. Cuomo signed it into law on August 15, 2011.

[7] See pages 10 and 7-A of Government Exhibit 922 from both of Silver's trials.

[8] See page 10 of Government Exhibit 923 from both of Silver's trials.

[9] See page 8-A of Government Exhibit 923 from both of Silver's trials.

[10] News release, "Speaker Silver Statement on Assembly Passage of Historic Ethics Reform Legislation," issued by Assembly Speaker Sheldon Silver on June 13, 2011, accessed December 6, 2018, https://nyassembly.gov/Press/20110613/.

[11] Taub testimony at Silver's first trial, November 4, 2015, 414.

[12] This information comes from the author's analysis of several government exhibits from both Silver trials, including 512 and 522. Another government exhibit, 1509, says Silver received $170,060 in fees from this case. The reason for this discrepancy is unclear.

[13] State of New York Joint Commission on Public Ethics, "In the Matter of an Investigation of Assemblymember Vito Lopez," February 12, 2013, 2.

[14] Joint Commission on Public Ethics' investigation of Lopez, 6–10.

[15] Al D'Amato testimony at the Skeloses' second trial, July 3, 2018, 1927–28.

[16] Curcio testimony at the Skeloses' second trial, June 20, 2018, 199–201.

[17] Anthony Bonomo's account of his dealings with Adam Skelos comes from the transcript of his testimony at the Skeloses' second trial, July 2, 2018, 1558–704.

[18] Government exhibit 1912 at Skelos trial.

[19] News release, "Former Assemblyman Eric Stevenson Sentenced in Manhattan Federal Court for Taking More than $20,000 in Bribes in Exchange for Proposing Legislation and Performing Other Official Acts," United States Attorney's Office, Southern District of New York, May 21, 2014.

[20] News release, "81% of Voters Say More Arrests of Legislators for Corruption Are Likely; About 1/3 Say *Their* Legislator Could Be Arrested," Siena Research Institute, Loudonville, NY, April 22, 2013, accessed January 10, 2019, https://scri.siena.edu/wp-content/uploads/2018/07/SNY_April_2013_Poll_Release_-_FINAL.pdf.

[21] Carl Campanile, "Shelly: My Hands Are Clean," *New York Post*, April 10, 2013, 6.

[22] Author's analysis of Silver's "Annual Statement of Financial Disclosure for Calendar Year 2012," filed with the State Ethics Commission on May 14, 2013. Government Exhibit GX 923 at both of Silver's trials.

[23] Glenn Blain and Kenneth Lovett, "NY Assembly Speaker Sheldon May Be a $6 Million Man, Financial Disclosure Says," *Daily News* (New York, NY), July 3, 2013, accessed January 4, 2019, https://www.nydailynews.com/news/politics/ny-speaker-sheldon-6m-man-disclosure-article-1.1389871. All the media accounts of Silver's form seem to have different interpretations of the size of his income and portfolio.

[24] Paulin testimony at Silver's first trial, November 3, 2015, 108–9.

[25] Kathleen Rice, Milton Williams Jr., and William Fitzpatrick, "The Commission to Investigate Public Corruption Preliminary Report," December 2, 2013, 6–7.

[26] Indictment, "United States of America v. Sheldon Silver," February 19, 2015, 6, 17.

[27] Author notes of Paulin testimony at Silver's second trial, April 30, 2018.

[28] Chris Bragg, "Cuomo on Moreland Tampering: It's My Commission," *Crain's New York Business*, April 24, 2014, accessed December 2, 2021, www.crainsnewyork.com/article/20140424/BLOGS04/140429924.

[29] Ronan Farrow, "Andrew Cuomo's War Against a Federal Prosecutor," *New Yorker*, August 10, 2021, accessed August 11, 2021, https://www.newyorker.com/news/news-desk/andrew-cuomos-war-against-a-federal-prosecutor.

[30] Untitled speech by Preet Bharara at New York Law School, January 23, 2015, accessed March 20, 2019, https://www.citylandnyc.org/video-citylaw-preet-bharara/#more-22655.

[31] Sealed Complaint, United States v. Sheldon Silver, Case 15 MAG 0170, filed in U.S. District Court for the Southern District of New York on Jan. 21, 2015, 14.

Chapter 14

[1] Transcript of Silver's second trial, May 7, 2018, 1149.

[2] Transcript of Silver's second trial, May 8, 2018, 1406–7.

[3] See "Annual Statement of Financial Disclosure for Calendar Year 2013, filed with the State Legislative Ethics Commission on May 15, 2014. Government Exhibit GX 924 at both of Silver's trials.

[4] Kenneth Lovett and Glenn Blain, "Speaker Silver Earned up to $750K for Work Outside Legislative Duties — More than Prior Year," *Daily News* (New York, NY), July 2, 2014, accessed February 12, 2019, https://www.nydailynews.com/news/politics/silver-earned-750k-legal-work-albany-article-1.1852888.

[5] Kenneth Lovett, "Sheldon Silver Earned up to $750G in 2013 Working a Few Hours per Week at Law Firm," *Daily News* (New York, NY), July 3, 2014.

[6] This email is Government Exhibit 239, used at both of Silver's trials.

[7] Whyland testimony at Silver's first trial, November 17, 2015, 2231.

[8] Transcript of Silver's first trial, November 5, 2015, 604–5.

[9] Transcript of Silver's first trial, November 5, 2015, 575–76.

[10] Transcript of Silver's second trial, May 1, 2018, 283

[11] Thomas Kaplan, William K. Rashbaum, and Susanne Craig, "After Ethics Panel's Shutdown, Loopholes Live On in Albany," *The New York Times*, December 8, 2014, A1.

[12] Transcript of Silver's first trial, November 5, 2015, 684.

[13] Transcript of Silver's first trial, November 5, 2015, 696. Cohen made these remarks in a nonpublic sidebar conference with the Judge Valerie Caproni and other lawyers.

[14] This exchange comes from Government Exhibit 5-T, used at both of Silver's trials.

[15] Government Exhibit 1433-T presented at both of the Skeloses' trials.

[16] William K. Rashbaum, Thomas Kaplan, and Susanne Craig, "U.S. Said to Investigate Sheldon Silver, New York Assembly Speaker, Over Payments," *The New York Times*, December 29, 2014, A1.

[17] Aaron Short and Carl Campanile, "Sheldon Silver Money Man Dons Soviet Hammer & Sickle Cap," *New York Post*, January 1, 2015, http://nypost.com/2015/01/01/sheldon-silver-money-man-dons-soviet-hammer-sickle-cap/.

[18] Kenneth Lovett, John Marzulli, and Greg B. Smith, "Sheldon Silver Accused of $4 Million Bribery and Kickback Scheme, Dems Continue to Support Him," *Daily News* (New York, NY), January 22, 2015, https://www.nydailynews.com/news/politics/assembly-speaker-silver-arrested-report-article-1.2087758.

[19] Todd Kaminsky, interview by author, February 4, 2021.

[20] Paulin testimony at Silver's second trial, April 30, 2018, page JA 0424 of Joint Appendix filed by the prosecution and defense in Silver's second appeal, United States v. Silver, et al., Index No. 18-2380.

Chapter 15

[1] Evans v. United States, 504 U.S. 255, 260 (1992).

[2] United States v. Silver, Document 262-1 in the case's PACER file, filed April 20, 2016.

[3] U.S. motion in limine presented before sentencing at Silver's first trial, Document 241 in his PACER case file, April 14, 2016, 3.

[4] U.S. motion in limine of April 14, 2016, 12–13.

[5] Defense motion in limine, filed April 14, 2016, 4.

[6] John Aretakis, interview by author, August 9, 2018.

[7] Kenneth Lovett and Dareh Gregorian, "Sheldon Silver Had Affairs with at Least Two Women — One a Lobbyist, the Other a Former Assemblywoman, Court Papers Show," *Daily News* (New York, NY), April 15, 2016, accessed July 29, 2019, https://www.nydailynews.com/new-york/sheldon-silver-cheated-women-court-docs-article-1.2602375.

[8] Transcript of Silver sentencing hearing, May 3, 2016, 53–54.

[9] Transcript of Silver sentencing hearing, May 3, 2016, 56–57.

[10] United States v. Silver, No. 16-1615, slip op. at 34 (2d Cir. July 13, 2017)..

[11] United States v. Silver, transcript of jury charge of May 10, 2018, found in Joint Appendix to 2nd Circuit Court of Appeals Case No. 18-2380, JA 1144.

[12] United States v. Silver, transcript of jury charge of May 10, 2018, found in Joint Appendix to 2nd Circuit Court of Appeals Case No. 18-2380, JA 1143.

[13] Document 439-4 in the Silver case's PACER file. The letter is dated July 19, 2018, and was filed with the court July 20, 2018.

[14] Transcript of Silver sentencing hearing, July 27, 2018, 34–35.

[15] Transcript of Silver sentencing hearing, July 27, 2018, 37–38.

[16] Transcript of Silver sentencing hearing, July 27, 2018, 42.

[17] United States v. Silver, No. 18-2380 (2nd Circuit Court of Appeals), Jan. 21, 2020, slip op. at 64.

[18] United States v. Silver, No. 18-2380 (2nd Circuit Court of Appeals), Jan. 21, 2020, slip op. at 71.

[19] Slip opinion, United States v. Silver, 83.

Chapter 16

[1] Maggie Haberman, Kenneth P. Vogel, and Dana Rubenstein, "Trump Prepares Pardon Wave for Final Hours," *The New York Times*, January 18, 2021, https://www.nytimes.com/2021/01/18/us/politics/trump-pardons.html.

[2] "Trump Should Not Pardon Ex-Politician and Criminal Sheldon Silver," *New York Post*, January 19, 2021, https://nypost.com/2021/01/19/president-trump-should-not-pardon-criminal-sheldon-silver/.

[3] Docket No. 20-30, Sheldon Silver v. United States, "Emergency Application to Recall and Stay Mandate, or in the Alternative Release on Bail, Pending Disposition of Certiorari Petition," filed by Silver's lawyers with the U.S. Supreme Court on April 20, 2020, page 3.

[4] From the text of the Hobbs Act: "The term 'extortion' means the obtaining of property from another, with his consent, induced by wrongful use of actual or threatened

force, violence, or fear, or under color of official right." Read the statute here: https://www.law.cornell.edu/uscode/text/18/1951.

[5] Denis Slattery, "Speaker Heastie Says Albany Lawmakers 'Laser-Focused' on Rent Regulations," *Daily News* (New York, NY), April 2, 2019, which can be found at this link: https://www.nydailynews.com/news/politics/ny-rent-regulations-20190402-vwwkvddqsbgblbkqy4zw5cjiza-story.html.

[6] Sandy Galef, interview by author, August 24, 2021.

[7] Clayton Guse and John Annese, "Two Dozen Assembly Members Skip Oversight Hearing on MTA's $51.5B Construction Plan," *Daily News* (New York, NY), November 23, 2021, https://www.nydailynews.com/new-york/ny-mta-capital-plan-construction-delay-covid-janno-lieber-attendance-20211123-7rl2as3hjneqtpwxpk53xvg63e-story.html.

CPSIA information can be obtained
at www.ICGtesting.com
Printed in the USA
BVHW051657210223
658946BV00012B/487